A President's
ODYSSEY

BY A. **MERRIMAN SMITH**

Harper & Brothers, Publishers, New York

BOOKS BY MERRIMAN SMITH

A President's Odyssey
Meet Mr. Eisenhower
A President Is Many Men
Thank You, Mr. President

A President's Odyssey

Smith, A   Merriman, 1913–
   A President's odyssey. ₁1st ed.₁ New York, Harper ₁1961₁

272 p. 22 cm.

   1. Eisenhower, Dwight David. Pres. U. S., 1890–   2. Visits of
state. 3. U. S.—Relations (general) with foreign countries.   I.
Title.

E835.S55   923.173   61—6198 ‡

"Is it not a noble farce, wherein kings, republics, and emperors have for so many ages played their parts, and to which the whole vast universe serves for a theater?"

Montaigne

A PRESIDENT'S ODYSSEY

CONTENTS

A WORD OF PURPOSE   xi

A clue to why President Eisenhower failed to behave as a lame duck should and, instead, went out campaigning the world with the zeal of a salesman behind in his orders.

CHAPTER 1
"Long Live the King of America"   1

"Zindabad" in India. What it was like to be caught in the midst of a million howling Hindus.

CHAPTER 2
Sugared Fruits and Persian Rugs   12

The problems. What gifts do you take to a dictator who has everything? How do you get a live gazelle back home?

CHAPTER 3
Safe Journeying   25

How can the Secret Service get him there and back alive? Watch out for bombs and hidden microphones.

CHAPTER 4
"Ike, We Trust You"   37

West Germany, the beginning of the goodwill tours. On the edge of the Iron Curtain for the first time.

CHAPTER 5
"Just Folks" in Britain   48

> The British behave like bobby-soxers as personal diplomacy moves between London, Balmoral and Chequers.

CHAPTER 6
"The Heart Is Full"   62

> Ike in Paris, the scenes of triumph revisited.

CHAPTER 7
In the Footsteps of Alexander   72

> Start of the longest tour in presidential history. The Vatican, and on to the warriors of Turkey.

CHAPTER 8
Under a Velvet Parasol   85

> Pakistan. Speeding lancers, snake charmers and slums sprayed with chlorophyll.

CHAPTER 9
A Hatful of Confetti   96

> Afghanistan. The King wants his own TV station as much as new jet fighters.

CHAPTER 10
Angel in India   105

> New Delhi. The tumult of Ike's arrival continues into his greatest personal triumph.

CHAPTER 11
A Realm of Wonder   117

> Iran, Greece and Tunisia. Tommy guns and rug-paved streets.

CHAPTER 12
Three Wise Men   128
The Western Summit. Preparing for Khrushchev. Off to Spain, Morocco and the gunslinging Berbers.

CHAPTER 13
Hail to the Chief Cha-cha-cha   143
Personal diplomacy in Latin America. Brasilia, the world's newest and muddiest capital.

CHAPTER 14
"We Are Not Saints"   158
Argentina and Chile. Ike tires in the foothills of the Andes and the Peronistas jeer him.

CHAPTER 15
Ike Weeps—Thousands Cheer   176
Violence and tear gas in Uruguay and Air Force One plane loses an engine over the Brazilian jungle.

CHAPTER 16
A Shuddering Thing   188
The Summit. Khrushchev kicks Eisenhower in the teeth and tells him to stay out of Russia.

CHAPTER 17
Stay Out of Japan   209
Off to the Far East and riots. The President gets the bad news in Manila.

CHAPTER 18
End of an Odyssey   224
Bayonets on Okinawa and a mob that hurts with kindness in Korea. Curtain calls.

CHAPTER 19

Was It All Worth It? 244

The diplomats frown, the experts deplore, but
they tend to forget about the people.

CHAPTER 20

The President Sums Up 256

Eisenhower thinks the world has grown too
small for future Presidents to stay at home.

A WORD OF PURPOSE

Dwight D. Eisenhower astounded his critics, amazed his friends and captured the attention of the world during his last two years in the White House.

Instead of functioning in the minimal manner expected of a lame-duck President, he toured abroad with the zeal of a salesman trying to make a quota—a quota of peace and understanding. He was selling, and selling hard, the difficult and highly perishable commodity of good will. He combated anti-Americanism where he found it with his charm and hundred-watt grin—in dusty streets, ancient palaces, cricket fields and across the table from his principal adversary, Nikita S. Khrushchev.

Eisenhower made four basic foreign good-will trips: his journey to West Germany, Great Britain and France in the summer of 1959; his eleven-nation tour to Asia, Europe, the Middle East and Africa in late 1959; to South America in the late winter of 1960; and to the Far East the same year.

He talked with virtually every ranking head of state except the rulers of Red China and the Iron Curtain countries. Naturally, his electric presence could not remedy nor quickly improve many of the deep-down diplomatic problems between nations. But despite rather humbling setbacks involving Russia and Japan, his jet-paced ventures in personal diplomacy may have accomplished more than some of his critics believe.

For one thing, he forced an up-to-date picture of life in other countries into the living rooms and schoolhouses of America. He may also have set a pattern for future Presidents. Because of Khrushchev's tactics at the attempted 1960 Summit conference in Paris and the forced cancellation of Eisenhower's trips to Russia and Japan, many Americans came to believe that personal diplomacy by a President would have to stop. This, however, seems to be a shortsighted appraisal.

Perhaps superficially but nonetheless energetically, Eisenhower ranged about the world in the belief that men who come to know each other personally are less likely to wage war than if they remain, as did too many statesmen of past decades, in relatively one-sided ignorance behind the high walls of their chancelleries.

A lesser personality in the White House, a President without the glamorous background of a war hero, might not be able to bring millions of foreigners into the streets of their cities throwing flowers and shouting *"Vive!"* Also, the diplomatic value of these applauding hordes might be exceedingly short-lived.

But as Ike traveled from the remote, icy peaks of the Hindu Kush Mountains in Afghanistan within sight of Russia to the humid jungles of Surinam, as he bowed and waved his way from Scotland to Korea, from Madrid to Manila, from Rambouillet to San Carlos de Bariloche, it was a moving, colorful and sometimes painful spectacle.

More than a travelogue, this book will deal with the amazing change in the presidency since the fairly recent days when Teddy Roosevelt was assailed for violating the Constitution simply by going to the Panama Canal Zone. This is written in the belief that an American President must be a participating citizen of the world and not an absentee benefactor.

Francis Bacon said, "It is generally better to deal by speech than by letter." And Thomas Macaulay said, "A man who has never looked on Niagara has but a faint idea of a cataract."

So it is with the presidency and diplomacy. In the last forty years of this swiftly moving century, no man in the White House can be ignorant of the people and their voices, the sights, sounds and smells of the rest of the world and still conduct foreign affairs with anything like the understanding he so urgently needs.

M. S.

A President's Odyssey

CHAPTER 1 *"LONG LIVE THE KING OF AMERICA"*

A powerful Democratic Senator sat in his office, clinking the ice of his twilight highball and studying a late edition of the Washington *Daily News*. It was late 1959 and a columnist friend sat across the desk from the political leader skimming the Washington *Evening Star*.

"Look at that," the Senator said glumly. "And it'll be like that on every front page of the world this afternoon—Ike—Ike—Ike. How in hell are we expected to build up a Democratic candidate with this sort of thing blanketing the newspapers and television?"

"If you're irritated now, how do you think it will be just before the convention with Ike in Russia?" inquired the columnist.

But Democratic jitters turned out to be premature and needless, thanks to Nikita S. Khrushchev, who, in his rage over the U-2 plane incident, called off the Eisenhower visit to the Soviet Union.

On this same December afternoon in 1959, far across the American Continent from the Senate Office Building, a nine-year-old boy sat at his nicked, scarred desk in a rural Oregon schoolhouse, painstakingly putting down on rough, cream-colored paper a communication to the White House: "Dear President, You do good for Peace. Please come to our town."

In a severely plain office of the Kremlin, an aide placed before one of Khrushchev's assistants the latest dispatches from Tass, the Russian news agency, along with a memo saying that

1

American news agency accounts of Ike's visit to Kabul, Afghanistan, earlier that day varied sharply with the Soviet news service as to size and behavior of the crowds in the Afghan capital.

In Paris, London, Rio de Janeiro, Capetown and Casablanca, radio loudspeakers crackled with superlatives and excited descriptions of a distant scene that sounded in the telling like wild, almost uncontrolled jubilation.

Slowly cruising units of the American Sixth Fleet in the Mediterranean outside the harbor of Athens also followed the story by radio and piped the broadcasts into the mess areas so the men at lunch could hear and possibly learn. An officer in the wardroom of the carrier *Essex* said, "By God, that old flag is really flying today."

This effusion of comment, reaction and attention around the world stemmed from what was happening in the pungent Indian dusk on Kitchener Road leading twelve miles from the Palam Airport into the center of New Delhi.

At the moment, the President of the United States was clutching the shoulders of a husky Secret Service agent, James J. Rowley, seated before him in an open Cadillac convertible. Eisenhower rocked under the impact of large bunches of flowers hurled at him from the mighty press of people around the car. He held his right arm over his forehead to shield his eyes and mouth as he tried to stay on his feet in a vortex of screaming, wildly gesticulating Indians and their smothering floral offerings.

Behind the shield of his arm, Eisenhower looked out at a scene never before witnessed by an American chief executive, the mass adulation of India that almost killed with its kindness. Men, women and children, crushing against the cars of the President's motorcade in what approached mass hysteria, had poured into New Delhi for days by train and truck, in rough lorries and overloaded busses, by camel cart and thousands simply by foot.

They jammed Kitchener Road in numbers never seen before by a world leader under similar circumstances. True, Eisen-

hower was the first American President to visit Asia. True, the Indian government had encouraged and even facilitated the turnout. But also true, the people of India turned out in masses that no one foresaw.

Beside Eisenhower in the besieged automobile that moved only inches at a time sat a man with a rosebud on his shoulder, a man whose face throughout the world symbolized peace and gentleness, a modest white cotton cap over his deep brown eyes, India's Prime Minister Jawaharlal Nehru.

Nehru was worried. He nibbled at his upper lip and stroked his chin, hunched down in the wild melee of flower blossoms and warily eying the intense young men in turbans and shirt-sleeves leaning into the car to roar the Urdu welcome, *"Hind Eisenhower ki jai!"* (Hail Eisenhower.) The Prime Minister looked up apprehensively at the standing Eisenhower as the visitor reeled and ducked under the impact of the heavier bouquets and garlands.

Lean, hard Indian police, turbans askew and their starched khaki shirts and shorts beginning to wilt with sweat, shouted and swung at the crowd with *lathis,* a slender wooden stick much like the old swagger stick of the American Marines but longer and partly covered with leather. Much of the time, the only light on the turbulent scene came from the ceremonial lantern bearers from small villages whose ancient beacons wobbled and sometimes disappeared in the rolling waves of humanity.

The long procession was bound for Rashtrapati Bhavan, home of India's elderly President Rajendra Prasad and once the regal palace of British viceroys.

The police tried to keep the sea of shining, sweaty faces from engulfing Eisenhower and Nehru completely. The officers swung with their clubs first at the shins, then at the heads. When swinging threats failed to work, the police flailed at any body target available.

On the rear of the car bearing the two leaders, deadly serious American Secret Service men clung awkwardly to the bumpers and trunk area in such a manner that any exuberant Indian who tried to climb in with Eisenhower and Nehru had first to broach the American security barrier, thin as it was.

One of the agents was bleeding noticeably about the hands as he warded off the backswing of the police clubs flashing dangerously close to the President.

Indians crushed to the front of the crowd used what English they knew in calling out to Eisenhower. Dusk had turned to night, but some of the Indians proudly shouted "Good morning, Ike," and with all the smiling dignity possible under trying circumstances, Eisenhower replied, "And good morning to you, sir."

The President bent down toward Nehru to say, "I've never seen anything like this in my life," when a heavy bouquet arched over the car and dropped in a sticky clump on the back of the visitor's neck. Ike straightened up and smiled nervously.

The procession inched into Connaught Circus, a famous, central area of shops and restaurants and a large, circular park. A massive electric display sign glowed atop one of the higher buildings, but some of the gleaming, hot letters were obscured by Indians clinging precariously to the iron structure of the sign that rocked slowly under its load of humanity.

Motorcycle police ahead of Nehru's car tried vainly to bore a hole in the crowd, but the people spilled over the motorbikes and between the legs of the club-swinging police, who were forced back to a protective line up against the Cadillac. A police jeep lost in the mob beamed a loudspeaker into the jam while an officer pleaded with the crowd to avoid injury.

Fever-eyed men, their jet-black hair gleaming in sweeping movie floodlights at Connaught Circus, thrust their grinning faces as close to Eisenhower as possible to screech, "*Zindabad, zindabad.*"

Two cars away from the President, a veteran Indian journalist said, "They're wishing him long life. Some of them are saying, 'Long live the king of America.'"

As far as the eye could see, in front and behind, to either side

of the President's car stretched an undulating crush of human bodies buckling under pressures from the rear of the crowd. One thought of newsreel pictures of asphalt pavement in an earthquake.

Five young Hindus in turbans of green and orange and yellow locked arms and burrowed beneath the police to come up beside the President's car yelling, "Gude day Aye-zen-huer, New Yawk, New Yawk." The President bowed and replied, "New York."

An angry swarm of police regrouped, rammed through the crowd and descended on the five young men with clubs. The youths retreated, still chanting and laughing uproariously. One of them reached to his forehead where a club had landed, felt blood and whooped joyously, *"Zindabad."*

At this point, the Cadillac was mired tightly in the crowd beneath a cotton archway proclaiming in foot-high letters, "The Prince of Peace." An American official trapped in a car behind the President looked up at the banner and said, "Christ never drew a crowd like this."

Ten minutes, then fifteen minutes passed with no noticeable progress around the circular park. The crowd was becoming more volcanic and Nehru decided to act. He leaped to his feet beside Eisenhower and began to tongue-lash his people in Hindi. His voice was all but lost in the storm.

I was watching from about fifty feet away, literally imprisoned inside an ancient American-made car. It was stifling hot, but it was necessary to keep the windows closed to avoid torrents of marigolds. With the windows down, hysterical Indians reached inside to snatch half-smoked cigarettes, jacket buttons, scraps of notepaper, anything for a souvenir.

An Indian friend explained, "This is a religious experience in a way. Our word for it is *drashan*. I cannot translate it exactly, but it means generally spiritual betterment for having been in the presence of a great man."

"If I didn't know better," I told him, "I'd swear these people were half-drunk."

"One can become quite intoxicated just from the excitement

of contact with other humans," he said softly. "That is what is happening now."

Nehru suddenly disappeared from our vision. A security car blocked a clear view from our car and I tried leaning out the window, but had to retreat from the clutching, snatching people in the street. It was not until later that I learned why Nehru vanished. He had leaped from the car down into the crowd and sailed into the police for not doing their utmost.

One particular policeman seemed to have displeased him. Nehru tore the officer's *lathi* stick from his sweaty hands and shoved him angrily toward the jerking, pushing spectators.

Shouting shame and disapproval at the crowd, he took a few swings with the stick himself before tossing it back to the startled policeman, then plowed like a zealous halfback toward the police jeep with the loudspeaker, pulled himself up into the open vehicle and stormed at the crowd—they were behaving frightfully in front of visitors and they'd better fall back or get hurt.

The cars began to creep out of the circle and when I could see the President's convertible again, Nehru was back in the car and troops on horseback were rearing and prancing into the crowd to open a narrow traffic lane.

It took only a few minutes more to reach the red stone corridors leading into Rashtrapati Bhavan and the cars swept through the heavily guarded gates into a peaceful cobblestone courtyard. It had taken us two hours and ten minutes to come twelve miles from the airport. I ran over to the side of the President's car as he and Nehru alighted. The floor of the open convertible was more than a foot deep in orange-yellow blossoms.

"What did you think of that welcome, Mr. President?" I asked.

He turned, brushing flower petals from his dark jacket, and looked fleetingly at Nehru, who seemed much more weary than Eisenhower.

"You saw it." Eisenhower smiled. "You write it."

Between the car and the palace door, there was a narrow aisle

of brilliantly uniformed Indian men and women in electrically purple, orange and rose saris. The air was heavy with the odor of flowers, smoke from nearby cooking fires, spices used in outdoor kitchens and the dust stirred by millions of feet.

Beside the President an ancient Hindu priest came out of the darkness into a flickering rim of torchlight to chant a high-pitched hymn that began the traditional rite of *Arthi,* an old Hindu ceremony to banish evil spirits that might attend the arrival of a visitor. A slim maiden in a shimmering white sari and a vermilion dot gleaming from her forehead began a slow undulating dance before Eisenhower.

She held out a silver tray bearing five small candles and floating white blossoms as she swayed sinuously in the shadow of the President. I found myself standing next to a stalwart Sikh in a long gray coat who seemed so quietly self-assured (he wore no identifying insignia) that I assumed he was a ranking police official (he was).

"What is she doing?" I whispered.

"This is an old ceremony of welcome," he replied softly. "They're blessing the President and taking steps to see that the evil eye does not gaze upon him while he is a guest at Rashtrapati Bhavan."

The girl shifted her tray of soft light and delicate blossoms to one hip and with her free hand placed six garlands of vari-colored flowers over Eisenhower's bald head to which several marigold blossoms still clung. She kissed him gently on the cheek and slithered back behind the palace guard while Ike colored up as he must have done when he played spin-the-bottle back in Abilene.

It was well into the evening and, the ceremonies over, Nehru said his good-bys at the door. Prasad, an impressively big man with a luxuriant white mustache standing out from his choco-late-colored, kindly face, showed Eisenhower to his expansive apartment on the second floor of the palace and then departed for his own quarters in another wing, knowing that the President was in an advanced state of fatigue and ready for bed.

The chief executive disappeared quickly into his personal quarters with his valet, John Moaney, while other members of the close personal staff gathered in a large circular room designated as an office for Brigadier General Andrew J. Goodpaster, the White House staff secretary, and Mrs. Ann C. Whitman, the President's private secretary. Major John S. Eisenhower and his wife Barbara wandered in and Dr. Kevin McCann, the Ohio (Defiance) college president, Eisenhower biographer and speech writer, joined the group. Their excitement broke through their fatigue. They babbled to each other about never having seen anything like the trip in from the airport.

The other staff members outside the President's suite could not see how he could be anything but exhausted, a sixty-nine-year-old man who still had to watch himself because of a 1955 heart attack. The staff started to drift into another large room for a late supper. They assumed the chief executive had flopped right into bed, but they were standing by for any last instructions before he closed shop for the night.

Suddenly, the President burst out of his suite, as someone later described, "a bouncing bundle of grinning energy." It was Eisenhower freshly showered, freshly shaved, a Scotch and water in his hand and wearing, just for this few minutes with his staff, a crisply pressed dinner jacket which he had donned impulsively just for the elated hell of it.

He was talking a blue streak, ten feet tall emotionally, as he relived his two hours in the convertible with Nehru. Naturally no record was made of the conversation, but those who were there were flabbergasted at his zest.

As later reconstructed, the talk seemed to be mostly unintelligible, with everybody jabbering at once, "I never saw anything like it . . . and did you see Nehru, himself, get out of that car . . . did those people try to crawl in your car . . . Barbara was terrified? How about me?"

An eyewitness to the intimate scene in the palace said later, "He was just like those people down in Connaught Circus—carried away. I've never seen him quite as excited and my God —talk, talk, talk."

While the emotionally charged President sat down to supper with those closest to him, a group of Indian and American security officials stood in the courtyard below replaying the events of a few hours before.

"I knew we'd have a big turnout and I knew it would be a bit sticky around Connaught Circus, but we did not expect what we saw tonight," said Balbir Singh, the chief of Indian security. "When he speaks Sunday at Ramlila grounds, we'll simply have to bring in more men."

U. E. Baughman, chief of the U.S. Secret Service, listened intently, the golden lamps over the palace doorway flickering in the evening breeze. Standing nearby, we got the full musty aroma of Mother India, an eternally pregnant mother discharging thousands of new human beings into her jungles, mountains and plains with every tick of the clock.

"I thought I had seen crowds," Baughman said. "But this one—"

"Chief, was there ever any real danger tonight?"

Baughman's opposite number in the Indian government was chatting with someone else, but turned prudently silent when he overheard my question.

"All I can say," Baughman replied, "is thank heavens it was a friendly crowd."

Beside a fountain in the courtyard, a fountain where two ceramic cobras rose on a slender pedestal to spit soft streams of water into the pond below, two Americans sat slumped on a stone curbing.

These men, trying to gather their strength before going on to the next chore, were two veteran Secret Service agents, Deeter (Dick) Flohr and John Campion, who had struggled with crowds since the days of Franklin D. Roosevelt. They were the pair riding the rear bumper of the convertible bearing Eisenhower and Nehru.

Campion's hands were hanging down toward the cobblestones and he was attempting to keep blood from several small cuts away from his clothing. Flohr, normally the agent assigned to driving the President, had one hand pressed against his side.

He was breathing heavily, in obvious discomfort. I asked Campion about his cuts.

"Those police sticks, when the fellows took their backswing, and the flowers. Some of the larger bunches had sharp sticks or thorns in them."

"Did you hurt your back?" I asked Flohr.

I've known Flohr since the time of F.D.R. and he is such a strapping stoic that his appearance in the courtyard was alarming.

"Brother Smith," he said slowly, "you're looking at the tiredest man in the world. I don't know what I hurt. I just want to get to bed."

Later, the official Secret Service log on the painful procession contained only this entry of police understatement:

5:37 P.M.   The motorcade departed Palam airport for Rashtrapati Bhavan.
7:47 P.M.   The presidential motorcade arrived at Rashtrapati Bhavan.

In the second-floor dining room, the President continued to express his gratification and amazement. He thought he had seen a record crowd in London shortly after World War II when he made his famous Guild Hall speech, but New Delhi was unique, something that would be forever a base of comparison.

In downtown New Delhi at the cable headquarters and in radio studios, the story was sped to every spot on the globe capable of reception.

In our stories for United Press International, Stewart Hensley, our chief diplomatic correspondent in Washington and an old India hand, and I quoted police officials, Indian and American, and settled for a crowd estimate of more than one million. My theory is that to estimate a crowd at one million is merely a journalistic—or police—method of conveying a superlative, of saying it was the largest crowd anyone recalled having seen or

heard about. Once crowd estimates range to two million, they become rather hazardous because it is doubtful that any expert or group of experts can tell with any degree of accuracy whether a crowd strung out over twelve miles is one or two million.

Many of the men who made the New Delhi crowd estimates had seen vast crowds in various parts of the world, from Nazi Germany during the forced turnouts for Hitler, to the religiously inspired multitudes that communed with Mahatma Gandhi. I had not seen the crowds for Hitler and Gandhi, but one thing was certain in my mind: from the days of F.D.R.'s greatest throngs to the present, I'd never seen anything approaching New Delhi. The actual figures made little difference. Most of my colleagues agreed simply that it was The Big One.

Other potentates, presidents and generalissimos along Ike's line of travel read the stories from New Delhi and heard the frenzied broadcasts. They set to work immediately to be sure of optimum reception when the President visited their countries.

The entire trip of some 23,000 miles became known as "the Indian trip." From Teheran to Tunis, from Madrid to Morocco, "largest ever" became a stock phrase. This carried over, too, into Eisenhower's later trips to South America and the Far East.

Anti-Americanism obviously was present in most of the places he visited, but who could see it behind the parade flags or hear it over the roar of the crowds? Eisenhower adherents can maintain with some justification that the "Yankee Go Home" signs were flyspecks on a vast billboard of "We Like Ike."

"We Like Ike" and "We Like America" do not necessarily equate. It seems fair judgment, however, that as of December, 1959, Eisenhower was the world's best-known and most popular figure.

CHAPTER *2* *SUGARED FRUITS*
AND PERSIAN RUGS

The President's decision to tour the world, show the flag in far-off lands and preach the doctrine of peace through friendship was easier to reach than the solution of the many problems this decision created—problems of protocol, logistics and personal safety; detailed, minute-to-minute schedules to be worked out with foreign governments. Even in an era of instantaneous communications, these things take time. An American tourist in Rome can pick up a telephone and within minutes tell his wife in Utica, New York, that he plans to buy her a car, but it may take hours, even days, for the American Ambassador to transmit to the White House the guest list for a luncheon to be given for the President during his visit to Italy.

A President of the United States, even in the jet age, cannot order his bags packed and simply head for the Washington airport without staggering stacks of advance paper work, ground-laying advance trips by protocol and security experts and much, much diplomatic conversation with the host government about where and when the distinguished visitor will eat and sleep, to say nothing of talking business with his hosts.

A presidential itinerary outside the country must be carefully balanced. Not too much time can be spent in any one nation. Also, there is a practical limit on any trip as to duration and areas covered.

During his first four years in the White House, Eisenhower talked privately about the need for good-will travel. He was

willing to undertake far-ranging journeys provided they could be held to about two weeks. He did not mind staying in Denver or Newport during the summer for weeks at a time, even months, because his plane could whisk him back to Washington in a few hours if a pressing emergency developed.

More than the time factor, however, Eisenhower feared what might happen when he got to picking and choosing the countries to be visited. He felt for a long time, as an example, that he could not go to France without visiting Italy or Belgium on the same trip; that he could not go to West Germany without traveling on to Scandinavia.

He wondered about visiting Japan without going to other friendly spots in the Far East. He did not like the firmly established custom that sprang up after World War II, as far as Washington was concerned, whereby visiting heads of state were expected to remain in the host capital a minimum of three days and attend at least two state banquets.

This was fine for ceremonial monarchs who had prime ministers running their countries, but Eisenhower boggled at the thought of being forced to visit ten or twelve countries just to see one or two close friends, of having to consume tons of banquet food in the cause of friendship.

In fact, there seemed to be a period early in Eisenhower's second term when the myriad difficulties or unattractive aspects of international travel seemed to outweigh his feeling that these were trips of necessity.

At least one man in the State Department felt that most of the fearful pictures being drawn for Eisenhower were extreme. He was Wiley Buchanan, chief of the protocol division and a well-mannered, rich Republican with a somewhat unusual streak of practicality for a man in his teacup and champagne-glass world of diplomatic niceties.

At a Washington banquet one night, there was considerable table talk of a possible Eisenhower trip to Asia and the Far East. A Senator mentioned Eisenhower's objection: that he could not go to India without tagging bases all over Southeast

Asia and being gone for four or five weeks. Buchanan said this reasoning was not justified. He said he could put together an itinerary for Eisenhower to travel to any part of the world and still limit the journey to virtually any time period he selected. Buchanan maintained this involved nothing more than the President making clear early in the planning of such a venture that he could devote X number of days to a specific trip and no more.

Some of the men around Eisenhower did not share Buchanan's views at first. They asked, of another trip, "How can he spend three nights in France and get away with only an overnight stop in West Germany?"

Buchanan proved to be right. Once Eisenhower decided to travel, the time and places were not beyond solution and amicable settlement. Of course, the State Department and the White House were under heavy pressure to expand a tour once it was announced, but they found by setting the schedule firmly before making it public, they could placate the by-passed nations to an acceptable extent by saying that the President could not spare additional time from his constitutional duties as an operating head of government.

It may have been difficult for the people of Belgium or Scandinavia to understand in the summer of 1959 why Eisenhower, after winding up his official schedule in Bonn, London and Paris, flew back to Scotland for several days of golf.

A similar difficulty in understanding may have arisen in some of the Southeast Asian countries in 1960. They wanted to have Ike visit, but were told his schedule could not be enlarged. Then Eisenhower flew from Korea to Hawaii for a week of golf before returning to Washington.

Behind the scenes, the State Department coped with these outwardly embarrassing disparities by explaining gently that while Eisenhower was in good health for a man of his age and medical background, there had to be a limit on the rigors of travel to which he was subjected. The White House, itself, became less sensitive on this point and by the time Ike reached

Hawaii, Press Secretary James C. Hagerty was frank to say that the President was tired and needed the rest.

Along with Hagerty, one of the chief architects of Eisenhower's travel plans was a canny Irish-born lawyer, Thomas E. Stephens, appointments secretary to the chief executive. Stephens and other members of the staff hit on a plan for encasing a presidential trip within a rigid framework and not hurting too many international feelings. Their technique was to select or create arbitrary time barriers or cut-off points.

Despite the golf dates in Hawaii, the terminal point of the Far East trip was pinned to the situation in Congress, then rushing toward recess ahead of the 1960 nominating conventions.

The Indian trip presented a more knotty situation. Eisenhower had pondered plans for going to India at some length and not come up with anything satisfactory. He did not want the trip to become an all-Asia tour. The problem solved itself, however, when the Indians scheduled the World's Agricultural Fair for December in New Delhi and the Western foreign ministers worked out plans for their chiefs of state to hold their own Summit meeting in Paris the same month. This gave Eisenhower a terminus at either end of this particular trip. It also left the White House in a position to tell the nations clamoring to be included in the President's itinerary that he was sorry, but his time was limited by the two major international commitments.

In the case of his South American trip, Eisenhower and his advisers decided on Argentina and Chile as the geographic termini. In fact, in South America, the President made the point publicly that while he was unable to visit many of the countries that invited him, he had selected the two most distant from Washington. This, however, did little to salve the feelings of Venezuela and Peru, particularly when Ike finished off the trip in typical style by several days of golf in Puerto Rico.

Within rather impossible limits, Eisenhower tried to keep his trips abroad from being classed as formal state visits. This was to cut down on ceremonial formality and time involved, plus permitting a freer, more personal relationship with the host. One way of doing this was to send word along diplomatic channels that the President preferred no white tie or full evening dress affairs. Black tie or dinner jacket only. This may seem to be a trivial matter in a world trying to avoid destroying itself with thermonuclear weapons, and it may seem a bit foppish to Americans who entertain at the backyard broiler in sports shirts and slacks.

To the diplomat, however, evening clothes are work clothes. White tie denotes the fullest formality whereas the dinner jacket is something one wears for an evening of bridge.

It should be noted that coincident with Eisenhower's declassed clothing policy, Khrushchev was bustling around the world almost belligerently plain in his crudely tailored Soviet business suits with their factory-style lines. Even when Ike entertained for Khrushchev at a state dinner in Washington, the Russian, despite his host's resplendent white tie and tails, showed up in a dark blue business suit, conventional white shirt and four-in-hand tie.

A major complication in planning Eisenhower's trips arose from the fact that the First Lady had, of necessity, to be a stay-at-home. Mamie is *not* robust and the grueling pressures of fast-paced travel and split-second schedule, plus her aversion to flying, eventually killed any hope that she might go along.

It was decided that John's attractive young wife, Barbara, would be the ranking woman member of the party on the eleven-nation India tour. Although the White House pointed out carefully that Barbara was not in the group as a substitute for the First Lady and did not have to be ranked as such, the younger Mrs. Eisenhower turned out to be one of the stars of the trip and entered into the swing of the host capitals much more actively than her mother-in-law would have been able to do.

The long jet caravan to India—and caravan it was, with as many as seven transport planes and a dozen helicopters involved

at a time—was Barbara's first venture into personal diplomacy. The President would have enjoyed having her on all trips, but Barbara, a dedicated mother of four growing children, and her husband looked askance at her long absences from their home in Gettysburg, where they had moved to get the children away from the spotlight of the White House. She made only one other trip—to the Far East.

To help with the numerous social chores involved in dinners and receptions given by the President in South America and the Far East, Mamie sent along her social secretary, Mrs. Mary Jane McCaffree. Ann Whitman, Ike's personable personal secretary, traveled with him constantly but her duties with the main stream of presidential business were too many and complicated to allow her participation in much of the social planning. She also had to keep track of the gifts. Ike and his people had no idea of the treasure trove he would acquire and the President was openly embarrassed in some countries by receiving so much more than he gave. Cargo planes were hauling the stuff back to the United States weeks after a trip ended.

Being staunchly dedicated to courtesy and custom, Eisenhower laid in a store of silver-framed pictures of himself (heads of state would not think of meeting for the first time without exchanging pictures suitably inscribed), handsome and especially engraved bowls and vases of Steuben crystal (which Ike described in the Far East as "something we do very well in our country"), super-deluxe ballpoint pen desk sets, transistor radios, Polaroid cameras and other American-made luxury items. These were the stock presents, augmented occasionally by personalized gifts for leaders he had known previously.

On his first major swing, Ike livened up an intimate gathering of the British royal family at Balmoral Castle by presenting Queen Elizabeth with a noble badge of America—a super-everything-transistorized, all-wave, portable radio produced by one of America's leading manufacturers. The Queen and her husband, Prince Philip, were delighted and the President beamed proudly—until they tried to cut it on. No one in the President's party or the palace household could coax the first sound out of the magnificent, dispatch-case-sized marvel of the American electronics industry.

At the first opportunity, the President excused himself and had a few words with his son John. And a few minutes later, Captain E. P. Aurand, the President's naval aide who was back in London at Grosvenor House, froze at the ivory-colored White House telephone beside his bed with the glum inquiry, "You say it won't work at all?"

Within seconds Aurand was on the direct transatlantic telephone to the White House in Washington. It was early evening in the United States, but the honor of the President and American industry was at stake.

Aurand and the White House switchboard tracked down the staff member responsible for getting the radio.

"I know the factory is closed at night," Aurand barked into the telephone, "but get the manager's name, get him at home, get him down to that damned factory and let's have one of those radios on the way over here on the very next plane. I want that thing here by tomorrow because the boss has got to have it before he leaves for France. And this time, be sure the thing works before it leaves the factory."

With each country, the President was the recipient of more and more treasure—an Arabian stallion and two live gazelles in Tunisia, an elephant in India, plus an ornately carved teak chest about as long as a limousine and half as high, a tissue-delicate, four-foot tree of silver filigree work in Pakistan (which required a stout chest about the size of a piano to get it back to this country without damage), jeweled sabers in Morocco, jeweled shotguns in Spain.

In addition to these direct presentations by the host, there were countless native gowns and robes, saris and sheaths, smocks and blouses, necklaces and bracelets and bolts of precious fabric delivered to the President, John and Barbara or Mrs. Whitman for Mamie. There were ivory toys for the grandchil-

dren, illuminated tomes for the White House library, rare wines, cases of sugared fruits and nuts, fabulous Persian rugs, priceless fans, models of buildings executed in silver and gold.

All of these had to be accounted for and acknowledged when possible by individual notes of thanks from the chief executive. Ann Whitman's typewriter clattered late every night trying to stay current with the more important gifts, trying to keep a record of even the humble squares of native embroidery left on the embassy steps for the famous visitor.

Members of the Eisenhower staff will disagree for years to come as to who had the more arduous duties on the major foreign trips. The baggage handlers (Army sergeants from the White House garage) bowed to no one in claims to exhaustion as they unloaded the aerial caravan night after night, and loaded it again in the morning. With aircraft bomb scares running high back in the United States because of some demented travelers, the White House took extra pains with the luggage and would not allow it to be handled by hotel bellhops, or even palace porters.

For long hours, constant conversation and meeting complicated problems, however, Jim Hagerty had few, if any, equals. The press secretary had had enough experience on earlier trips to the Geneva Summit, to Big Three meetings in Bermuda and brief journeys to Mexico and Canada to know that once Ike decided to hit the big road, he would encounter press problems never before posed to the White House in such volume and complexity.

Hagerty, working with Stephens, the Secret Service and D. E. Long, veteran White House transportation officer, had to arrange transportation, working and living quarters, communications facilities and even medical care for the tremendous assembly of reporters and photographers who wanted to accompany the President.

There were some around the President who thought entirely too much attention was paid to the press arrangements; Hagerty, however, had powerful ammunition to use against this sort of incomplete thinking—what good was a good-will visit if it did not receive maximum public attention?

When Eisenhower gave the go-ahead for setting up a series of foreign trips, Hagerty knew that much of the territory to be covered would be seeing a free press in operation for the first time. A free press is not without its objectionable and annoying aspects—photographers fiercely battling up the steps of the Vatican for advantageous camera position, reporters completely free of the fear of state displeasure asking locally unheard-of, deeply probing questions of startled officials in such places as Madrid and Ankara. Hagerty felt firmly, however, that along with the President, the American press with its concomitant pictures and sound was pioneering new areas and letting in new light.

To be sure, many of Eisenhower's stops were so brief—five hours in Iran, less than that in Okinawa—that the reporters had little time for more than dispatching relatively sketchy accounts of the public reception and what the President said to the local parliament.

But Hagerty knew there were benefits in the presence of a large, traveling American press corps—benefits for Eisenhower, benefits for the United States and, hopefully, an influence toward greater freedom of the local press without seriously flouting local custom. He insisted in each country that local correspondents be given the same access to Eisenhower as the men from Washington.

In Madrid, the correspondent for the Spanish news agency was shocked to find himself riding with his American, British and French counterparts only two or three cars away from Eisenhower and Generalissimo Francisco Franco. This veteran Spanish reporter had never before been that close to Franco in public.

Journalists in Spain, Turkey, Iran and Tunisia watched apprehensively, wonderingly, as reporters from Washington in press room conversation were openly critical of something Eisen-

hower had said in a speech or spoke of him with rough familiarity as "old bullet head"; or as a bedraggled, equipment-laden photographer roared at a uniformed symbol of a police state, "Get your God-damned Tommy gun outta my stomach or I'll let you have it with my camera."

Ugly Americanism? The local reporters of most countries did not think so. It was the powerful process of free information in operation, grumbling like hell over any interference. Poor taste? At times. But nothing like the poor taste of an occasional (not many) American Embassy official who cursed a restaurant waiter in his native tongue or blabbed openly his critical opinion of local conditions, this done in English and on the insulting theory that the local residents were too stupid to understand.

Hagerty originally hoped for conditions to permit the President to hold free-swinging, Washington-style press conferences in many of the countries he visited in 1959-60. This, however, was just too much for most of the local cultures to take.

When Ike got to London, the British reporters clamored for a press conference, even to the point of staging daily shouting matches with Hagerty over the failure of Ike to meet with the journalists. The arguments ended rather abruptly, however, when some American reporters asked Peter Hope, Hagerty's opposite number from the British Foreign Office, for a press conference with Prime Minister Harold Macmillan. The Prime Minister does not engage in press conferences and under the circumstances it was better for Eisenhower to go along with Macmillan's custom.

In India, Eisenhower and Nehru were on such frequent public display and speaking so often that there wasn't much left to be said in a question-and-answer session. In other countries, quite aside from the touchy situation caused by the resident potentate's refusal to answer questions, Hagerty ran into other press conference roadblocks.

The process of journalistic accreditation in other countries frequently is a rather loose affair and Hagerty ran the risk of exposing Eisenhower to pamphleteers and causists along with the legitimate reporters. If Eisenhower had gone to Russia, however, he would have had several press conferences and attempted to field the pointed inquiries of Soviet newsmen in a less tempestuous manner than Khrushchev displayed when he was in the United States and France.

In many countries, Hagerty was the voice of the President when Ike was not before an audience himself. And Jim frequently was almost as lavishly displayed in the local newspapers, although he rarely went beyond extant knowledge or previously stated positions in coping with the deeper questions of foreign policy. This annoyed some of the local editors and correspondents and brought Jim something less than total approval in certain areas of American journalism. The British particularly pilloried Hagerty for knowing what the President had to eat, but little of what he had to say to Macmillan.

At times, Hagerty looked worse on public display in foreign capitals than he deserved. The local papers prior to Eisenhower's arrival, and often with the co-operation of the host government, built up the visit as a meeting in which the President would tackle a lengthy agenda of specific business problems with his host and, inferentially, not leave without supplying some specific solutions. To have to let the air out of these inspired balloons without offending the resident government took delicacy and luck, which on occasion seemed to elude Jim.

If Eisenhower had undertaken his good-will trips earlier in his White House tenure, the foreign service of the United States might have benefited immeasurably. Not so much the President, because he usually was too well insulated, but members of his staff ran into just enough malperformance on the part of embassy personnel to make them wish they had encountered it early enough to do something about it.

This is no blanket indictment of the foreign service. Most of the embassy personnel working with the traveling White House was a credit to the country, but there were some bad apples, ranging from officious fops who regarded Ike as a boob and the people under him as vassals to some pitiful types who had gone

so completely native that they had come to regard the United States as something gauche, uncultured and to be avoided except when forced back by home leave or dreadful reassignment.

At the time this book was written, Hagerty and others close to the President would not discuss this situation for publication. But I was there—in not many, but enough countries where the White House staff was ripped by real rage at the high-handed or sometimes simply stupid behavior of a depressingly high embassy official.

There was one deputy chief of mission who still may not know how close he came to being fired right on the spot for giving the White House an incredibly erroneous list of local cabinet officers and other ranking officials of the host government who were to receive personal letters of thanks from the President. What could be more offensive than having a foreign cabinet officer receive a warm note from a President—with his name misspelled and his title wrong? Yet this happened in a large and important country, the letters typed and signed and on the way to mailing before the *faux pas* was discovered, largely by chance and thankfully in time. The miscreant fought back under an unpretty cover of Martini-shaded bellicosity and somewhere in the State Department today it can be hoped that some record exists of this man's loutish inefficiency.

Most of this sort of trouble, however, seemed to originate with a second- or third-echelon man; an idiot trying to stay under the President's heels in the hope it might help him back home; an information officer trying to tell Hagerty how to run his business and committing Eisenhower to engagements never before discussed with the White House; an expatriate bragging about having successfully avoided going back to stateside supermarkets and frozen dinners.

There is another side, however, to the relationship of our embassies to presidential travel abroad. To repeat, most of these people seem to be dedicated Americans trying to represent their country fairly and effectively. But they're human beings and thus susceptible to the shock of having a President visit their faraway outposts. They live for weeks, from the ambassador on down to the doorman, in terror of these words, "We can't have anything go wrong." White House officials whip into town, plaster the place with directives and fly out again, leaving some lonely, uncommunicative Secret Service agents behind to see that the schedule is prepared according to plan and without hitches.

The ambassador is waked at night by secret cables saying all food for the President must be "purchased, prepared and served in the usual manner, yet under close supervision of competent authorities." In other words, the ambassador is told, "Don't make any fuss over his food, but if he gets poisoned, you're to blame."

Or a classified letter in the morning diplomatic pouch asks, "What time would this reception start and what time would it conclude? Is this a stag reception? How many people would be involved and how many people would the President have to shake hands with?"

Or the embassy information officer tries to mollify editors of the powerful local papers by saying, "I'm sure he'll have a press conference if it is at all possible and we're leaving some time in his schedule for it, but of course, we'll have to await word from Secretary Hagerty." Then to his horror he picks up the afternoon paper to read that Eisenhower definitely will hold a mass press conference. When the President comes to town Hagerty says no, there never have been any plans for a meeting with reporters because the schedule is so tight. And the local papers scream editorially about the "canceled" meeting and Hagerty goes gunning for the man who started the story in the first place.

CHAPTER 3 *SAFE JOURNEYING*

Working out the ceremonial and diplomatic details of Eisenhower's foreign travels was nettlesome and complicated, but there was a far graver area of planning—getting him there and back alive and uninjured.

Unfortunately for them, the men of the Secret Service under Eisenhower did not occupy the position of influence and control at the White House when it came to presidential travel that they exercised in previous administrations. Under Roosevelt and Truman, and due largely to World War II, the Secret Service was consulted from the very inception of a trip and the agents were in full control of advance planning, subject always to revisions ordered back at the White House. The field work, however, was solely the province of the protectors.

Under Eisenhower, however, policy changes within his staff led to a diffusion of Secret Service authority in travel planning, particularly in the preliminary work. Much of their work was taken over by nonpolice officials of the White House and the State Department. This may seem like hair-splitting attention to detail, but slow removal of the Secret Service from the policy area of planning Eisenhower trips abroad produced complications.

The Secret Service is charged by a law passed shortly after the assassination of President William McKinley with seeing to the personal safety of the President, his wife and their children. It was thought for years by many Americans, including some members of Congress, that the Secret Service held a veto power over movements of a President. This is a myth.

Only in a true and sudden emergency could the Secret Service arbitrarily take over and control the President's movements; for example, hustling him out of an unsafe building or removing him from a leaky ship. If a President wants to go to the North Pole, however, he can do it and the Secret Service will have to accommodate itself to his plans, keeping him as safe as possible under the circumstances.

When Eisenhower began to put together plans for good-will travel, the Secret Service came in on the planning only after the trips were outlined in considerable detail. The agents were given the task of working out security arrangements within an established itinerary and time schedule, and they had to dove-tail their arrangements with the armed services involved in transportation and with the State Department.

Thus, in a way, it was somewhat suddenly that the President's legally designated protectors found themselves up against the gravest security potential in their knowledge. Could he make it through the Middle East into Asia and back again without being shot at, poisoned or bombed? What about foreign nationals bound to be injured in the crush of civic receptions? Was it possible to get him from Point A to Point B in a given capital and still keep a tight schedule written by men who would not have to carry it out?

What about fire escapes and elevators in some of the palaces? What about politico-religious fanatics who might get their ticket punched for the Elysian Fields with one well-placed bomb?

After the President returned from West Germany, England and France, and there were early discussions of the forthcoming trip to Asia, a high school boy shook some of the august officials of the federal government by a simply stated proposition, a crystal-clear statement of danger.

Eddie Gilkey, a high school student in Compton, California, apparently was asked by his teacher to join his classmates in writing to the President about his travels that had filled their newspaper for days. Most of the letters from Compton were praise and hopeful rote. But not Eddie. He wrote Eisenhower:

I feel that your extensive traveling is of no value in strengthening the cause for peace; in fact, I believe it will be more of a detriment than a help. If something should happen to you on any of your foreign trips, the United States would have to be ready to do something about it. And this might lead to most unfortunate circumstances.

Obviously motivated by much more than a high school boy's letter, top security men of the government—the Secret Service, the Federal Bureau of Investigation, State Department security, the Central Intelligence Agency and collateral groups—had examined this point at some length. Vice President Nixon was warned in advance that his 1958 South American trip probably would encounter anti-American violence of serious proportions. He brushed this intelligence aside and went ahead with the trip, and the violence came off as predicted in Venezuela, with some Secret Service men getting bunged up in the rioting.

The various federal agencies studied the eleven-nation itinerary closely and while there were some doubts about South America and grave doubts about the Far East, the consensus was that Eisenhower could be properly protected.

There had to be certain basic attitudes at this end. One was to rely heavily on the thoroughness of foreign police methods. The Secret Service could concern itself only with the tight perimeter immediately around the President.

His plane would be guarded every minute it was on the ground overseas and guarded by Americans, White House Americans. Actually, these plane guards were Air Force Police under command of the White House air aide and the President's pilot, Colonel William G. Draper.

How to guard the plane in the air? This was best accomplished by having it in the best possible mechanical condition and followed by a duplicate plane, plus a supply ship loaded with replacement parts. During overwater travel, American naval vessels were spotted strategically beneath the flight path.

There seemed to be no fear that Russian forces would try

to harm the President as he traveled along the edge of the Soviet
Union on the Asian trip, but this did not apply to Communist
agents in other countries. Host governments were encouraged
to keep known agitators and anti-Western fanatics as far as possible from the President's vicinity.

Then there had to be hard-headed preparations made in each
foreign country to cope with emergency if it arose. In each city,
American agents, working in consultation with embassy officials,
lined up the best available hospital space, surgical facilities and
English-speaking doctors. The names of the doctors and nurses
were checked with local authorities, then a complete file on
emergency medical plans was sent back to the White House
well before departure.

If Eisenhower knew about some of the plans being made for
him "in case," he accepted the situation as the way of presidential life. He seemed to have thought little about his personal
safety, accepting the fact that those charged with his protection
could and would do their jobs.

They could and did, but at an effort Eisenhower still may not
know about.

Not all of the danger facing a President abroad is physical.
Some of it involves new wrinkles in cloak-and-dagger intelligence.

For example, when Eisenhower still expected to go to Russia,
his security men had to assume that many of the rooms he would
occupy from Moscow to Siberia would be wired for secret sound.
There was talk of a new type of Russian sound siphon—a simple
light bulb that could transmit audible conversation through
radiated heat waves to a receiver some distance away. The
Secret Service could not have changed all the light bulbs in
Russia, but they would have warned the President to watch
what he said in living quarters outside the American Embassy.

Khrushchev may have felt the same way when he visited
Camp David, Maryland, in September, 1959. His agents prowled
the Maryland hideaway, usually within view of American personnel, for days before the Soviet Premier arrived.

While he was at Camp David, Khrushchev was as safe as he would have been back at the Kremlin, possibly safer since any internal enemies would have had difficulty getting by the U.S. Marines at the gates of the camp and around its fences. The White House felt much the same way about Eisenhower's presence in the so-called police states. Military control was so tight in such places as Madrid, Ankara, Teheran and Tunis that a murder-minded malcontent would have had exceeding difficulty getting within miles of the visitor.

When the President was in Teheran, a man tried to step from a curbing to shout something at Ike as he drove by with the Shah of Iran. The man uttered one word, unintelligible, before a policeman swiftly clasped his hands over the fellow's mouth and two other officers hoisted him into the air, over the crowd and away. An American agent saw the incident and asked, "Suppose he was just trying to say 'Hi, Ike'?"

Part of a President's security when he is outside the country is communications. He and his staff must be able to pick up a telephone and get Washington within a matter of seconds. His encoded cables must be sent and received as promptly as they would be handled at 1600 Pennsylvania Avenue. Mail and state documents must be flown to him from Washington, sometimes daily, in complete security and without delay.

His communications away from the United States are handled by a special detail of the Army Signal Corps assigned to the White House and, in recent years, commanded by Lieutenant Colonel George J. McNally.

On March 14, 1960, when Eisenhower still expected to go to Russia on June 10, a memorandum was sent from the White House to the American Embassy in Moscow, listing the telephone, radio and teletype requirements for the President. These requirements were minimal and customary in world capitals previously visited by Eisenhower, but their scope was astounding to the officials of some countries where one is fortunate if able to complete a local telephone call and be understood. The White House system as outlined:

A. One full period voice circuit [a 24-hour direct telephone, in lay language] via cable from the United States Embassy in Moscow to Washington, D.C.

B. One full period, full duplex [24 hours and two-way] four-wire teletype circuit via cable from the United States Embassy in Moscow to Washington, D.C.

C. One full period voice circuit [24-hour direct telephone] from the United States Embassy in Moscow to each Soviet city visited by the President [including Kiev, Stalingrad and two towns in Siberia].

D. One full period single sideband, high frequency, 1,000 watt [short wave] radio circuit from the United States Embassy in Moscow to provide backup [in case of failure] for the full period voice circuit via cable from the . . . embassy in Moscow to Washington.

E. One full period single sideband, high frequency, 1,000 watt radio circuit from the United States Embassy in Moscow to each Soviet city visited by the President. This circuit to be used as a backup for the full period voice circuit from the U.S. Embassy, Moscow, to each Soviet city visited by the President while he is in each city. Equipment and operating personnel to be provided by this agency [the White House Army Signal Agency].

F. One full period radio network operating portable, short range equipment [walkie talkies] for convoy vehicles and personnel coordination. Equipment to be provided by this agency.

G. Extension telephones in each Soviet city which the President will visit. The exact number and location to be determined by the length of stay and the number in the President's party. [This would have meant the installation of from 50 to 100 telephones for members of the White House party and connected with a special White House switchboard in each city.]

H. One line from the U.S. Embassy, Moscow, to the local telephone exchange.

I. An additional switchboard within the United States Embassy at Moscow to terminate the circuits requested in this correspondence. This equipment can be supplied by this agency if technically compatible with existing Soviet Communications systems.

The Signal Corps working on plans for Moscow ran into one difficulty—there were no Russian telephone books available except in central libraries. By White House standards, the Russian requirements were normal. In fact, when Khrushchev visited the United States, a similar communications system was set up and made available to him, but the Russians made little use of it, apparently distrusting any telephone system that worked perfectly and particularly an American system. The Russians had their own theoretically secure phone line from inside Camp David, plus a special circuit for the Tass news agency.

It was impossible to have this direct telephone service from areas of Asia and the Middle East because telephone communications from India, Pakistan, Afghanistan and similarly distant nations are handled over radio circuits instead of cable and thus are subject to heavy, frequent atmospheric interference which makes around-the-clock circuits useless.

As a protection, however, the Navy stationed a powerful communications ship in the harbor at Karachi for the entire period Eisenhower was in the Middle East and radio transmission was possible through this vessel.

But the scope of Secret Service planning was even more detailed and encompassing than the electronic intricacies of the Signal Corps.

In setting up the five-day visit to India, five agents arrived in New Delhi nearly a month ahead of the President on what the Secret Service calls a "joint protective survey." Between November 16 and December 9, these agents had to check and report back to Washington on nineteen different locations where the President would sleep, eat, speak and inspect.

Before the President's plane touched down at the Palam Airport, the five agents—Mampel, Kelly, Knight, Roth and Meredith, all veterans at this sort of thing—had to co-ordinate their security arrangements with eight branches of the Indian government and five units of the American government in addition to the White House and its subdivisions.

Their field report on Rashtrapati Bhavan, where Eisenhower

and his immediate staff lived, included such nuggets as "The basement houses the electrical kitchen, the silver and gold stores, the ice factory, the cold storage, the cinema, the wine cellar—no more in use, the soda water factory, and the laundry, carpentry shops, etc."

They also reported that the estate covered 330 acres, the house itself 5 acres; 500 yards of covered carriageways, 1½ miles of halls, 340 rooms, 227 columns, 35 loggias, 37 fountains "including the fountains on the roof," and 10 elevators.

Arrangements were made for the Signal Corps to set up their switchboard in the west wing of the Ashoka Hotel, some distance from the palace. There was one leased long-distance telephone circuit from New Delhi to Paris, where calls could be relayed to Washington, but the circuit was so poor that calls were understandable only during two or three evening hours. The code machine was set up in a guarded area on the second floor of the embassy chancery.

It seemed to the Indians like many more, but only twenty-five Secret Service men were used on the Indian trip, even after Eisenhower arrived and was moving around extensively in the New Delhi area.

The Secret Service had decided long before Eisenhower went to India that when a President dined outside the White House, it was considerably safer to have him eat standard fare with nothing prepared especially. Special food preparations call attention to the recipient, so in India and in other foreign countries, the agents requested that the President be served right along with his host and other members of the party.

The advance agents in New Delhi along with Indian security agents checked all kitchen personnel at the palace and methods of food handling before Eisenhower arrived. The Americans asked only one exception for the President—his drinking water. He drinks the same American mineral water even in the White House and cases of it followed him around the world. This requires tact on the part of the agent, whose job it is to see that a

bottle of the special water always is available for service at a foreign banquet table, and even on the rostrum of a foreign parliament.

Preparing food for the President's plane while it is in foreign territory requires advance planning. In India, meals for Air Force One, as the jet transport assigned to Eisenhower was known, were prepared at the Imperial Hotel under the supervision of Pan American World Airways. In this way, no one in the kitchen could possibly know which portion was destined for consumption by Eisenhower. When the food was packed in big metal warmers, a Secret Service agent who had been waiting unobtrusively in the wings emerged to accompany the meals to the waiting aircraft.

The Secret Service also saw to it that the electrical wiring in all buildings where Eisenhower was involved checked out for fire safety shortly before his arrival. This applied to American embassies as well as buildings of the host government. In Brazil, for example, every room of the embassy from basement to attic was searched by Secret Service agents minutes before the President entered.

The over-all security force for the President's visit to Rio de Janeiro included 27 Secret Service agents, 4 U.S. Marines from the embassy, 2 State Department security men, 2,500 members of the Brazilian armed forces, 800 federal district police and 150 palace guards. One agent was assigned full time to examining gifts for the President as they arrived, using a portable fluoroscope on some of the packages.

Much of the planning and protection is not so romantic as peering into mysterious packages with a suitcase X-ray. Witness the Secret Service report on the President's brief visit to a luncheon at São Paulo, Brazil, in the modernistic Conjuncto Nacional Building:

From the presidential limousine directly ahead through entrance passageways and upon reaching the center lobby, bearing slightly to his right to elevators (210 feet); enters the center elevator and ascends to the second floor; turns right and walks eighty (80) feet and enters Fasano's Winter Garden Restaurant; upon entering turns right and ascends a circular stairway, carpeted, consisting of two (2) flights of stairs of 16 and 15 steps; walks straight ahead fifteen (15) feet and enters the main entrance to the banquet hall; turns right and walks about twenty (20) feet to the center aisle; turns left and walks sixty-five (65) feet around the head table to seat (470 feet—estimated travel time, 10 minutes).

In the same building, the elevators were checked and placed under police control until Eisenhower had arrived and left the restaurant; also, each fire extinguisher was located, identified, tested and marked on a chart.

It was in São Paulo that Secret Service protective research, conducted through the Brazilian government and possibly with some leads from the United States, turned up the fact that two known members of the Communist party who also were identified as "members of the confederation of Cuban workers," one of them having lost both hands in a bomb accident, and believed to have grievances against the United States, had shown up in São Paulo. The two Cubans were placed under secret Brazilian surveillance and local authorities were prepared to arrest them at any time. As far as known, it was not necessary to take these men into custody while Eisenhower was in Brazil.

In São Paulo, the security around the President, in addition to the Secret Service men, included 1,000 uniformed police (more than in Rio de Janeiro), 400 plain-clothes detectives, 700 military police and 3,000 troops on the auto route between the airport and town.

During the South American trip, the President switched from jet plane for part of the journey to his old prop-powered *Columbine III*, a Super-Constellation. At Santiago, Chile, there was only one surface fuel tank at the airport for the type of high-octane gasoline used by the *Columbine*.

Therefore, the Secret Service and the Air Force, not liking the idea of fueling the President's aircraft from the single, easy-to-spot source of supply, hit on this protective system. A regularly scheduled commercial airliner was fueled in the normal course of field operations just ahead of the *Columbine;* then the President's ship was gassed; a member of his crew with a special portable inspection kit took a gas sample to test it for purity.

An advance report on this check-and-recheck system then said unemotionally: "If nothing happens to the commercial flight and if Major Foss finds no impurities in the gasoline, then the assumption will be that the gasoline is safe and of a quality acceptable for the use of *Columbine III.*"

The Eisenhower administration also was responsible for employment of another new security device—the helicopter. Whirlybirds by the dozen were used on each foreign trip, manned always by the same crews drawn from the armed services and stationed in Washington as a regular pool for the White House under the supervision of Aurand, the naval aide.

The helicopter reserved for the President was equipped with automatically inflatable pontoons packed around the landing wheels to slow down the sinking of the ship and provide some rescue surface if the plane was forced to land in water.

In daylight hours, American helicopters also hovered frequently not far from the route of a presidential auto procession. Aurand's men had rigged a special harness for the President at the end of a long cable. If he had encountered severe difficulty in a crowd, the 'copter could have hovered over the President's car, lowered the harness and hauled him up to safety. This might have saved the President from an uncomfortable situation, but what it would have done to relations between the United States and the host country is a bit dizzying to contemplate.

Possibly the closest Eisenhower came to use of his sky-hook was in Korea, where a wildly receptive crowd overran police and halted the President's car in front of the Seoul railroad station. The helicopter was waiting overhead, but instead of resorting to car-to-sky hopping, the White House motorcade turned from the prescribed procession route and chased up back alleys to the sanctuary of the American Embassy residence. And again, this was a friendly crowd.

CHAPTER 4 *"IKE, WE TRUST YOU"*

What really triggered Eisenhower into personal diplomatic action during the summer of 1959 was the development of a high degree of sensitivity in the West toward his announced exchange of visits with Khrushchev.

In Bonn and Paris, the idea smacked too much of unilateral negotiations. In London, Prime Minister Harold Macmillan was facing a general election in the autumn. He had advocated an early Summit and plans for one were not immediately forthcoming.

Also, there were widespread fears in Europe of West German ambitions. The British were keenly interested in a permanent ban on nuclear tests before France joined the select group of nuclear nations by firing her first tests. In Paris, President Charles de Gaulle was coping with a nasty Algerian crisis and causing trouble by pulling French naval units out of the NATO Mediterranean fleet, refusing to accept NATO stockpiles of atomic weapons and medium-range missiles and asking some of the NATO air units to cease using French bases.

Macmillan was stressing the need for a better timetable for East-West negotiations, a subject on which Eisenhower had some fixed ideas himself. The President wanted to exchange visits with Khrushchev before going to the Summit. After the talks with Khrushchev, he wanted a Western Summit, then the big Summit.

At the same time, there was mounting trouble in Asia. Nehru was taking a firmer attitude toward Red China and this needed encouragement from the West. Chancellor Konrad Adenauer was deeply concerned about Berlin and East Germany and feared that Eisenhower-Khrushchev talks might involve some new plan for solution of the off-and-on Berlin crisis without West Germany being represented in the talks.

Russia wore a relatively kind face during this period as a prelude to Khrushchev's trip to the United States, but Eisenhower could see behind the scenes that the Soviets were using every possible break to exploit even the smallest crack in the Western alliance. An exploitable Western split had long been Russia's hope.

Eisenhower came to the conclusion that as preparation for his Khrushchev talks he would have to do everything possible to ease European fears. What was needed was a series of pep talks and after determining the need, Eisenhower assigned himself to the task. His relatively new Secretary of State, Christian A. Herter, was a man of earnest competence, but he lacked the drive of the late John Foster Dulles and he was scarcely known to the public in many foreign countries. The President decided to leave for Europe in the latter part of August, taking Herter with him to discuss specifics with his counterparts, but leaving Eisenhower reasonably free to concentrate on a needed job of public relations.

Before the timetables were drawn, however, the White House ran into difficulty. The President understood that Adenauer would be visiting London in late August and tried to set up a meeting there with the German Chancellor, then eighty-three years old. True, Adenauer did have plans for going to London but not in late August. And he also wanted to meet Eisenhower on German soil, not in England. This portion of the program had to be changed as delicately and quickly as possible.

Settling on an itinerary, the President, shortly before taking off for Bonn, London and Paris, tried to make it plain that he was not going abroad to negotiate treaties, nor would he be a party to any decision involving a third nation during his talks with the Soviet leader.

The purposes he outlined for making the trip were so lofty that some of his critics inclined to poke fun at the venture and there were questions asked at the White House and at No. 10 Downing Street about whether he planned to take his golf clubs. The trip, however, drew a much more serious reception in Europe, where tension was greatest.

Before leaving Washington, Eisenhower talked of his trip at a press conference and among his purposes he listed these points:

"To pledge once again in the several capitals I shall visit, America's devotion to peace with honor and justice; to support Western unity in opposing, by force if necessary, any aggression; and to preserve the defensive strength required for our common security.

"To suggest to each of the responsible officials whom I shall meet that we, together, re-state our readiness to negotiate realistically with the Soviets on any reasonable and mutually enforceable plan for general or special disarmament.

"To make a real beginning towards solving the problems of a divided Germany; and help in reducing, otherwise, tensions in the world."

A reporter reminded him former President Truman had said in a syndicated article that he thought Ike's trip to Russia might damage the prestige of the presidency. The President bristled at this, saying he was tired of people worrying about the prestige of his job when all mankind was at stake.

"What we are talking about now," he said, "is finding some little bridge, some little avenue yet unexplored, through which we can possibly move to a better situation."

Europe, it seemed to many of us when we got there, was tired of tension, weary of bickering, fed up with wondering when and where the next Soviet-created crisis would erupt. The Europeans wanted someone to cheer, and moreover they wanted assurance that somehow everything would work out. Eisenhower could not have received a friendlier build-up abroad, particularly in the British press.

"There is an obvious tendency, more perhaps in France and Germany than here, to fear that President Eisenhower is going to sell us all out when he meets Mr. Khrushchev," wrote Sir William Hayter, former British Ambassador to Moscow, in the London *Observer*. "It is not very sensible to feel like this. To begin with, any such action would be highly dishonorable. President Eisenhower has his critics, but no one has ever suggested that he is anything but an honorable man."

Eisenhower's stated desire for a greater show of Western unity in strengthening NATO was received somewhat differently than his over-all goals. France was suspicious. The British thought Ike might have a stormy time with De Gaulle.

In all three countries, the officials were somewhat overwhelmed by the Hagerty-Stephens advance party. American efficiency and briskness did not sit too well. The British particularly were disturbed by the presence of Secret Service agents, whom most of the London papers insisted on calling either F.B.I. or G-men. One newspaper insisted that the agents were "dressed identically," and there was some expression of public horror at the thought of "Hagerty's hustlers," as the agents were christened in London, invading the Queen's well-ordered security at Balmoral. There were cartoons of the agents dressed in tartans and kilts and carrying submachine guns. The French did not like Hagerty's insistence that a certain number of reporters and photographers should accompany Eisenhower and De Gaulle through the streets of Paris.

The London *Observer* said of Hagerty:

> The correspondents who meet Hagerty in Europe will not see him at his best. He is no analyst, but a "hard news" man. His philosophy of practical politics is "they slap us; we slap them." He is uneasy in foreign affairs and devotes himself to selling the President's performance rather than to the issues and their implications. But even when he is uneasy, competing with the smooth liquefaction and intelligently directed asides of the Foreign Office spokesmen, his authority, his single-mindedness, his bristling, barbed personality, still dominate. He has brought

the cultivation of the relationship between the President and the mass media to a fine Machiavellian art. Whether such an art is wholly desirable is quite another question.

There was little of this sentiment in Bonn. Hagerty himself said later that at no other point on an overseas trip did he receive such efficient co-operation and such quick perception of his problems, which involved not only the best possible presentation of the President, but the care and confidence of his traveling press party of about seventy. The Europeans insisted that all of these were White House correspondents. Less than half could be classified as reporters or photographers regularly assigned to the White House. The others came from a number of American cities and several foreign countries, too.

The President used the military version of a Boeing 707 jet transport for the trip, one of three assigned to the Military Air Transport Service for use by ranking government officials. It was the same plane Vice President Nixon used on his earlier trip to Russia.

Aside from his own staff, the principal policy-level officials flying with Eisenhower were Herter; Thomas S. Gates, Jr., then the Deputy Defense Secretary; Livingston T. Merchant, Deputy Undersecretary of State, and John N. Irwin, II, Assistant Secretary of Defense for International Security Affairs.

Eisenhower flew from Andrews Air Force Base outside Washington before dawn on Wednesday, August 26, arriving, after a brief refueling stop in Newfoundland, in the late afternoon of the same day at Wahn Airport, outside Bonn.

The bright orange safety paint on her nose and tail structure standing out in the summer sky, the powerful 707 roared over the field in a gray haze draping the low, wooded hills around the airfield. Adenauer had not reached the field and Colonel Draper, at the controls of Air Force One, made a second pass at the strip in order to time his landing perfectly.

When Eisenhower stepped from his silvery speed plane onto the soil of the nation whose destruction he had directed less than fifteen years before, a pattern was set; a pattern of effusive reception, of warmth and of what had all the evidence of affection; a pattern that recurred in varying degree everywhere he visited.

The Germans were amazed at the President's healthy appearance. They had expected much worse. Eisenhower struck a jaunty figure as he came down the landing ramp nimbly to greet the eighty-three-year-old Chancellor, whose seamed face resembled in many ways the countenance of a revered Indian tribal chief who had seen many hard winters in the American West.

The general public was not admitted to the airport, but one could see just outside the gates a crush of humanity bristling with American flags.

While the President and the Chancellor greeted each other at the bottom of the ramp, a field battery banged out a twenty-one-gun salute and a mixed honor guard of Federal Republic armed forces froze at attention. Ike met with the German Cabinet, bowing as he walked down the reception line. He was pink-cheeked and apparently no worse for his flight of over nine hours.

Mounting a small, red-carpeted speaking stand, Eisenhower was quick to offer reassurance of his high esteem of the aged Chancellor.

"In my country," Eisenhower said, "the name of Adenauer has come to symbolize the determination of the German people to remain strong and free. In the implementation of that determination, the American people stand by your side."

The cheers from the largely official audience seemed almost proper, but nothing explosive.

A motorcade of gleaming new cars wheeled slowly onto the field. The Germans had suffered some embarrassment about two weeks earlier when it became known that the West German government had no open car which would seat three comfortably in the rear seat (Adenauer, an interpreter and Eisenhower). The manufacturers of the Mercedes came to the rescue,

however, with a custom-built model complete with handrail for Eisenhower to clasp while standing during the procession.

As the procession started from the field, a crowd of about a hundred persons sped through the police lines and raced toward the wings of the President's plane. Previously warned German guards quickly cut on fire hoses and doused the sight-seers, who turned and fled.

Outside the airport gates, the cars moved through walls of cheering Germans. Eisenhower seemed almost surprised and pulled himself to his feet to answer the loud greeting.

The black Mercedes was surrounded by an escort of motor-cycle police in shining white leather coats, but at times the crush of the crowd and the narrow highway made traffic difficult. Families had come from as far away as Frankfurt and made the day an occasion for picnics beside the road. Hampers of sausage and beer scattered underfoot as the noise of the motorcade heralded the approach of one of the more curious heroes of German history, the man who had presided at the German surrender after history's most terrible war.

In the village of Sieburg, a banner, "We Like Ike and Konny," stretched across the highway. There were hundreds of "We Like Ike" signs, some printed, some hand-painted.

Entering Bonn over the Rhine bridge and onto a street called "Berlin Freedom," the President passed under another large sign, "It is not too late, open the [Brandenburg] gate." Near the weathered university buildings, a group of young socialists held up a sign apparently reflecting fears that Adenauer might try to talk Eisenhower out of meeting Khrushchev. "Ike, go on—don't let him slow you down," it said.

It was dark when the procession reached the American Embassy residence at the suburb of Bad Godesberg. The narrow street was choked with people and the cars could move only inches at a time. On a tree-lined sidewalk across the street, a chorus of German children sang in admirable schoolroom English, or tried to, "The Battle Hymn of the Republic." A gowned choir also attempted to sing, but the push of the crowd

was too much and their wine-velvet vestments were pulled askew
as the police shoved vainly to clear a path for the motorcade.

Eisenhower alighted and Adenauer saw him to the front
walk of the residence. In the movie floodlights, Ike's face was
cherry-red and beaming with excitement as he threw his arms
into the air in a closing gesture of thanks.

Police on horseback were brought in to clear the street and
as the crowd ducked for safety from the sharp hooves of the
animals, a disturbed figure could be seen in the background, a
tall man trying to maintain his footing in the shifting shoals of
excited spectators. It was Christian Herter, deposited some distance from the residence door, trying to make his way through
the crowd on crutches.

In the Bundespresseamt Office down in the government section of the city, the best crowd estimate for the evening seemed
to be in the neighborhood of 250,000, more than twice the
population of Bonn. What was more interesting than the size
of the crowd was its attitude. Eisenhower could not have been
received more warmly or enthusiastically in his own home town
of Abilene. In fact, Abilene has yet to show the enthusiasm for
Ike that Bonn demonstrated.

In the latticed, terrace dining room of the Bad Godesberg
hotel that night, journalists from all over the world sat with
members of the American and German staffs, going over the
afternoon. One of Adenauer's aides said, "You can search until
doomsday for explanations, but I think the reception was
summed up in one sign over the street right after we entered
Bonn."

Most of us remembered. The sign said, "Ike, We Trust You."

After spending the night at the residence of Ambassador
David Bruce, the President drove into Bonn the next morning
at eight o'clock to call at Palais Hammerschmidt, the residence
of President Heuss, ceremonial head of the German government; then to an imposing residence nearby, Adenauer's Palais
Schaumburg, for the business of the day.

The President, the Chancellor and their aides were together

during the day for about six hours and the meeting produced a mild sort of communiqué into which the Germans could read a variety of encouragements, but which in essence did not change the international picture largely because it was not intended as that type of document. What was more interesting to most Germans was that Eisenhower at midday interrupted his conferences of state to hold a press conference, a meeting of about three hundred reporters in a large hall of the Foreign Ministry.

The conference was short of a howling success. American reporters dominated the conference from the start and the Germans were hesitant to jump into this new form of communication between head of state and the public.

The German newsmen were intensely interested, quite naturally, in their own problems and how these might be affected by the Eisenhower-Khrushchev talks.

"I, myself, am not conducting negotiations for anybody else with Mr. Khrushchev," Eisenhower told the conference in syntax that frequently caused the Germans to check notes with their American opposite numbers. "I am trying to explore his mind to see whether there is any kind of proposal or suggestion that he can give that would make him a real leader in the search for peace. If we could do that, it will be a tremendous achievement in itself. Therefore specific plans are not something that I'm particularly interested in as far as those conversations are concerned."

At one point in the conference, the President, a bit awkward about appearing on a stage, peering down at the reporters and being unable frequently to hear or understand the questions from the Germans, said jocularly that the Americans had asked enough questions, that he could see and talk with them any time; he wanted to have some inquiries from his German friends.

But by the time the Germans thawed and began to ask about something other than how Ike liked West Germany, the President's time was running short. Also, Hagerty made a mistake in a foreign country, trying to run the conference on White House rules which specify that no one leaves the room or dispatches news stories until the conference has ended. Hagerty did not know it at the time, but the Germans forgot to disconnect a loudspeaker in the hall outside and about half the conference was out on the news wires of the world before someone discovered the error. And inside the room, there were reporters who had brought in short-wave radio senders under their coats.

After the conference, the leaders had lunch and resumed their talks. Each time Eisenhower drove through the streets of Bonn during the day, the curbs were jammed with cheering Germans. Seldom had the White House travel party seen such sustained interest throughout an entire day. Some spectators stood before the embassy residence all during the night.

Soon it was time to continue on to London. Before the President and his host flew by American helicopter to the airport, they issued a soft communiqué which said in part, "The mutual co-operation of both their countries within the Atlantic alliance, which alliance is of the utmost importance to world peace, will . . . continue to be one of the pillars of the foreign policies of the two countries."

Soft words or not, newspapers at home and in Europe called the Bonn visit a personal triumph. Adenauer, at least, was measurably happier after having heard Eisenhower talk persuasively about his hopes for Berlin, for disarmament, for a generally more relaxed world; all as possible results of his forthcoming talks with Khrushchev.

In Bonn, as it was bound to happen later on in a number of world capitals, Eisenhower's personality—the British and the Germans differed over whether he was a father or an uncle image—overshadowed the world problems which were so pressing as to cause the visit in the first place.

Whether Eisenhower transacted a scrap of enduring business, the West Germans were highly honored to have him in Bonn and, justifiedly or not, many of them felt that because of his presence and his outward interest in their welfare, the Com-

munist shadow over Berlin was not quite so dark as it had seemed a few weeks earlier.

As Air Force One painted fleecy jet contrails in the sky speeding Eisenhower to London and a still greater personal triumph, he sent a radio message back to Adenauer saying, "When . . . I look back on the last 24 hours, I believe we have attained much."

It certainly looked that way then, but this view could not have foreseen that an American U-2 would fall in Russia, bringing the cold war to the most frigid point since the days of the Berlin blockade. In hindsight, it can only be said that the trip to Bonn was better made than not. Eisenhower lost nothing by it, even in the light of later developments with Russia. At the time, it was a most hopeful beginning.

CHAPTER 5   *"JUST FOLKS" IN BRITAIN*

It is still difficult to realize that the British behaved very much like American bobby-soxers over Eisenhower. The staid English unstiffened their upper lips. They raced from their pubs to slosh ale in the air and shout "Good ole Ike" when he passed. Their newspapers hailed him as "Conqueror Ike" and their commentators on the telly described him not as a well-preserved old gent with a magnetic smile, but as a handsome, broad-shouldered, powerful leader of the free world.

His visit to England had everything—monster crowds in Piccadilly, a visit to Balmoral where the pregnant Queen Elizabeth came to her front gate to meet him, a weekend at Chequers with the Prime Minister, an astonishing Ike-and-Mac telecast from 10 Downing Street, Churchill, Montgomery and roast beef with Yorkshire pudding in Winfield House.

There was Sunday church in the countryside of Buckinghamshire, where the penny press of London reported breathlessly that Ike dropped "a big bundle of DOLLAR BILLS" in the collection plate; there was a quiet visit to Oxford in a dove-gray Rolls-Royce; a thirty-minute visit to the American Chapel at St. Paul's; and, of course, a certain amount of diplomacy.

This was a presidential personal appearance tour at its peak. Eisenhower had been well received in London before, but nothing like August, 1959. And little of it was lost on the French, preparing to welcome him in Paris a few days later. They got the message and went to work on making their show even better.

Macmillan well understood that Eisenhower had no intention of attempting to deal with Khrushchev in the name of the Western allies as a whole; thus the tinge of suspicion that preceded the President's arrival in Bonn and Paris was not present in London.

Macmillan, facing an election, did want to get on with a Summit, possibly before the elections, but there seemed to be increasing doubt as to whether this would be possible. A material move toward the Summit would suffice. There were other matters, however, pending between the President and the Prime Minister, not as to decision but certainly warranting across-the-table conversation, which on occasion can promote speedier understanding of policies and positions than the exchange of notes through normal diplomatic channels.

Macmillan did not need to hear it from Eisenhower, but London was a strategic spot from which the President could reiterate the dedication of the United States to the North Atlantic Treaty, and, as Eisenhower put it: "to say again to every free nation with which our country is associated in bilateral or multilateral treaties that we seek to be a loyal partner in our common enterprise, which is the advancement of freedom and human standards and the furthering of a just and lasting peace."

These things had been said many times over in Washington, in press conferences and speeches, but from the platform of Europe Eisenhower's words at the moment seemed new; they commanded attention they never would have received if uttered against the familiar scenery of Washington. This, incidentally, is a point future Presidents would be wise to mark: a speech, a theory, a policy stated and restated many times at home takes on a new sense of urgency and importance when put forth in a new and dramatic setting.

There was no specific target of anti-Americanism in Great Britain. To be sure, many Englishmen felt much more keenly than many of their American cousins the need for reducing the possibility of nuclear war. Many Britons were apprehensive about the presence of nuclear weapons on their soil. After all, they were much closer to the threat than the people of the United States. There was not, however, the intensity of feeling against this country that showed like angry sores in other parts of the world.

Thus viewed from a number of aspects, the President's trip to the United Kingdom was more than a lavish gesture of good will. It was revisiting the scenes of World War II triumph, the selection of an advantageous forum, an opportunity for man-to-man discussion of new problems cropping up to harass the West (the fighting in Laos; trouble in India; the French and NATO), and if in the course of the meetings Macmillan's domestic political fortunes benefited, so much the better from Ike's standpoint. This was palsmanship.

It was said in some London circles that Eisenhower on his arrival attracted a crowd larger than the multitudes on the streets for the Queen's coronation. Scotland Yard men and journalists who thought this was true expressed their thoughts only to intimates because to have this sort of thing in print would have been a discourtesy to Her Majesty. And lest even this brief reference offend any stout son of the Commonwealth, it should be pointed out that London gave Eisenhower a reception never matched in size and vocal expression in his own country.

In the late afternoon of Thursday, August 27, 1959, after a brief flight from Bonn, Eisenhower landed at the London Airport, where Macmillan, a graying man whose frequently sad face was relieved by flecks of humor in his shrewdly intelligent eyes, waited in a nest of Foreign Office officialdom, furiously intent military officers, a lord in waiting representing the Queen and ranking Americans led by Ambassador John H. (Jock) Whitney.

After standing quietly in the pale lemon sunshine of a British summer evening while the proper salutes were rendered, the two old friends faced a battery of microphones and cameras to exchange greetings. Normally these airport affairs have about as much feeling as the opening of a new bank, but there was some

thing different on this afternoon. For one thing, Macmillan and Eisenhower looked at each other as they spoke. They had their notes, but the prepared sentences were not needed.

"The programs which face our two countries, together with our allies, are difficult and complex," Macmillan said. "Your initiative towards their solution is a source of immense satisfaction to us all in Britain. . . . We feel them all the more because you, sir, are a President whose name was a household word to all of us, even before you were elected to your high office."

Eisenhower seemed to mean it when he spoke of his "true enjoyment at being once more back again in this land that I have learned so much to love.

"Let me say," he continued, "I did not have to come here to assure you or the British people that the American people stand with them, strongly, firmly and determinedly, in the defense of freedom, liberty and the dignity of man. You people know that we feel that way."

Then they were off to the center of London. In the suburbs the spectators were relatively restrained and thinly spread, but the crowd developed enormous proportions as Eisenhower and Macmillan proceeded behind a motorcycle escort that had rehearsed for days on a secluded race track.

Standing in the rear of the Rolls while Macmillan remained seated, Eisenhower literally shone with pleasure as he bowed and waved. People pointed excitedly to the "USA 1" plate on the front of the Rolls, the silken American and British flags whipping in the wind from the gleaming front grille. A uniformed civilian driver and a somber Scotland Yard man rode in the front seat, disappointing some of the British who had expected a bulletproof vehicle draped in crew-cut Secret Service men.

It was a late-shopping night in London and this helped the turnout. In Hammersmith, stout men and their red-cheeked women strode from the pubs to cheer "ole Ike." Hundreds of men and boys tried to keep up with the motorcade on their bicycles and there were several painful pileups in view of the President.

Thousands were gathered around Grosvenor Square, site of the American headquarters during World War II and known jokingly at the time as "Eisenhowerplatz," and the early evening darkness was brightened by thickly massed American flags. In Hanover Gate, many hoisted and waved "We Like Ike" signs and in Regent's Park, outside Winfield House, the embassy residence, a crowd of better than five thousand clustered around the gates and clung to the iron fence of the embassy's twelve-and-a-half-acre estate in the heart of London.

In the calm of the Winfield House courtyard, Eisenhower brushed the travel dust from his Oxford-gray jacket and then bounded up the steps to greet Mrs. Whitney with a less-than-fatherly bear hug and kiss. Macmillan came in for a drink and left quietly by a back gate rather than plow through the crowd at the main entrance.

Mrs. Whitney, the former Betsy Cushing who was once married to Elliott Roosevelt, and her husband had arranged a quiet evening for the traveler. The house, a fifty-room dwelling with steam cabinets in the marble bathrooms, was built in 1936 at a cost of about $2,500,000 for Barbara Hutton when she was the Countess Reventlow.

The President, beginning to feel the pace of the trip but still bubbling with enthusiasm about his welcome to London, sat down for a late dinner with the Whitneys, Herter, John Eisenhower and Major General Howard McC. Snyder, the staunch but aging White House doctor who went everywhere with the chief executive, even the golf course.

Down in Fleet Street, the newspapers of London seemed to be competing in enthusiasm for the visitor. Crowd estimates for the arrival parade ranged from 750,000 to 1,000,000.

As far as the British public was concerned, the biggest news the following day, August 28, was the President's flight to Balmoral to spend the night in the Highlands as the guest of the royal family. For the diplomats, however, this was a workday. While Ike went to Scotland, Herter and Foreign Minister Selwyn Lloyd met with their undersecretaries and specialists

to prepare the way for talks between Eisenhower and Macmillan on disarmament, nuclear tests and East-West tensions in general, plus preparations for the United Nations General Assembly which was to meet in New York the following month. Laos and Algeria also came up, but their spokesmen were loath to admit these specifics.

Hagerty set up shop at 10 Carlton House Terrace, a rambling old structure once used by the Germans prior to World War II. There was no room for press conferences, so the British put up a large tent across the street in a small park. There Hagerty held forth once or twice daily with Peter Hope of the Foreign Office, Harold Evans of the Prime Minister's staff, and Andrew Berding, the Assistant Secretary of State for Public Affairs.

It became evident quickly that these spokesmen would have little in the way of substantive diplomatic news until the end of the visit. What business there was between Eisenhower and Macmillan would not be discussed until the weekend at Chequers, the country estate of Prime Ministers for generations, and until then, or even then, the hard facts of diplomatic life tended toward menus and costumes rather than issues and agreements.

The first full-scale briefing in the tent, which became known as the "Hagetorium," concerned some sparse details of the meeting of the foreign ministers, some crumbs of description from Balmoral, a kindly lecture by Hagerty on why the President had to have Secret Service men with him (many Britishers resented this deeply) and some notes on tree planting. There were these exchanges during the course of the press conference:

Q. I didn't see any Secret Servicemen at Balmoral. Are there any there?
HAGERTY: Sure. A few.
Q. Do they wear kilts?
HAGERTY: Do they wear kilts? No!
EVANS: Well, gentlemen, perhaps I could wind up the fun and games by adding one item of news. During his visit to

Chequers, the President will plant a tree to commemorate his stay there. The name of the tree you had better listen to hard. I shall probably not announce it correctly, the Metasequoia Glytostroboides.

The skirmishes of 10 Carlton House Terrace may have been important to those involved, but not to the British public, whose eyes were turned to Balmoral, the 24,000-acre personal estate of the Queen fifty miles from Aberdeen. Overlooking the river Dee, the pale gray granite castle was built in Scottish baronial style by Prince Albert for his wife, Queen Victoria, who often took three days to make the trip from London; Ike made it in two hours.

The President, son John and Dr. Snyder with Ike's valet, Moaney, flew from London to Dyce Airport outside Aberdeen, where the Duke of Edinburgh greeted him in the cold and misty weather that makes Scots dour. The President flew in a Comet jet of the Royal Air Force, which pleased the British.

The London *Evening Standard* printed a cartoon that day showing a furious Scottish shepherd with his flock on a mountainous road between Balmoral and Dyce and a motorcade bearing down on the animals. The herder was saying angrily to an arm-waving policeman, "Ike who?"

Reporters and photographers, many of them from the Eisenhower party, swarmed around the castle entrance, a fact in itself rather unnerving to the people of the ordinarily untroubled rural community. A man in a deerstalker cap was proceeding determinedly on his business down a road near Balmoral when a policeman stopped him with the polite inquiry, "Are you press?"

"Good God, no," roared the outraged Scot. "Are you mad, officer?"

Riding over the Highlands with Philip and a small motor entourage, the President spotted a group of children at the village of Peterculter holding up a fifty-star American flag. On

the roadside beyond Aboyne, Scots held wooden-shafted golf clubs to salute Ike, and not far from Balmoral a sporran swung in solitary decoration from a telegraph pole.

The Queen was expecting her third child, the news of her pregnancy having been announced only a short time before, and the public had seen virtually nothing of her, even in pictures, since she retired behind the gates of Balmoral for the summer.

As the President and the Duke arrived before the gate, Queen Elizabeth, a radiantly healthy-looking young matron in a soft blue wool suit and a tiny white hat with upturned brim, stepped from a car just beyond the gatehouse and walked out into the road with her sister, Princess Margaret.

The President bowed from the waist, but kept his head up, looking at the Queen.

"How nice of you to let me come," he said, and she murmured that she and the family were honored, indeed, that he could spend a brief time with them. While the womenfolks watched, the President inspected the Queen's Guard and a band of kilted bagpipers played what the London *Star* identified as "The Mist-Covered Mountains." The London *Daily Worker* said flatly it was "The Green Hills of Tyrol," while the *Daily Telegraph* settled for "Loch Nivar No More."

Walking to the automobiles after the guard inspection, the President took the Queen's arm as they entered the grounds of Balmoral. It is English custom that one never touches the Royal Person in public, but this gesture of Eisenhower's was acccepted. First the Queen met him at the gate, and then he took her arm. The London *Sketch* devoted its front page of one edition to the photograph of their walking into the grounds with the President holding her elbow, and the black display-type head across the first page said "UNCLE IKE." Somewhat carried away, the next edition of the *Sketch* had a new streamer headline, "GODFATHER IKE?"

Inside the castle itself, the President was shown to his apartment and then he had lunch with the family, passing through the great halls studded with deer antlers from another century, the coloring dominated by the red, black and lavender tartan which Prince Albert designed for himself.

After lunch, with the Queen driving the car, Her Majesty took the President, John, Dr. Snyder and Princess Margaret in a shooting brake (a Canadian Ford station wagon type of vehicle) around the estate. Prince Philip took his two children, Prince Charles and Princess Anne, in another car to Glas Allt, an old summerhouse of Queen Victoria's, beside Loch Muick, where the entire party gathered for a late afternoon picnic.

The Queen then drove the President on to Birkhall, about ten minutes away by car, to the private house of the Queen Mother. There they had cocktails at dusk and returned to Balmoral.

Leaving Balmoral the next morning, Saturday, August 29, the President showed signs of having shifted from uncle, past the possible godfather status, to the friendly grandfather.

Standing on the castle lawn, he patted little Princess Anne on her shining hair and asked, "Are you going to learn to cook?"

The Queen laughed and said in jesting threat, "I'll send you some samples."

"If you don't, I'll be bombarding you with letters," Eisenhower replied.

Princess Margaret, tiny but beautiful in an open-necked pink blouse and tartan skirt, was standing nearby taking pictures. Prince Charles suddenly looked up and spotted one of Margaret's dogs, a spaniel named Rolly, standing on a battlement thirty feet overhead.

Feeling the situation called for some sort of comment, the President said uneasily, "He's really looking things over, isn't he?"

"He's just stupid enough to jump," added Prince Philip.

Family visit over, the President headed for the airport and a quick Comet flight to an airport near Chequers, where Macmillan waited.

The day before, the Prime Minister for the first time in

history had admitted the press to his estate and permitted them to wander about the first floor for a preview of the rooms in which he and Ike would confer. The *Daily Express* noted that Ike's hope to "melt a little bit of the ice" in the cold war was melting British protocol, too.

There were crowds in each of the Buckinghamshire country villages on the way to Chequers and they crowded the narrow, twisting roads so closely that the motorcade had to move carefully. Chequers could not have been calmer, but the *Sunday Pictorial* called the atmosphere "electric" and dubbed the weekend "Summit for Two."

Eisenhower arrived in time for lunch and the afternoon was devoted to a meeting of the two principals with Herter and Lloyd, Whitney and Sir Harold Caccia, the British Ambassador to Washington; Sir Norman Brook, secretary to the British Cabinet; Brigadier General Andrew J. Goodpaster, the White House staff secretary; and John Eisenhower, along in his capacity as Goodpaster's assistant.

During the afternoon, the cables from Asia told of new fighting on the northern border of India as Red Chinese troops strayed or shot their way into Indian territory, ostensibly chasing Tibetan refugees.

The Queen sent five brace of grouse from Balmoral for dinner that night, and in the late afternoon, the President and Macmillan went out on the front lawn to hit some golf shots with clubs borrowed from Whitney.

The next day, Sunday, the President and the Prime Minister went to the tiny Ellesborough church not far from Chequers.

Macmillan, following his usual custom, read one of the two Scripture lessons of the day, reading from the book of Romans, "Let us not therefore judge one another any more; but judge this rather, that no man put a stumbling block or an occasion to fall in his brother's way."

The rector, the Rev. C. N. White, a former platoon sergeant in the light infantry, injected a note that made it difficult for the British cartoonists to rib entirely everything Eisenhower and Macmillan did together. The pastor said, "I bid you in the name of Christ to consider the significance of this occasion, which will be indelibly impressed on our minds because two of the greatest men in the world have broken off their conference for a while in order to turn to God."

During the late afternoon, the President and the Prime Minister with no prior announcement took a quiet drive to Oxford to see Magdalen and Christ Church College. They were together in this manner for more than two hours, talking constantly and possibly doing more diplomatic business in that brief but undisturbed interval than at any other time of the visit to Britain. Since there was no one else in the car but a chauffeur and a Scotland Yard man, it made it most difficult for the British or American newspapers to develop any kind of source, authentic or otherwise, on details of their conversation.

The Manchester *Guardian* did not quite like the situation and said:

> Mr. Eisenhower and Mr. Macmillan in the Chequers weekend have practiced golf shots, they have eaten grouse sent specially by the Queen from Balmoral, they have attended matins in the local church, they have paid a lightning visit to Oxford (while the rest of the company played croquet on the lawn), and they have talked over the future of mankind.

Eisenhower and Macmillan arranged an entirely new departure in diplomacy for the following evening, Monday, August 31, in London: a two-man telecast from the drawing rooms of 10 Downing Street, the small, historic residence of Prime Ministers. On Sunday, Hagerty, Evans and Hope shuttled between Chequers and London by helicopter in an effort to produce some sort of news, but there was none forthcoming except the broad subjects discussed by the men and some of the social details. It was quite obvious that if Eisenhower and Macmillan had anything to say, they were saving it for their TV audience, which was to include a number of countries on the continent.

The situation produced an angry revolt by some of the British reporters in Hagerty's tent that Sunday night, but all the press secretary could do was fight to keep his temper and ask for sympathy.

On August 31, the day of the historic telecast, Hagerty and the Prime Minister's spokesman, Evans, caught hell from both sides every time they saw reporters. The British were in the vanguard, demanding an Eisenhower press conference and some objecting that Eisenhower and Macmillan were setting a "deplorable precedent" by going on TV together where they could not be criticized on the spot.

Principally the British seemed peeved because Ike held a conference in Bonn and none in London. This argument raged through most of the day, but quieted when time neared for the broadcast. The great men of the Commonwealth—Churchill, Attlee and others—rolled up narrow Downing Street that night for dinner and to watch what stands to this day as one of the more amazing public performances of two heads of state: Eisenhower and Macmillan resting comfortably in drawing room chairs and approaching vast world problems in public much in the manner of Huntley and Brinkley. An American cameraman cracked, "Which one is Chet and which is David?"

The program began at 7:20 P.M., British summer time, with a view of the two men, comfortable in well-cut dinner jackets, and lounging in chairs with two small microphones on a low table between them.

"Well, Mr. President," Macmillan began, "I want to start by saying how much we all welcome you here—hundreds of thousands of our people have seen you on the streets, and millions of our people will be watching you tonight.

"In the seventeen years of our friendship, which I think started in North Africa, we have had many frank talks together. And I think we can have a frank talk this evening. We have had good talks at Chequers, and here we are at Number Ten."

The conventional diplomats who cut on their TV sets in Europe that night must have blanched a bit as Ike took over.

"Well, Harold," he said with Kansas heartiness, "let me tell you right away and tell to all those good people out there who have been so kind to me and my party, that we are mighty glad to be back visiting again this lovely country."

Where I was watching in London, in the home of some friends, a British man called it "indecently naked diplomacy." An American said, "I keep waiting for the commercial." Eisenhower's voice cut through, "Well, Prime Minister, I would like to say a personal word about this business of Anglo-American relations."

Back and forth the two men talked, praising each other and each other's country. Then they talked of goals. Macmillan said frankly he wanted a Summit meeting. Eisenhower said that if there was to be a Summit, Khrushchev had to understand beforehand that "peace is an imperative." Macmillan dropped in unabashed election season plugs for his administration.

"Don't let anyone in America think it's the sun setting on the British Empire," the Prime Minister said. "It's the dawn rising on the new Commonwealth and it's all part of the same story."

Later, Macmillan, in following up Eisenhower's remarks about improving the economic lot of the world, said, "You helped us very much with the heavy engineering. I wish you could do something for us on wool textiles." The President returned the favor somewhat obliquely by saying of the pound sterling, "We want to see it just as strong as you want to see it."

With the homey back and forth, there was serious talk, disturbing possibly to some diplomats in the informal treatment, but still meaningful. Eisenhower said the people of West Berlin could not be abandoned, that he thought a Summit without some indication of fruitful results from Khrushchev might be depressing and discouraging.

"Our great strength is our dedication to freedom," the President said, "and if we are sufficiently dedicated, we will discipline ourselves so that we will make the sacrifices to do the thing that needs to be done. And that is exactly what you and I, I think,

are trying to teach ourselves, our friends, our own peoples and, hopefully, Mr. Khrushchev."

"God save your gracious Queen and all her people," the President called out as the show went off the air.

The experts with some justice could find much fault with what the two principals said that night. It was vague although hopeful, it was disorganized but entertaining. Khrushchev possibly could not perceive that many Westerners probably liked and understood this low-pressure A-B-C approach to world problems. Judging from man-in-the-street comments printed by the British papers and from the people with whom the American travel party came in contact, the high point of the speech for the British viewer was Ike's good night—"God save your gracious Queen and all her people." This they liked very much and for the moment, with the flags flying and "good ole Ike" buzzing around London in his shiny gray Rolls and him being so nice about the Queen, the foreign affairs expert who would have expounded anti-Ike philosophies in London pubs that night might have had his face pushed in.

CHAPTER 6 *"THE HEART IS FULL"*

As President Eisenhower left the warmth of London and departed for Paris where De Gaulle was supposed to be waiting somewhat unenthusiastically, the Manchester *Guardian* gave "Uncle Ike" a parting salute:

> His journey, of course, is not over. The most delicate part lies ahead in Paris. There he will have to tackle the thorniest of his allies and, although again his own warmth and charm cannot fail to help, the duration and domesticity of his stay in Britain may itself prove something of a handicap. To come so obviously from a happy British embrace is perhaps not the best introduction to a coolly distant French government; but, just as the storm clouds seem to have disappeared before Ike's presence in Bonn and London, so all may go smoothly in Paris.

De Gaulle may have been sulky, but he had no intention of letting it show. He had marked well the lavish receptions in West Germany and Britain and he was determined that France, too, would stage a monumental welcome for the visitor. This was not difficult to do because the French, being a sentimental and demonstrative people, had strong, favorable, wartime memories of Eisenhower. The French people, also, did not seem to like the idea of dissension between traditional allies.

The Paris newspapers drummed up interest and sentiment in the Eisenhower-De Gaulle talks by hailing them as "the Old Soldiers' Summit," and joined in urging the public to save their biggest turnout for Ike, not for his arrival procession, but later

the same day when he was to appear before the Hôtel de Ville, the City Hall of Paris.

The French Ministry for Posts and Telegraphs also announced that beginning with Ike's arrival and for the duration of his stay, citizens could send the President ten-word telegrams of greeting from any part of the country for half price or about twenty-five cents.

On Wednesday, September 2, 1959, Ike and his party arrived at Le Bourget, where the stalwart De Gaulle, towering in a severely cut gray suit, awaited his wartime colleague in a tented La Salle d'Honneur beside the airstrip.

The airport ceremonies were cordial but within the normal bounds of diplomacy. Eisenhower seemed quite happy as he greeted De Gaulle, but the French leader was composed, even reserved, as he escorted the President to their waiting touring car.

De Gaulle had wanted a minimum of interference from reporters and photographers during the processions about Paris and the presidential car was surrounded by sixty-four motorcycles. The crowds from Le Bourget to the entrance to the city were friendly, but hardly enough to warrant the policemen stationed every twenty feet.

Once they were in town, past the Madeleine, however, the sidewalks were thronged. Eisenhower stood to acknowledge the cheers. The motorcycles pulled out and gave way to a majestically colorful mounted band and honor squadron of the Garde Républicaine, dazzling in their silver helmets, flashing lances and sabers and on their immaculately groomed white steeds.

Driving slowly down the Rue Royale toward the Place de la Concorde, Eisenhower bent down and tugged at De Gaulle's sleeve, asking him to rise and join in receiving the applause. De Gaulle seemed reluctant, but he pulled his towering bulk up and saluted the crowd gravely while Ike held his arms over his head and flashed his best uncle smile.

They bumped into the cobbled courtyard of the French Foreign Ministry on the Quai d'Orsay, paused briefly for a piercing bugle salute in the brilliant summer sunshine and De Gaulle departed. Eisenhower went to his suite in the ministry, and after a brief rest, motored to the Élysée Palace across the Seine for lunch with De Gaulle, De Murville, Herter, French Prime Minister Michel Debre and other ranking members of both governments.

After lunch, the principals got down to business in a conference room on the second floor of the palace, looking out over the magnificent gardens of the Élysée and its handsome tree-lined driveways. The business meeting could not have lasted much more than an hour and a half, and the leaders parted again.

It was late afternoon when Eisenhower returned to the Élysée and the midtown streets were jammed. Stores and businesses, with government encouragement, had closed early. Thousands of school children were brought back to Paris from their summer camps. And the city also was jammed with the peak load of summer tourists, including thousands of Americans.

Leaving the palace, the two Presidents drove slowly up the broad Champs Élysées to the Arc de Triomphe. For this solemn occasion, De Gaulle had shifted from civilian clothes into his familiar khaki service uniform and Ike was in a dark business suit.

Beneath the towering arch and a mammoth tricolor flapping slowly in the evening breeze sweeping up the Champs Élysées, Eisenhower accepted a shining ceremonial sword from a French officer and rekindled the eternal flame at the base of the monument. A bugler sounded "taps" and, unbelievably, the heart of Paris was hushed. Veterans, some with empty sleeves, stood beside the Arc, caps in hands, and their battle standards from two wars lowered while Eisenhower and De Gaulle stood at silent attention.

The ceremony over and the two men back on display again, the Champs Élysées came alive with screaming kids, flag-waving women and cheering men.

They drove back down the Champs, across the Place de la Concorde and into Rue de Rivoli, the crowded shopping center, where so many people hung from the upper stories of buildings that the structures seemed to be leaning over the street. Driving slowly beside the somber gray-black walls of the Louvre, they came to the large square in front of the Hôtel de Ville, which was covered for the day with American flags and tricolored bunting.

M. Devraigne, the Mayor of Paris, was on hand with an enormous gold key to the city and a mighty cheer went up from the square where a crowd of fifty thousand was jammed.

As De Gaulle rose to speak, there had been no news of substance from the afternoon talks other than the obvious: the men had talked about NATO, Algeria and Ike's forthcoming meetings with Khrushchev. Unless De Gaulle was putting on an enormous show, however, his relations with Eisenhower had not been marked by the coolness so widely forecast in advance.

"Since the times are difficult, naturally America and France have to see each other and hear each other," De Gaulle said. Then he added quite emotionally and with a wave of his large hand toward Ike, "I can tell you this: that all has gone well between us."

There was a riot of applause and the crowds buckled the flexible wooden fencing as the French President then presented the visitor.

Almost falteringly, the President began to speak, turning to De Gaulle for understanding, it seemed, as he said, "When the heart is full, the tongue is very likely to stumble. Should I try to express to you today the true feelings, the true sentiments that now inspire me, I should be completely unable to speak at all."

Eisenhower's amazingly talented, multilingual interpreter, Lieutenant Colonel Vernon Walters, was on hand. Walters is an exceptionally fine interpreter because he is able to capture the emotions of the speaker, and also, on this day, Eisenhower was speaking without text. Walters' talent, however, was for once extraneous because the French caught the emotion in Ike's voice and showered him with applause.

Eisenhower rambled a bit, going back to the days of Lafayette to trace the strong friendship between the two countries, and praising De Gaulle, saying what a privilege it was to be working with him again in trying to find the right path to peace and security.

"People that love liberty will never let it slip away from them, either by neglect or under threat," the President said.

Eisenhower normally was most reluctant to attempt even a word in a foreign language, but on this day, on the steps of the Paris City Hall, he wowed the French with a closing line in much the same way he captured the British by closing his television speech with blessings for the Queen and her subjects.

"To all the people who lined the Champs Élysées, who were along the streets and boulevards as I came down here," he said, "I have one small French phrase that I think expresses my feelings: *Je vous aime tous* [I love you all]."

The American reporters whooped with laughter, one of them saying, "Ike's gone southern on the French." Public sentimentality of this sort produces little more than yawns among the diplomatic negotiators and the foreign policy theorists, but it captured the French front pages that night and countless Frenchmen parroted the phrase for days.

That evening, in the great dining hall of the Élysée Palace, nearly two hundred leaders of the French Republic gathered for dinner in Eisenhower's honor. The Foreign Ministry also began to pass the word that the leaders were getting along progressively on many, but certainly not all, matters of substance. The French got the idea that Eisenhower had agreed essentially with De Gaulle on his basic approach to the Algerian independence problem. There also seemed to be a better understanding about Eisenhower's plans for talking with Khrushchev (who also wanted his own meetings with De Gaulle). While Macmillan wanted a speedy approach to the Summit, the ideas of Eisen-

hower and De Gaulle on extensive groundwork seemed to be closer than many had expected.

Some differences remained, however, and Eisenhower referred to the situation in his toast at the banquet that night:

"Unless we have the stubbornness, the courage, the resolute persistence of General De Gaulle, we shall not win. I think that with that kind of courage, we shall never fail. I would call him stubborn, but as long as he is stubborn in support of principle and right and peace, this is a powerful inspiration for all of us."

The next day, Thursday, September 3, there was some strictly American business for Ike. He moved from the Quai d'Orsay out to the U.S. Embassy residence of Ambassador Amory Houghton and began a series of conferences not directly connected with his De Gaulle talks.

He first met for an hour with M. A. H. Luns, president of the North Atlantic Council, and Paul-Henri Spaak, secretary general of NATO. Then he saw Italy's Prime Minister Segni and Foreign Minister Pella with Herter. He had seen the Spanish Foreign Minister in London before leaving. These side conferences were matters of courtesy, and also, they concerned future moves of the President.

Ike reported to Segni on his plans for exchanging visits with Khrushchev and promised to keep the Italian government well informed on all developments. Eisenhower and Segni issued a communiqué reporting that "full identity of views resulted as to all questions examined." Here is an intriguing bit of diplomatic jargon. In truth, it means virtually nothing. It sounds and reads as though the men were in "full" agreement, but it does not mean that at all. Simply translated: they understood each other.

They did agree, however, "that a controlled and balanced limitation of armaments represents the most appropriate means to guarantee peaceful relations between East and West." This was part of a continuing American effort to show the Russians that the West really meant business in wanting to start down the road toward at least a practical beginning of disarmament, a goal which eluded Eisenhower throughout his White House career.

Later in the day, Eisenhower dropped in on the NATO council, then he and De Gaulle motored about thirty-five miles outside Paris to the quaint town of Rambouillet and the historic château of French kings and presidents, a solid, fortlike structure with sections of its masonry dating back to the ninth century.

De Gaulle had prepared a second-floor suite for Eisenhower, a stone-walled apartment in the Tower of Francis I, the oldest section of the building. The suite was filled with pink roses to relieve the stern architecture, and the host thoughtfully provided a television set and special wiring for an electric shaver.

The Rambouillet château looked more like a castle than anything Ike had seen, even Balmoral. A large stony courtyard dominated one side of the building, with a fence of high, black iron spikes surrounding the yard, a stone hut for detectives of the Sûreté and the Secret Service and the operatic splendor of the Garde Républicaine, with long streamers of black horsehair trailing from their gleaming silver helmets that shone like traffic signals in the lights of arriving limousines.

On the other side of the building, an expansive, emerald green lawn led down to a floodlighted lake where hundreds of ducks bobbed at ease and a leather-upholstered punt waited for distinguished passengers (who never ventured beyond the lawn because the night was too chilly).

The two leaders and their top advisers talked most of the evening, over cocktails in a ground-floor drawing room once used by Napoleon for his bedroom, and over dinner in a blue-walled dining hall with narrow tapestries running to the ceiling between the long windows.

Late that evening, Eisenhower and De Gaulle sent their spokesman back to Paris to release a communiqué written in the arch third-person style of such documents, saying that the principals were in complete agreement on Berlin and that "a summit conference, useful in principle, should take place only when there is some possibility of definite accomplishment."

As for Algeria, they would admit only that they discussed it, but from private briefings by foreign ministry representatives of both countries, it was learned that Eisenhower would have something to say about Algeria after his return to the United States. The communiqué spoke of their devotion to the Atlantic Alliance and how it could function more efficiently, but if there was any major De Gaulle back-down, it did not show in the communiqué or for any appreciable time thereafter.

Next morning, September 4, Eisenhower said good-by to De Gaulle at Rambouillet early in the morning, and then took a helicopter over the misty roofs of Paris to Le Bourget.

"I feel that the visit of General De Gaulle and myself has been mutually profitable," he said before getting on Air Force One, "and in my opinion will mark another further step in our co-operative effort to achieve a just peace."

And then he was off to Scotland for a few days of golf at Turn-berry, church outside the village of Shanter, immortalized by Robert Burns, and a few nights of rest in Culzean Castle, where he had an apartment given to him as a World War II tribute by the people of Scotland.

While Ike golfed, the Western world set to evaluating his trips to Bonn, London and Paris. Newspapers that had been almost hilarious in their excitable reporting of his first impact on Europe began to take a more guarded view. The consensus at home and abroad seemed to be: Okay, Ike. Your friends understand now what you're up to with Khrushchev. And we wish you all the luck in the world. But we still don't see much indication of a Russian change.

He landed back in Washington the evening of September 7.

"Everything is going splendidly," he said at the airport. He conceded that "troublesome" differences as to "procedure, method and tactic" existed, but he added that problems of this nature had been satisfactorily talked out during his journey. Members of his staff thought the West was unified as never be-fore in the cold war.

Three nights later, the President went on television to report on the trip. He still had a noticeable ruddiness from the Scottish fairways.

He said there had been no retreat from the fundamental principles of NATO; that he was gratified by the face-to-face affirmation of Atlantic Alliance principles and purposes; that the various units of the French Community would have the right to make their own final decisions as to their political destinies.

Most of the speech, however, was devoted to the talks with Khrushchev scheduled to begin in Washington in another three weeks. He spoke again of his "hope that serious exploratory efforts may reveal new opportunities for practical progress toward removal of some of the causes of world tensions.

"I know that neither America nor her allies will mistake good manners and candor for weakness; no principle or fundamental interest will be placed on any auction block," he said.

"It is my profound hope that some real progress will be forthcoming," Eisenhower told the American people, "even though no one would be so bold as to predict such an outcome."

Thus concluded the President's first major venture in diplomatic diplomacy. He had been responsible for a Western show of unity ahead of his talks with Khrushchev. It was a dramatic show, too; more effective, more demonstrative than any combination of communiqués or joint statements.

Undeniably the trip was a distinct personal triumph for Eisenhower. The quarrels and suspicions of Western Europe seemed to dim under his charm and personality.

Much of the welcome for Ike was a nostalgic tribute to the man who typified victory in World War II. And being a victory symbol in one war, his very presence offered promise of success in a new era of warlike tension.

But in the great offices of Whitehall, the Quai d'Orsay and the State Department, men still worried. How had the Kremlin really reacted to Ike's triumphal procession across Europe? Communist propaganda outlets had played the trip with only a moderate amount of jaundice and depreciation, even less than

usual. Quite obviously the Soviet policy makers would not attempt to tear down Ike on the eve of Mr. K.'s arrival in Washington. Thus, missing from the world picture at the moment was a reliable measurement of Soviet reaction to the tightening unity of the Western leaders.

Ike, however, was in business. Regardless of how the Khrushchev talks turned out, Europe had convinced the President that the free world needed rallying. He was convinced by the trip that his name, his face and his physical presence could be used not only in the general quest for peace, but to generate a better understanding of the United States. And, in net effect, Ike came home from Europe a confirmed traveling man.

CHAPTER 7 *IN THE FOOTSTEPS*
OF ALEXANDER

In the early autumn of 1959, Khrushchev had come and gone, leaving behind something called "the spirit of Camp David" and a feeling in the United States, however temporary, that relations between Russia and the West had improved as a result of the Soviet Premier's visit with Eisenhower and his on-site view of the American people.

Khrushchev at Camp David had removed any timetable for a unilateral move in Berlin and this was regarded by Eisenhower as sufficient promise of fruitful negotiations to go ahead with plans for a Summit meeting. The President put over his own trip to Russia until the spring of 1960. Khrushchev suggested the weather might be better.

While Eisenhower never said it to my knowledge, I had the distinct impression that even after Camp David the President had some misgivings about his ever going to Russia. In fact, this impression was so strong that on November 30, 1959, I told the executives of United Press International in New York that regardless of what might be announced later I would have to see Eisenhower in Russia before I believed it. This is not literary hindsight. My reasoning was this:

An Eisenhower trip to Russia in the spring or early summer of 1960 would have to presume that Khrushchev avoided any new crises with the West for a period of at least seven or eight months. And there was nothing in the past to indicate that Russia's Premier would behave himself for that long. Also,

Eisenhower left himself plenty of escape hatches. Arrangements were under way for a Western Summit in the winter. And Eisenhower planned separate conferences with Macmillan and De Gaulle in Washington before meeting Khrushchev again.

Disarmament and nuclear test ban talks in Geneva were alive, but not lively. Congress had quit for the rest of the year and a serious steel strike slowed American industry.

Shortly after Khrushchev departed, Eisenhower flew out to Palm Springs, California, to catch his breath and try to throw off nagging symptoms of a cold he picked up in Europe.

On October 14, 1959, he observed his sixty-ninth birthday. At an age when many men were puttering around in their carpet slippers, he was putting. On the day of his birthday, he was speeding by jet back to Washington from his boyhood home of Abilene, Kansas, where he had attended a ceremony in his honor the day before.

To the amazement of many medical men, Eisenhower had survived three grave illnesses in his middle sixties and gone on to the most active period of his life since the days when he commanded the Allied Forces against the Axis.

From external evidence, he was in good health, possibly better than at any time since his 1955 heart attack. He still had to rest each day after lunch and use an electric cart when playing golf. He also had to watch his diet, staying away from fats, starches and sweets.

When Eisenhower returned from the California desert, he and his staff began constructing one of the more spectacular feats ever undertaken by a chief executive in office—a tour of eleven nations of Europe, Asia and Africa. He wanted to complete this trip, plus a journey to South America, before going to the Summit. Not only was he out to sell peace and good will, but he wanted to tell as many of the smaller nations as possible that he would take their views to the conference table once he, Khrushchev, Macmillan and De Gaulle could get down to face-to-face discussions.

His itinerary—Italy, Turkey, Pakistan, Afghanistan, India,

Iran, Greece, Tunisia, France (for the Western Summit), Spain and Morocco. People of the Middle East and Asia quickly pointed out that he would follow the invasion paths of Darius, Alexander, Genghis Khan, Tamerlane and the Moguls. The distance was close to 23,000 miles.

It took weeks of hard work to put this one together. The logistical problems were maddening (How to get demineralized water for the jets in countries where there is no demineralized water? Answer: Ship it in ahead. How to get new batteries for the walkie-talkie radios in Afghanistan? Answer: You don't unless you take them with you). Files began to pile up in the offices of Jim Hagerty, Tom Stephens, John Eisenhower and General Goodpaster as ambassadors deluged the White House with questions and answers about the trip (the type of clothing to be worn at an audience with the Pope; the voltage and type of current available in the royal palace at Athens).

Eisenhower's slogan was to be "Peace and Friendship in Freedom." He had hundreds of medallions made with these words imprinted on one side, and "In Appreciation, D. D. E." on the other. These were to be handed out by members of his staff to their opposite numbers in the host countries.

There was a speech-writing chore of mammoth proportions and the President sent for one of his favorite writers, Kevin McCann, who had to leave his college duties in Ohio and undertake a giant research job before departure. (The chief White House speech writer, Malcolm Moos, was along, but occupied with the State of the Union message to Congress in January.)

The most ambitious undertaking in personal diplomacy ever attempted by a President, a three-week journey halfway around the world, began on the night of December 3. The Washington stores were decorated for Christmas but the newspapers were depressed by stories of fruitless efforts to end the steel strike.

Before motoring in the early evening to Andrews Air Force Base to board his jet transport, Eisenhower went on the air to tell the American public about the trip.

"During this mission of peace and good will, I hope to pro-

mote a better understanding of America and to learn more of our friends," he said. "In every country, I hope to make widely known America's deepest desire—a world in which all nations may prosper in freedom, justice and peace, unmolested and unafraid."

My diary for the departure showed a rather unexcited entry:

Dec. 3—Washington. The reporters piled aboard three big Army busses parked on Pennsylvania Avenue outside the White House in the late afternoon rush hour. Everybody going aboard with small overnight bags and typewriters and dressed in sports clothes for the long trans-Atlantic flight to Rome. A passerby surveys the scene and says, "They look a little old for the draft." Press-photo-radio-TV party over 70 men and one woman, Elaine Shepard, who writes for a women's syndicate.

At Friendship Airport, a big, gleaming Pan American 707. No dinner until after we left Goose Bay, Labrador. I filled up on canapes and went to sleep. Across the aisle from me, Capt. George Burkley, a Navy doctor along for our benefit. He lectures us on the importance of taking our anti-dysentery pills.

And for the next day:

Dec. 4—Rome. We got into Ciampino Airport two hours ahead of the President. Hard, cold rain. The President came off his plane in a topcoat, no raincoat. Thank heavens someone told the band to cut it short. Both national anthems highly truncated, but not enough to keep Ike from getting his head wet.

First impression of Rome—dismal. Gutters gurgling with dirty water. The Appian Way looks like a soggy back alley. Ancient ruins squirting streams of clay-colored water. No crowds at all braving this sort of weather. Only thing resembling a reception for the President was in the center of town and there the people darted out of buildings long enough to wave and shout, then back in again out of the cold downpour.

The Associated Press reported from Italy that "ancient Rome gave President Eisenhower a rainy but warm welcome. . . ."

Rainy but friendly, yes; rainy but warm, no. A heavy overcast and driving rain kept Air Force One above the field twenty minutes after scheduled arrival time, while President Giovanni Gronchi and Premier Antonio Segni huddled in the entrance of an airport building and aides tugged at microphone cables to move the arrival ceremony indoors.

Handshakes and band salutes over, Ike and the Italian leaders moved inside the airport waiting room, where the President made his first speech of the trip. Gronchi responded with praise for Ike's "great political sagacity" and then the party set out in a dishearteningly damp motorcade for the cavernous Quirinal Palace, which was to serve as the White House for two nights.

The procession into town was a ride, not a parade, because of the weather. The Colosseum, the Forum and Piazza Venezia were shrouded in gloomy rain and Ike could only wave, half-seen, from behind the raised windows of his car when he eventually encountered street crowds near the palace.

Umbrella-carrying Romans in the Piazza Venezia hoisted their bumbershoots long enough to scream "Viva Eekay" beneath the balcony where Mussolini once held forth.

At the palace, the President discovered there were no elevators and he walked slowly up an enormous, maroon-carpeted stairway into a great hall, where he inspected the guard before retiring to his apartment.

The Italians, with their love of ceremony, were a trifle annoyed by Eisenhower's insistence on having some of his office staff with him. General Goodpaster, who was at the President's side probably more than any other staff member with the exception of Mrs. Whitman and John Moaney, the valet, was assigned to a cloakroom—and with Ann Whitman. The Italians would not countenance a secretary, even a President's personal secretary, living in the palace, so she worked in the cloakroom with Goodpaster and joined most of the staff down at the Grand Hotel for what few sleeping hours there were in Rome.

Largely because of the weather and the lack of crowds, there was no "feel" of a major trip. It seemed almost as if Ike was

trapped in a drafty old castle on his way to something better. The picture changed that evening, however, as Eisenhower and Gronchi held their first business meeting in a tapestried drawing room of the Quirinal. Segni and Foreign Minister Giuseppe Pella sat in on the conference with Robert D. Murphy, Undersecretary of State for Political Affairs, who was along as the ranking foreign policy adviser (Herter was busy preparing for the Western Summit in Paris).

Eisenhower immediately let Gronchi and Segni know that he sympathized with their desire for a greater voice in the deliberations of the larger powers; in fact, the President told the Italians he would be happy to relay their feelings on a number of subjects to the Western Summit, as well as to the Big Four meeting later on.

There was about an hour of business, then the two Presidents went into a glittering, mirrored hall for dinner with a group of carefully selected guests. The Italians kept the dinner small, but afterward there was a spectacular reception for about three thousand leading figures of Italian government, society and culture—chubby cardinals moving sedately past Roman beauties in their flamboyant hair styles, pink-over-white lipstick and gowns so attractively cut that it was difficult to keep one's eyes on their faces.

Eisenhower, with Signora Gronchi on his arm, strolled through fourteen drawing rooms, stopping occasionally to chat with an old friend or a distinguished Roman.

During his strolling chat, the President said he was not at all dismayed by the absence of a crowd for his arrival; in fact, he said, he was highly complimented that as many Romans did brave the rain. There seemed to be nothing to rumors sweeping Rome that he had caught another bad cold in the rain. He scoffed at worries over his well-being and said he was feeling fine.

At one point in his promenade with Signora Gronchi, an American reached out of the throng, grasped her hand and roared, "Hello, Barbara."

The well-wisher thought the Italian President's wife was

Eisenhower's young daughter-in-law and, in the best of civic pride, wanted to show some of his Italian friends that he was in solid with the Eisenhower family.

Eisenhower bowed gravely to the man and waited until he was about ten feet away. Then the President exploded with laughter. He called for his interpreter, Colonel Walters, to explain why he thought the incident was so funny and to tell Signora Gronchi how complimented she should feel. Then Ike realized how that might sound, and quickly corrected himself. He said he wanted to tell Barbara right away what a fine compliment had been paid *her*.

The next day, Saturday, December 5, from my journal of the trip:

> Rome—Rain and more rain. None of us able to beat the fatigue born of that overnight flight across the ocean. Little or no sleep now for two nights. But today not without its light moments. We drove with the President by the North American College not far from the Vatican and several hundred young seminarians were standing in the rain to cheer him. My colleagues won't support me, but I'd take an oath I heard the seminarians shouting, "We liketh Ike."
>
> When the President went to the Council of Ministers building for his late morning meeting with Prime Minister Segni, some of us explored the huge complex of government buildings around the Viminale Palace. They have coffee bars much like the snack stands in federal buildings back home, but over here the coffee hour runs all day.
>
> To get a tiny cup of espresso, one must first fight through a dense crowd to a cashier's booth, buy a ticket, then fight across the room again, easily as crowded as a going-home bus, to a gooey counter, present ticket and eventually get a jigger of coffee with a smear of sugar paste across the lip of the cup. Coffee strong enough to be chewed, not sipped.
>
> To the Villa Madama (Foreign Ministry guest house) with the President for lunch by Pella. Grand house. Lousy lunch. Ate in pantry beneath stairs. Hope Ike did better. Then went to sleep in drafty lobby in hard oaken chair with back eight feet

high. In the late afternoon, shopping for religious objects to take to the Vatican tomorrow for papal blessing.

The day was not so superficial as the diary indicated. Eisenhower paid a traditional visit to the tomb of the Italian Unknown Soldier, stood bare-headed for several minutes in a chilling rain, and swirled on through the miserable weather in a small Italian limousine to a series of business meetings that occupied the rest of the day. The talks between the Italian and American officials continued on an informal but apparently effective basis. By the time the day ended at the historic Quirinal, once the home of Popes, those around the President felt much better about the trip. Ike, Gronchi and Segni were hitting it off fine. Absence of crowds seemed to matter less. Possibly the continuing downpour contributed more to diplomacy than the history books will ever record.

By nightfall, the two Presidents issued a communiqué that seemed to have more meat in it than these frequently limpid documents often contain. Eisenhower agreed to support Italy's desire for a greater voice in shaping the policies for East-West negotiations; both spoke of determination to get on with disarmament (although the Italians had precious little to disarm); and outside the language of the communiqué, Eisenhower promised to talk to Macmillan and De Gaulle about having an Italian spokesman appear at the Western Summit later in the month.

Diary notes for Sunday, December 6, in Rome:

Up at 5:15, baggage in the lobby before 6:30. The White House says to accompany each bag to the hotel ground floor to keep the luggage from being misplaced (also to keep anyone from sticking a strange bomb in a bag).

The first sunshine we've seen this trip, en route to the Vatican by bus. Up a million cold stairs to the Consistory Chapel where we waited 30 minutes for Pope John XXIII. Sunday private audiences most unusual. He's seeing the press and members of the White House staff, then the President.

For our audience, His Holiness came in through a small red door. A most engaging, friendly man. Corpulent but very small feet in red slippers. Graceful. A chamberlain tucked a small satin pillow under his feet when he sat on his gold and red throne, a brilliant picture in snow white robes. This man has great taste and presence. Of course I'm not a Catholic, and looking at him, I get a feeling of genuineness rather than holiness. He joked with us in Italian about his attempts to learn English, but the monsignor translating for the Pope took out the levity and left us wondering what the Italians were laughing about.

The President arrived at Vatican City about the time we were leaving (we had to get to the next stop ahead of him) but Italians and tourists were pouring into St. Peter's Square. The still-wet paving stones glistened in the morning sun as Eisenhower drove in a top-down blue convertible through the Arch of Bells into the Court of St. Damasus, where the Swiss Guards, their spotless steel pikes shining above their yellow, blue and red uniforms, rendered honors and a band of the Palatine Guards played "The Star-Spangled Banner."

Luxurious carpets, used only on the highest state occasions, covered the path of the President from the car to a small elevator that took him to the Pope's apartment. John and Barbara were with the chief executive, Barbara in a dark suit and black lace mantilla. Barbara photographed beautifully in the soft glow of sunshine reflected from the red satin walls of the papal library.

Naturally, the remarks exchanged by the President and the Pontiff were relatively stilted and dictated by the formality of the occasion. Only one other President—Woodrow Wilson—had conferred with a Prince of the Church and that was in 1919 when Wilson visited Pope Benedict XV.

Pope John, even within the limits of formality, seemed trying to convey all possible support for the President's mission without putting a church stamp on it. They talked for twenty-seven minutes in the Pope's private library and in his halting English,

he Holy Father sent Eisenhower on his way into Asia with
hese words:

"We earnestly invoke the powerful assistance of God upon
ou in your noble efforts as the untiring servant of your people
nd of the cause of peace in the world."

They exchanged inscribed photographs and the Pope had a
pecial present for Ike—a gold medal inscribed simply "John
XIII—Obedience and Peace."

A helicopter whisked the President, John and Barbara from
he Vatican to Ciampino and the waiting Boeing 707.

His next stop, two hours and forty minutes away by jet, was
Turkey, a strong—police-state-strong—member of the Western
lliance, home of some of the world's best fighting men, the site
f powerful American bases closer to the Russian border than
Havana is to Miami. His destination, Ankara, and an overnight
ep meeting with President Celal Bayar (who was deposed a
w months later).

Bayar asked no special concessions, but he had his doubts
bout direct dealings with Russia. It was Eisenhower's job to
eassure him that there was no ground to be given before Khru-
nchev.

Diary notes on Ankara, December 6:

Amazing turnout over the 20-mile route from Esenboga airport to town. First few miles, virtually no spectators except
lonely riflemen silhouetted on hilltops overlooking isolated
narrow highway. But nearing Ankara, great bands of wild,
sword-swinging dancers from the hills. The men do the dancing
here. Belly dancers only in the cities.

Turkish people love bright, colored lights. String them all
over the buildings in honor of their distinguished visitor. Ike's
picture in lights on one building over 100 feet high.

The communiqué didn't come out until 2 A.M. Quite a scene
in the chamber of the Turkish parliament—reporters stretched
out sleeping on the desks of the lawmakers, waiting for the
communiqué. Turkish reporters not very talkative about the
39 editors and writers currently in jail here for publishing

articles that displeased the government. If Bayar could only hear what the Americans are saying about staying up all night to get a communiqué which was in virtually final form before Ike arrived.

Turkish officials seemed more amazed than the Americans at the turnout for Eisenhower. Ankara, a city of less than a half-million, had at least 400,000 on the streets that afternoon. The Turkish papers claimed as high as 700,000.

Eisenhower and Bayar rode into town in a 1934 Lincoln touring car that once belonged to Kemal Ataturk, the national hero of the country who established Turkey as a republic after the First World War and brought mechanized industry into the Moslem world for the first time.

The enthusiasm of the Turks for Eisenhower matched anything he saw in Europe earlier in the year. The main street, Ataturk Boulevard, was decorated with a series of red, white and blue arches with such slogans as "Turks Are Friends Indeed, Ike" and "Take Our Love Back, Ike." Troops with submachine guns lined most of the route, but we saw a small child wriggle through the armed guard to hold up a crudely lettered sign saying, "We Please Cheer Ike."

Turkish reporters talked during the ride into town about how Bayar always wanted more military aid and how the public associated this possibility with the President's visit. This was to be a familiar story in every country Eisenhower visited.

The general tone of the newspapers seemed more realistic than the conversation of the reporters. The Ankara and Istanbul papers seemed to accept that the importance of the trip was largely historical and ceremonial rather than of immediate, material value. The papers were particularly pleased, however, about Eisenhower visiting three member countries of CENTO on the eve of a Western Summit.

Arriving at the guest house, a comfortable residence on a hill overlooking the city, Eisenhower seemed genuinely surprised by the warmth and size of the welcome.

After a short rest, he was driven through the blue haze of a dusty, early evening to the impressive Ataturk mausoleum. Up three flights of stone steps, then into a sternly beautiful chamber, where he placed a wreath of fresh flowers beside a bronze wreath and stood for a few silent moments gazing up at the softly glowing star and crescent of Turkey behind a latticed grillwork.

Then he drove to Bayar's palace for the business of the day, while in the center of town the Turkish Army staged a colorful parade for the benefit of thousands who crowded into Ankara just to say they had been in the same city with Ike. The leaders were talking in a quiet paneled study, but outside their windows, in the darkening sky, skyrockets stitched fiery patterns overhead. Downtown traffic was hopelessly blocked as Army trucks strung with Japanese lanterns and colored lights lumbered down Ataturk Boulevard.

Multicolored lights blazed inside the ornate greeting arches and brilliant signs proclaiming "Turks Trust Ike" shone throughout the city. People on the street laughed approvingly at Eisenhower's few words of Turkish at the airport—"*Hos ulduk. Cok tesekkur ederim.*" (Welcome and thank you very much.)

At dinner that night, the President was lavish in his praise of Turkey's role in NATO. He called the country "a modern proving ground that democracy and stout hearts are a people's best instruments for the achievement of greatness," and he promised continued American aid, economic and military.

The late night communiqué was in the same vein, saying the two Presidents recognized that "*détente* like peace has to be considered as an indivisible entity" and that close co-operation between their two countries on a bilateral basis, as well as through NATO and CENTO, was paramount.

The joint communiqué also included special praise by Bayar for Eisenhower's efforts to reduce international tensions.

It was almost midnight before the President left his hosts, including Prime Minister Menderes (also since deposed) and

Foreign Minister Zorlu as well as Bayar, and returned to his quarters for a few hours of sleep before continuing on to Asia. The festival lights of the city were blazing brightly and as Eisenhower went to bed Turkish Army trucks rumbled through the city, dropping off rifle and submachine gun patrols at frequent intervals to mount a guard for the President's trip to the airport.

Before he left the guest house early the next day, gifts began to pour in on his harassed staff. Mrs. Whitman's small office in the temporary White House was overflowing with presents from cities which the President was unable to visit, including Istanbul and Izmir. There were silver boxes, rugs and meerschaum pipes, a smoking set from Skisehir and a portrait of Eisenhower made of Turkish and American stamps (it took the donor two years to make it).

Before boarding his plane, the President told Bayar and Menderes his reception in Ankara was extraordinary and that he was deeply touched.

"This country takes hold of my heart," he said.

He also spoke of diplomacy and the results of their talks.

"We stand together on the major issues that divide the world," Eisenhower said as Bayar nodded agreement. "We see together, and I know of no reason whatsoever why we shouldn't be two of the strongest parties standing together always for freedom, security and the pursuit of peace."

Speeding to his next stop, Pakistan, Eisenhower began to receive some of the early returns on his trip. The reaction in Rome and Ankara was excellent, but more important, excitement was begining to spread in Karachi and New Delhi. Countries not included in the schedule were urging that they be added; countries already down for brief visits were suggesting extensions. The President was beginning to show some slight evidence of physical fatigue, but it was lost in his exuberance over the way the Turks had turned out for him. He shucked off his coat, pulled on a light sweater and prepared to nap as much as possible during the five-hour flight to Karachi.

CHAPTER **8** *UNDER A VELVET PARASOL*

Flying between Ankara and Karachi, the President and those closest to him began to realize for the first time the punishing scope of their undertaking. On paper, the schedule had not seemed too wearying. But after four nights on the road, and those virtually without sleep for almost everyone in the party except the President, fatigue was beginning to manifest itself.

Eisenhower seemed to be standing the trip better than his staff. He got to bed from one to three hours earlier than most of his associates and he was able to stay in bed a bit longer than the rest of the party in the mornings.

He had no packing and unpacking of clothes to vex him, no files to be shoved into cases, no worry about his transportation or the plane leaving without him. And as Kevin McCann said, "Nothing to carry."

The long, mimeographed schedule became the arbiter of daily life. One would no more think of starting the morning without a schedule in pocket than strolling into the hotel lobby minus pants. At the end of one particularly grueling day, McCann saw some friends in a palace courtyard and observed grimly, "I don't know how many friends we made today for the United States; in fact, we may have lost a few, but by God, we kept the schedule."

Turkey added a little lift to the trip, but Pakistan promised the first real excitement—a twelve-year-old nation firmly on the side of the West, struggling under a tremendous burden of widespread poverty, a steady stream of Moslem refugees from largely Hindu India, and a gunpowder-sensitive position on the southern flank of Russia and Red China.

President Mohammed Ayub Khan awaited Eisenhower. Ayub was an urbane, British-trained general who found himself somewhat reluctantly in the role of a dictator while trying to develop a constitutional political system whereby he could step aside for a democracy. He had a host of problems, none of which Ayub really expected to have solved on the spot. Pictured by one diplomat as a man "trying to make the country pure by whacking it with the flat of his broadsword," Ayub, more than obtaining gains of an immediate material nature, wanted Eisenhower to get a well-balanced, if brief, look at Pakistan.

The Pakistani leader, a powerfully built man with more the look of a wealthy South American than an Asian dictator, wanted reassurances concerning American aid. The United States, from 1947 until the time of Eisenhower's trip, had spent more than one billion dollars in Pakistan, largely on economic assistance, but also to strengthen her armed forces. The Pakistanis were somewhat perturbed by rumblings in the American Congress and Eisenhower's constant battle to keep the aid program from being seriously cut.

The most sensitive problem awaiting Eisenhower, however, was the dispute between India and Pakistan over Kashmir, a vast area to the north held by Pakistan, and in it the mountainous Ladakh District where Chinese Communist troops had occupied some three thousand square miles. India had been quarreling with Peiping over this district and Ayub felt this was more properly the affair of Pakistan. He wanted Eisenhower to attempt establishing some area of settling the dispute with India when he went on to visit Nehru.

Eisenhower had read position papers on Pakistan prepared by the State Department and flying over the Arabian Sea to Karachi's Mauripur Airport on the crisply clear, sunny afternoon of Monday, December 7, he went over the situation again with Murphy, Goodpaster and John. The President was highly sympathetic to Ayub's feelings about foreign aid, but Ike knew

he could not risk offending the Indians by sticking his oar into the Kashmir argument.

At the airport, surrounded by enough troops to have settled a border dispute, the President got his first exposure to the color and humanity of Asia. A red carpet rolled up to the ramp of Air Force One and as Ike emerged from the plane, F-86 jets, Pakistani-operated but obtained from the United States, flashed over the field, which was surrounded, wherever the omnipresent military permitted, by thousands of dusty brown country natives, many of them squatting in the dirt and squinting almost doubtfully at the "Emperor" from so far across the world that many found it difficult to comprehend. After all, it took longer for some of these Moslems, lean to the point of knobby hardness, to trudge behind their donkeys from their villages to Mauripur than it took Ike to come from Washington.

Flanked by U.S. Ambassador William Rountree, one of the more able envoys Eisenhower encountered in his travels, Ayub was hearty in his welcome.

"You symbolize in your person," Ayub told him, "the dynamic manifestation and working of the principles of universal peace, freedom and good will."

"Before we leave, we are not going to be disappointed," Eisenhower said at the conclusion of his brief remarks.

The route of Ayub's white Cadillac convertible from the airport into town covered about ten miles, and the Pakistani President had scrubbed, polished and painted every possible part of it within the powers of his martial law. Even the light poles were freshly painted. The more unsightly buildings were either whitewashed or plastered with pictures of the two Presidents. Through the day and night before, sweepers had attempted to keep the streets free of blowing desert sands.

Once outside the airport, Eisenhower stood quickly in the back of the car and saw stretching before him on the flat highway a solid double-wall of flag-waving humanity.

The crowd was orderly. Desert and mountain people know better than to rush into the streets when a king is passing. The children seemed to make the most noise in the outlying districts. There were separate viewing areas for the Moslem women who were cautiously emancipated enough to venture into public, their dark eyes mere twinkles behind the small slits at the top of their shapeless burkas, a limp, black cotton head-to-toe shroud. The more modernized women were out in everything from their fat-bottomed slacks to fluttering saris, ornate jewelry sparkling in the intense sunlight.

There were thousands of Pathan tribesmen in ballooning white trousers, long-tailed shirts and tattered turbans. The police allowed the children to take the front row on the curbings —old-men-looking children with spindly legs and scabby heads. Ayub had done an excellent job of spreading hundreds of thousands of small American flags along the route and the children loved them.

There were countless banners—"We Like Ike—Dawood Cotton Mills" and "Long Live Eisenhower." Nearing the city itself, with a population of two million, the crowd became more enthusiastic. With the first mass cries of *"Zindabad,"* Eisenhower bent down to Ayub, who explained the people were wishing him long life.

The President and his host drove into the city through Bunder Street, normally teeming with sidewalk stalls, which had been ordered dismantled for the Eisenhower visit. Hundreds of refugee shacks had been bulldozed flat. My diary for that day noted: "When we passed one incredibly smelly section of the city, we were told by our driver, and quite proudly, that the area had been sprayed with a deodorant. Should have sprayed this a bit more. The fellows dub this 'Chlorophyll Heights.' "

In Elphinstone Street, the two Presidents stopped their convertible while mounted lancers of the presidential household guard kept the crowd from spilling over the line of police and military sentries at the curbs. Eisenhower and Ayub, accompanied by a Pakistani military aide and the ever-present Secret Service agent Rowley, climbed into a glittering black and gold

carriage drawn by six freshly combed white horses. Footmen in scarlet and gold tunics, white trousers and towering gray and gold turbans rode behind the leaders, protecting them from the sun with scarlet velvet parasols.

Here, the people were jammed forty deep, rammed in some areas far back into the lobbies of movie houses playing *Ilya the Mighty* with "4-track magnetic stereophonic sound system from Russia!" and Jerry Lewis in *Don't Give Up the Ship*.

A ten-year-old boy, later identified by police as Shahid Faridoon, wriggled through the streetside guards, dodged between the lancers' horses and shoved into the presidential carriage a crude pencil sketch of Ike with a laboriously printed legend, "You always did the best for peace and we all hope for something more in the future."

When the carriage pulled off the streets and into the calm, guarded grounds of the President's house, Ayub's rather wandering yellow-brick mansion, Eisenhower literally popped out of the vehicle.

"That was really something," he muttered to Rowley. Then he looked up and saw the American press association men standing nearby.

"I hope you hard-boiled boys were a little impressed by that," he said. And they were.

The government announced officially that the crowd was one million. If this was relatively accurate, then the later estimates at New Delhi of two million might not have been too far from right.

The two Presidents went to an upstairs parlor and chatted for about thirty minutes about the new threats in the north posed by the Chinese Communists. Then they went to their separate apartments to shift into dinner jackets and meet again before dinner to exchange presents.

Dinner that night took place under a large striped canopy on the lawn beside trees festooned with colored lights, and with 150 guests the President sampled his way through a long menu —*bhekti*, a fish from the Arabian Sea; *tikka kabab*, mutton broiled on a spit; *biryani,* heavily spiced rice with mutton, beef and chicken. And after dinner, bagpipe music on the lawn and wildly whirling men dancers from the hills with Buster Brown haircuts of polished black hair.

Hagerty and his public relations apparatus set up shop in another tent, this one in the garden of the Metropole Hotel, where grizzled snake charmers were doing such a business from our crowd that their flute-weary cobras at intervals slumped in exhaustion over the sides of their woven baskets. There was little interest in Hagerty's briefing that night; the spectacle was a far better story than Jim's crumbs from the thirty-minute chat before dinner.

Diary for December 8, the second day in Karachi:

With Ike to Ayub's polo grounds to watch mounted members of the palace guard in tent pegging, racing their ponies at break-neck speeds over hard, bare ground toward tiny wooden pegs which they speared skillfully with silver-tipped lances. Bravest man: guard who stood motionless over one of the pegs while a lancer hit the target and somehow retrieved the peg at full speed.

Palace people laid about a half mile of oriental rugs between Ayub's house and the polo field so two presidents could stroll in comfort. Obviously cheaper to use rugs than pave a sidewalk.

To cricket match before lunch. Not enough excitement having Ike in town, but he has to come when Pakistan's national cricket team is playing its "test" matches with Australia, the equivalent of our World Series. Ike put on a Pakistan blazer and tie when he got to the stadium. He rooted for home team but was completely puzzled as officials of the Cricket Association spoke of the effective blows in the first over.

Ayub asked the White House travel party to tea this afternoon, same tent where DDE had dinner last night. A loud-mouthed American woman who lives in Pakistan nearly ruined the afternoon by gushing over Ayub. He finally moved away from her physical clutches and had a nice chat with some of us. He says very frankly Pakistan has to go in for birth control clinics in a big way, but with the situation in the United States,

there's no reason to talk to Ike about it. I admired a beautiful book on the tea table, handsomely bound in rich Arabian leather, gold edged leaves. Asked Ayub the significance, thought it probably was a guest book. He laughed and said, "I'll have to tell my baker. He'll be most flattered. Here, try a piece." Turned out to be a fancy chocolate cake. Bitter by our standards. Only one thing stronger than Ayub's coffee. His cigarettes. So strong they feel like they're set to go off.

During the morning, the President also visited the embassy to say hello to members of the American community. He did this in each country. On this morning, he talked about prejudice and preconceptions, saying how necessary it was for Americans living abroad to understand more about the far-from-home land in which they found themselves, not judging local customs and conditions by American standards entirely.

In the afternoon, Ayub turned over his polo field to the public, a crowd of about 25,000, for a civic greeting to Ike. It was a punishingly hot day and the dust came up in clouds from the field. The President spoke of American aid and its continuance without saying whether the level would rise or fall, and he expressed hope that Pakistan and her South Asian neighbors would improve relations among themselves.

There was a ceremonial visit to the tomb of M. A. Jinnah, the revered founder of Pakistan, and that night—it seemed as though Eisenhower had been in Pakistan for days—he entertained Ayub at Rountree's residence.

The only substantial, purely business meeting had taken place that morning for little over an hour, and resumed at lunch. The free flow of expression between the two men seemed to surprise both. At dinner, Eisenhower in his toast said, "We think we learned something about your country that will be helpful to us—if we have done that, that is the real reason we should have come."

Ayub responded: "Our discussions have absolutely opened my eyes; that you put up with our frankness, and you, too, have very frankly expressed your point of view—it has been a matter of real education and information for us. We are most grateful indeed."

This remark by Mohammed Ayub Khan reflected one of Eisenhower's most telling techniques on his foreign trips. The President's breezy, almost locker-room manner of approaching some of the more volatile issues up for discussion struck many of his opposite numbers as amazingly frank. Eisenhower told Ayub, for example, that he simply could not butt into the family quarrel between Pakistan and India, certainly not as Nehru's guest, but he would be happy to tell one and all that a solution of their differences would be looked upon in the United States with great approval.

He also told Ayub frankly that he thought there would be no reduction in aid to Pakistan; in fact, he was ready to seek an increase when he returned to Washington but Ayub would have to realize that a Democratic-controlled Congress had the final say.

There did not seem to be the preoccupation with Eisenhower's upcoming participation in the Western Summit and later the Big Four that there was in Italy. The final communiqué spoke of the need for the non-Communist nations to stand together in strength. And it underlined "the urgent desirability of finding solutions to existing disputes" in Southern Asia.

While the President was getting along so well with Ayub and his associates, another member of the family began to shoot upward in public attention as a magnitude star of the trip and a superb advertisement for the United States. This was Barbara Eisenhower as she began to overcome her natural inclination for the background and stand out as an enjoying participant. Newspapers in each country devoted increasing amounts of space to her.

Barbara made no attempt at regality, but asked intelligent questions when she visited a native hospital or school. She was batting in a frightfully fast league of smartly groomed, Paris-

styled women of the international set and doing more than holding her own.

At Ayub's dinner for the President, the women of Pakistan and the resident diplomatic corps dazzled in evening finery, but Barbara stood out like a Miss America at a D.A.R. convention as she glided over the lawn on Ayub's arm to watch the Khattak tribal dancers. Her chaste, uncluttered, white evening gown projected dramatically against the background of flame-colored saris and the deep-dip models from France.

As the President moved around Karachi during the two days he was there, he attracted vast crowds. The schools were closed during his visit and his route was frequently lined by thousands of small children, squatting in the eternal dust and furiously clicking small stones together in an ages-old form of welcome.

Whether it came from within or whether it stemmed from the hot, enthusiastic public response to Eisenhower's presence, Ayub seemed to grow more lavish in his praise of the visitor with each public appearance. In their last major date together, at the polo grounds, Ayub called him an "extraordinary head of state" and said of his mission and the United States, "Never before in the history of men has one single country taken upon itself so much to preserve the peace and freedom of others."

Pakistani newspaper reaction to the trip was startling in volume and intensity. Part of this was to be expected on the first trip by an American President into Asia. It was to be expected, too, because Eisenhower and the country he represented had been Pakistan's principal benefactors since the establishment of her independence. But some part of the press reaction, as well as the public response, had to be attributed to more than Ayub's advance work and more than required good behavior while the man with the money was in town.

My colleague Hensley said that night as we were discharging thousands of expensive words on the world-wide subscribers of U.P.I., "These Pakistanis are good people. I'm speaking of the ones you can get to know. They probably think more like we do than any other people out here in this part of the world." And he tossed over an advertisement from a Karachi paper extolling the merits of a bookstore in Elphinstone Street and saying, "Our heartiest welcome to President Eisenhower—10% discount to his entourage."

As we worked through most of that night in Karachi, it was difficult to size up the stop in Pakistan with complete balance and detachment. This is a problem inherent in looking at and listening to raw history in the making.

Eisenhower was hailed as no chief of state before him and, in all probability, as no one had ever been hailed in Pakistan. It was true, however, that he had virtually no conversational contact with the general public. As far as the masses were concerned, it was a one-way relationship.

This situation, however, would seem to be inevitable, particularly in a country such as Pakistan with its vast chasms between population strata. And it also reflects the manner of presidential travel with its considerations of personal security and protocol.

It might seem ideal to have a President while abroad spend some time in sincere conversation with the ruled rather than the rulers; with a few dissidents instead of always the majority. Practically, this is next to impossible.

Suppose Eisenhower had insisted on striking out on his own in Pakistan even for an hour or two, seeking out the so-called average citizen to see how he felt about his life and times. The bare-legged water vendor with his scarred goatskin could not have conversed with him in the first place without an interpreter, and even then, a man of lowly station in Asia would be frightened by the mere thought of having to talk with a king.

A merchant in his store? Eisenhower during the Geneva Summit tried going into a toy store unheralded and such a mob developed that the trembling shopkeeper's place of business was in genuine danger of serious damage until alarmed Swiss police arrived on the scene and shoved the average citizens back into the street.

Doctors, lawyers, educators? The top ones got to the banquets and behaved about as expected, suddenly barren of any comments except those highly laudatory of the host, the honor guest and anyone else within hearing. Sin, poverty and the weather usually are about the only targets of criticism at such affairs.

Thus, how does a President learn anything but what his host wants him to learn? For one thing, he has, we must presume, a certain amount of prior knowledge based on reports from his diplomats. He can absorb something from the crowds if he is perceptive (if all the signs are trimly painted, if all the flags are exactly alike, then the host government, in consultation with the American Embassy, is largely responsible). One crudely crayoned "Ike Like We" is more encouraging than a hundred printed "We Like Ike" posters.

A President also has at his disposal a vast source of information in the voluminous reaction reports that flow into the White House, not only from the embassy and in newspaper editorials, but in mail from those of a foreign public able to write and able to pay postage.

Perhaps more important than all of the foregoing is that a President should be able to get the feel of a country through a process of sociopolitical osmosis while he is on the scene, and from this derive a certain amount of improved understanding when next a problem involving the particular country crosses his desk back at 1600 Pennsylvania Avenue.

On the night of December 8, it was close to midnight before Eisenhower got to bed in the ornate suite on the second floor of Ayub's house, and tired or not, Ike had to be up at five-thirty the next morning for one of the longer days of the trip, the high light to Afghanistan and on to India in the afternoon.

After a helicopter flight from the polo field over the pungent smudge of early morning cooking fires to Mauripur, Eisenhower grasped Ayub's hand beside Air Force One and said, "Our stay has been all too brief. We have had just a sample of your country and should like to come again."

CHAPTER 9 *A HATFUL OF CONFETTI*

Book-length examination of Eisenhower's personal diplo-macy in action naturally involves a good bit of picking and choosing on the part of the person conducting the examination and by the standards of some experts, his brief visit to Afghani-stan might not warrant inspection in detail.

He was there only about six hours. It would be charitable to say that he spent as much as an hour in concentrated attention to the problems of the country. But to many of us on the trip, Afghanistan was the most fascinating stop up until that point.

A remote, mysterious, jagged kingdom in the heart of ancient Asia, Afghanistan covers an area of 250,000 square miles from the twenty-thousand-foot peaks of the eternally snow-mantled Hindu Kush Mountains in the northeast to the wild, western deserts of the Helmand.

The capital of Kabul, Eisenhower's destination on Wednes-day, December 9, was a little more than a hundred miles from the Russian border, a twelve-hundred-mile border with Afghani-stan on one side and on the other the Soviet Republics of Tajikistan, Uzbekistan and Turkmenistan.

During the 1950's, the Russians and the United States had competed in supplying aid to one of the world's few remaining monarchies whose ruler, King Mohammed Zahir Khan, a hook-nosed, swarthy potentate, wanted even more—from both sides. For this distant nation of twelve million population, the United States had supplied assistance, largely economic, worth about $146 million since 1950. The Russians had done much more,

supplying arms, the country's one arterial paved highway, a grain elevator, a bakery. At the time of Eisenhower's visit, British sources estimated there were over a thousand Soviet technicians in Afghanistan.

Afghanistan, where some of the bloodlines run back five thousand years; where Alexander the Great drove his great Greek armies through a four-year invasion to set up a Greco-Bactrian rule that lasted for two centuries before it was wiped out by the Parthans and the Kushanis; where the national sport still is *buzkashi,* a wild autumn game in which as many as five thousand horsemen divide into two teams and attempt to carry the carcass of a calf several miles through opposing ranks.

Afghanistan, where the monotheistic religion of Zoroaster was dominant many centuries before Christ; where the Mongolian hordes in the thirteenth century led by Changiz (Afghan spelling) Khan murdered most of the Islamic population; where today Afghan parents place veils over the faces of infants before taking them out of the house lest the babies be harmed for life by the gaze of someone with an evil eye.

Afghanistan, where tribal youths fire ancient rifles before the doors of young girls as their way of asking their hand in marriage; where at the first snowfall in Kabul, people try to slip poetic couplets beneath the doors of friends without the deliverer being caught (the penalty is a feast); where the King is the spiritual as well as the temporal leader and to talk with him a few moments is to be blessed.

This was the land to which the President of the United States sped by jet over the snowcapped peaks between Afghanistan and Pakistan, once friends but now divided by suspicion and trade wars, yet characteristically permitting thousands of nomads to roam back and forth across the borders with the seasons.

A nation now entirely Moslem except for tiny minority groups of Hindus and Jews, Afghanistan under King Mohammed Zahir had remained relatively neutral in the East-West power struggle, but had accepted all possible military assistance from the Russians. Weathered and hardened by some of the world's most difficult geophysical conditions and with a history of having been pillaged by one foreign army after another, it was not surprising to find the Afghans generally suspicious of everyone from beyond their mountains and deserts.

The Afghans, through their ministers, made it plain before Eisenhower arrived that they would like more economic assistance from the United States. Soviet aid rose sharply after the 1955 visit of Khrushchev and Bulganin—oil storage tanks, power plants, small factories and improved communications. The United States at the time of the Eisenhower visit was building new highways, a modern airport in Kandahar to the south of Kabul, and dams, and was assisting in such not-readily-visible projects as teacher, nurse and doctor training.

Eisenhower was in no position to guarantee or even encourage the hope of substantial increase in American aid and whether the King was aware of this was debatable. In fact, some Americans in Kabul, who, incidentally, seemed to love the town and the people, said that what the King wanted most from America at the moment was his own television station, this despite the fact there were no receiving sets in his country and not much of a market for them, either. With a station, however, he might have placed government-owned sets strategically for communication with the nearby tribes. He was using his small state radio station for this purpose, and through this station had passed the word for the tribesmen to come to town on December 9 to see the great ruler of a powerful nation far across the mountains (Afghanistan has no coastline so it doesn't do much good to talk to the tribesmen about "far across the seas"; their trouble has always come from men on foot or on horseback).

King Zahir wanted the best possible turnout; if it proved to be better than that accorded Khrushchev and Bulganin, this was the will of the people. Zahir and his ministers wanted economic aid, but also, they were sensitive about having their country exposed to the world as more primitive and backward than absolutely unavoidable. So, the king sent his representatives and workmen to the little villages beside the thirty-eight-

mile, Russian-built highway connecting Bagram Airport, also Russian-built, and Kabul. For days there was a mass clean-up campaign. Fronts of century-old compounds were whitewashed, roadside areas brushed and raked.

Then, during the day and night of December 8, tribesmen drifted in from the hills to camp along the procession route and in the crude hostels open to travelers. They pegged their horses, donkeys and camels and squatted beside tiny, flickering campfires through the night, awaiting the two kings. These were the proud Pashtoons, the quickly spoken identification of all Afghans.

The weather had been questionable during the night and early in the morning. An American helicopter swirled high over Bagram and radioed the latest flying conditions to Air Force One. It was only a little before nine in the morning when the big jet appeared over the horizon, but it seemed scarcely daylight and the weather was bitter cold on the broad concrete runway built by the Russians.

The King, muffled in a khaki-colored military greatcoat, arrived in a dull-red, open Daimler and his honor guard, uniformed in the style of the World War II German Army, staged an elaborate salute.

As Eisenhower's plane approached, six Soviet-built MIG-17 fighters, flown by Afghan pilots, streaked through the cold, gray sky to escort the American plane to a safe landing.

The airport area was kept clear of the public and only the official party, including a small group of flower-laden children in native festival dress, was on the field. U.S. Ambassador Henry Byroade was on hand, along with the dean of the diplomatic corps stationed in Kabul, Soviet Ambassador Mikhail V. Degtyar.

When Eisenhower stepped from the plane and greeted the King, the formalities were brief—the national anthems, the review of the honor guard and salutations over a public address system totally unneeded in an assembly that could not have numbered more than a few hundred.

Strange was the word for the drive into town. Strange, in that

the President and members of his party looked upon sights
beheld by few Westerners. In the country, the crowds were made
up predominantly of men and children; tribesmen wrapped in
heavy woolen robes of brown and dirty white, many of them
covering the lower part of their faces in a protective reflex born
of mountain cold, desert dust and the presence of strangers.
What women there were in the rural areas watched from afar,
standing in shrouded, veiled groups (even though the King had
ordered veils abandoned) beside dun-colored village walls far
back from the highway. Aside from the white-faced king riding
beside Zahir, the tribesmen saw something else utterly new,
utterly confounding. Many of them quickly averted their gaze
to the ground. Others stared intently in seeming disbelief at
what was passing before their eyes—Barbara Eisenhower and the
women on the Eisenhower staff gaily waving and smiling to the
stern Pashtoon men, to whom this must have meant just so
much Western frivolity, letting women behave in such a brazen
way right out there on the highway built by the thick-necked
people from the north and which was not suited to the hooves
of camels and donkeys.

On the approaches to the town, dominated from a gracefully
landscaped hill by the King's Chilstoon Palace, the nature of
the crowd began to change. There were occasional groups of
rhythmically skipping male dancers, the wailing pipes of wispy-
bearded musicians, and confetti, first thrown somewhat self-
consciously, then furiously as the Afghans got the idea.

Diary notes show:

> Welcome in Afghanistan was amazing. People in country
> near airport out in force, but reserved; wrapped literally to the
> eyes against the morning cold. Wouldn't know man from
> woman, the way they're wrapped up. In Kabul, however, the
> place was wild. The Afghans took a little time to sense just
> what was expected, then they began rolling themselves into
> human balls and hurtling from the hillsides toward Ike's open
> Daimler. Dozens of smiling men literally tried to climb in with
> him. This may be a militarized monarchy, but the town people

seem friendlier with the police than about anywhere we've been.

Office and factory workers, men and women dressed in Western style, clogged the streets, throwing rose petals and other flowers, confetti and serpentine tape. The city women were unveiled, but they stood apart from the men. There were the customary thousands of American flags, the "We Like Ike" signs near the University. The sun broke through the overcast and the mile-high capital became more comfortable for the President in the open car.

The brim of his black Homburg filled with confetti, draining like a colorful gutter when he tilted his head. As the motorcade approached a bridge which led across an icy stream and up the hill to the palace, the crowd became so enthusiastic that the cars scarcely moved until policemen ahead pleaded with the people to stand back.

Crossing the bridge, Eisenhower looked down at the stream and to his laughing amazement, several dozen men and women were wading across the icy water without removing shoes or stockings, or even rolling up their trousers. The people seemed to be carried away by the occasion and wanted one more close-up of the visitor before he disappeared behind the heavily guarded gates of the palace.

Once inside, the President sat down for a luncheon conference with the King, Prince Mohammed Daud, the monarch's nephew, Premier and principal adviser; plus the ranking members of both parties.

At the airport, Eisenhower had told Zahir, "It is a sign of the age in which we live that I am able to travel the many miles involved in this journey in the short space of time available to me. It is a reminder of the fact that all of us live very close together in the twentieth century."

The New York Times reported the next day from Kabul, "Most of those along the route probably had no notion of who, or even what, 'Eisenhower' was."

At lunch over a plate of green-tinted rice with sugared raisins and bits of mutton mixed in it, the President did his best to encourage the Afghans as delicately as possible to stand clear of any close involvement with the Soviet Union; any involvement more binding than Afghanistan's current acceptance of the type of military aid the United States could or would not provide.

Repeatedly he praised the rugged Afghan spirit of independence, their courage and hardiness.

"And so, I propose a toast to the King," he said. "May he continue to enjoy good health and well-being and the benign guidance of the Almighty [this was a bow to Zahir's spiritual leadership of his people]; and to the people of Afghanistan, may they never falter in their steadfast determination to maintain their honor and independence. May they march ever forward in peace, progress and prosperity."

While the President was having lunch, we were working in another part of the palace (some of the copy Hensley and I filed was still coming into Paris nine days later when we arrived there for the Western Summit). Many of us had been in a great many places with one President or another, but seldom had we encountered friendlier people than Zahir's palace staff. Outside, the dark-eyed boys with the Tommy guns were rather insistent on their prerogatives, but under the King's roof, members of his court, during the hour and a half we were there, showered us with information, some of the world's more interesting stamps, boxes of raisins and nuts, American coffee of which they were exceedingly proud, even sharpened pencils.

Some of us were deeply impressed by the Americans on Byroade's staff in Kabul, which I certainly would have expected to be regarded as the boneyard of the foreign service. Quite the contrary, the embassy personnel to whom we were exposed spoke enthusiastically of their assignment. One young foreign service officer said he had been there six months, had eighteen more to go and hoped it somehow would be possible to extend his tour.

While the President talked at the small luncheon of his admiration for the industriousness of the Afghan people and their determination "to share in the dynamic achievements of our times; to enjoy the life which modern science and engineering makes today possible," I sat with a scholarly Afghan on the staff of the Premier while he spoke softly in excellent English of his people and their ways.

He said the population of Kabul was about 200,000 and his government thought at least twice that many turned out for Eisenhower. The Soviet leaders, he said, had attracted nothing like this response.

I spoke of fears in other parts of the world that Afghanistan, by accepting so much from the Russians in the military field, might slide slowly into the Russian sphere of influence and thus produce even greater problems in an already troubled subcontinent lying next to the Soviet Union and mainland China.

He answered by recounting some of Afghanistan's history; overrun time after time by foreign forces which always, even if it required centuries, had been disgorged. He said the lowliest Afghan herdsman might suffer all manner of discomfort and poverty, but he could never be made to accept foreign rule.

He said it was difficult to appreciate the ferocity of Afghan patriotism; how Afghans, faced with death in a foreign land, wanted if necessary their bodies dismembered and packed back to their native land for burial.

During our chat, I saw the deep sense of Afghan hospitality at work—the constant passing of plates; "Here, you've not had nearly enough—try some of the duck." We spoke of everyday living, how the housewife makes her bread dough (*naan*) at home and takes it to a nearby bakery for cooking; how the bundlesome clothing of the tribesman is essentially utilitarian with the heavy turbans and long black shirts providing centuries-tested protection against sun and dust.

After lunch, the King and the President returned to the Daimler and drove through another jam of people and rose-strewn streets to the Jeshyn National parade grounds for a ceremonial farewell before a helicopter rushed Eisenhower to Bagram and the waiting Air Force One.

Murphy and Afghan Foreign Minister Naim checked with Byroade and issued an agreed draft of a joint communiqué by the two leaders. In part this document said:

> Both sides also agree that in the present day it is imperative that international disputes are settled by peaceful means and further concurred in the need for world peace, especially so as to enable the energies of mankind to be channeled into constructive pursuits of development and human fulfillment.
>
> They endorsed unqualifiedly the principles of the United Nations Charter as standards for international behavior.

Then the King expressed his hopes that Eisenhower would achieve some concrete results at the Western Summit and from his forthcoming visit to the Soviet Union.

Air Force One roared down the long runway, built thoughtfully by the Russians at a length to accommodate jet bombers, and moments later, the President looked briefly out beyond the gleaming nacelles of his engines to the rocky, forbidding, chill Khyber Pass. He stared at the good-for-little expanse below while Moaney got his bunk ready.

Goodpaster and John were waiting with some papers to be read. Ike looked at them almost listlessly. The circles under his eyes seemed heavier. His day was then ten hours old, and only half done. He motioned to Moaney to shut the door of his compartment, pulled off his coat and slipped into a soft sweater. The President eased down on his sofa bed, one of two aboard Air Force One, and with the lullaby of jets pulling the ship up high over the Hindu Kush snowcaps, he dropped off to sleep. India was only an hour away.

CHAPTER 10 *ANGEL IN INDIA*

At the time of Eisenhower's triumphal arrival in India described at the start of this book, a number of other heads of state and chiefs of government were either traveling on missions somewhat similar to that of the President, or they had ambitious trips in the planning stage.

Adenauer had just conferred with De Gaulle in Paris about the upcoming Western Summit and Segni had been in London talking with Macmillan about coming to Rome in the spring. Khrushchev was planning a trip to France and to Southeast Asia. Gronchi was going to Moscow, Adenauer to Rome, De Gaulle and Macmillan separately to the United States.

Who stirred up all this travel? Eisenhower? Or was it Khrushchev? Actually, the President was rather late in the international travel derby. The Soviet Premier had traveled extensively within the Russian sphere of influence, but also, he had swung far afield to Asia and the Far East long before Ike's plans in that direction were on paper.

Eisenhower's trip and the Western Summit, however, must have accounted for some of the personal diplomatic missions undertaken at about the time he was in India. With the exception of Khrushchev, the trips of such leaders as Macmillan, Segni and Adenauer were more business than ceremonial affairs. The Russian was a tremendous crowd attraction wherever he went, De Gaulle was to become one, too, in London and Washington, but none of them had the box-office power of Eisenhower.

"Somewhere in all of this, time must be found for the summit meeting itself," the New York *Herald Tribune* commented. "One does not envy the keepers of the diplomatic engagement books."

In addition to the phenomenal nature of his welcome, Eisenhower's visit to India had other unusual aspects. He was in the country the better part of five days, one of the longer visits on record by a President to any foreign nation. During those five days, he spoke eight times. Little wonder he said to friends later that he talked so much in India he began to tire of the sound of his own voice. Perhaps it was Nehru's influence on the schedule, but Eisenhower also got a much closer view of India than any country he had visited, or for that matter, has visited since.

His presence could not have been timelier from his standpoint. The country was incensed over the Chinese border incursions, and the nagging threat of conflict to the north added a greater sense of urgency to India's other needs—a nation of 400,000,000 racked by poverty of such vast proportions that the average Westerner, even on the scene, found it difficult to comprehend.

For too many years, in India and in much of non-Communist Asia, the image of Uncle Sam was not particularly attractive. The United States was pictured as a protagonist of the cold war, using her wealth, including her aid to India, primarily to erect barriers against the tide of Communist ideology. Indian neutralism in East-West affairs seemed at times to many Americans to be approaching pro-Soviet sympathy.

The cruel Communist crushing of Tibet and the Chinese occupation of Indian frontier territories had a sobering effect on Nehru's people and these armed excursions came at a time when the United States was pleading for peace and a cooperative effort to better the bread and bed of all mankind.

Eisenhower in New Delhi thus faced a multipurpose task. He had to listen attentively and sympathetically to India's needs

and still keep the response to his presence from skyrocketing into unjustified hope. He also wanted to take fullest possible public relations advantage of being on Asia's center stage for most of five days. This required an even more punishing schedule than Pakistan.

With scarcely time to recover from the rigorous arrival night, the President on Thursday, December 10, left the Rashtrapati Bhavan for Rajghat, the beautifully simple memorial to Gandhi. The Rajghat, a large, flat, rectangular mosaic beside a peaceful grove of young trees, was covered with an intricately designed blanket of tiny blossoms. After slipping off his shoes as a matter of respect and putting on felt slippers, Eisenhower walked to the edge of the memorial, stood thoughtfully for a few minutes, then went to the grove of trees, where he planted another sapling to the memory of Gandhi.

This brief ceremony was over by nine o'clock in the morning and then followed a whirlwind day—a formal call on President Prasad, a business conference of nearly two hours with Nehru, a brief visit with a group of Indian Girl Guides and Boy Scouts, lunch with Nehru and their top advisers, an address to Parliament, and finally a ceremonial banquet given by Prasad followed by a long program of Hindu music and dances which did not end until nearly midnight.

Moving about the vast city of New Delhi, Eisenhower saw the amazing contrasts of India—goat herders leading their flocks over paved city streets beside streams of automobile traffic, new building beside dusty rubble containing the crude shelters of countless half-naked families; the chromed and carpeted majesty of the ultra-modern Ashoka Hotel; natives crouched beneath the trees outside the old Imperial Hotel offering crudely polished pieces of old glass as genuine star sapphires.

He saw the stately color of India—thousands of potted plants set out for sun on the broad steps of a government building; the dignified tea-bearers of the Mogul Gardens behind Rashtrapati Bhavan in their white turbans and white chin-whiskers, their calf-length coats of scarlet and gold and their stiffly starched duck trousers; the glittering gold nose screws worn by some of the more theatrical women.

Diary notes for December 10:

We seemed to be in and out of the stone-paved courtyard of Rashtrapati Bhavan all day and night. During the morning, some of us were invited into the Moghul Gardens to have coffee and cakes with Ike and Prasad under a striped canopy. The lawn is in better condition than most American golf greens. Counted a dozen fountains and gave up. Someone says, "He'll never play this course—too many water hazards."

In the several public appearances during the day with Nehru, the Prime Minister now seems to have his people under much better control than last night. Thousands move with just a gesture of his hand. When Eisenhower spoke to Parliament, Nehru stage-managed everybody before the President appeared. While Ike was speaking, Nehru lounged on one side of the rostrum and seemed almost bored. He applauded only at the end, but the members applauded frequently by whacking the palms of their hands on their desk tops. This would horrify Congress back home.

Got to the Rashtrapati Bhavan early tonight to watch some news pictures made at the reception before dinner. It was Prasad's dinner but during the introductions at the preceding reception Nehru seemed to think things were moving too slowly and he took over briefly. Never been in quite this kind of jam before. Got trapped inside the reception hall and couldn't get out. Dinner was in the next room, no reporters.

Had counted on being able to return to hotel to change into dinner jacket for after-dinner party, but instead, cooled heels for two hours in Prasad's diplomatic reception hall, a vast and beautiful room. Watched workmen erect stage for dancers and bring in chairs for dinner guests.

When Ike came back in for the after-dinner show, he spotted some of us in the corner trying to hide our four-in-hand ties and olive drab wash-and-dry suits; in stage whisper he asked, "How did you get in?" Program of Indian dances went on and

on. Ike watched from a sofa with dancers performing only a few feet from him. Some of the girls by the standards of any country are very elegant lookers. Their heavy eye makeup makes us wonder whether the current American trend might have started over here. We're told these girls are the country's top dancers and their standards of living and remuneration would compare favorably with our ranking Hollywood stars. Wonder how a boy kisses a girl with a large gold screw through her nose?

Eisenhower's speech before Parliament was his major appearance of the day, although his private talks with Nehru the same day probably had a more important bearing on relations between the two countries. Before Parliament, he was no American *"badshah"* (king) as the public has called him. He was the powerful leader of a powerful nation to which India was looking for help as she sought to embark on another five-year program of economic improvement, this one to require about $23 billion of which as much as five billion would be needed from the outside. Russia had promised $375 million and was expected to offer even more.

The President also had to bear in mind that Nehru, while deeply worried about conditions on his northern borders, was highly sensitive about India requiring military assistance. Nehru did not want his troubles with the Chinese Communists thrown into the over-all cold war picture.

"Our hope is that we are moving into a better era," the President told the Parliament, speaking from a white-railed rostrum between columns of glistening blue stone. "Over most of the earth, men and women are determined that the conference table shall replace the propaganda mill; international exchange of knowledge shall succeed the international threats and accusations; and the fertile works of peace shall supplant the frenzied race in armaments of war."

The hall, where most of the members wore jodhpur-type trousers and kept on their white Gandhi caps, was silent and thoughtful as Eisenhower spoke of America's own battle with prejudice and bigotry within her borders. The members were silent as he told of the world being trapped in a vicious circle of weakness and fear inviting aggression or subversion and military strength in one nation begetting even greater armed strength in another.

"In the name of humanity, can we not join in a five-year or a fifty-year plan against mistrust and misgiving and fixations on the wrongs of the past?" he said in a combined question and proposal. "Can we not apply ourselves to the removal or reduction of the causes of tension that exist in the world? All these are the creations of governments, cherished and nourished by governments. The peoples of the world would never feel them if they were given freedom from propaganda and pressure."

Public acceptance of Eisenhower in India manifested itself almost immediately and the Indian press was generally most enthusiastic. The *Hindustan Standard* printed a front-page cartoon in which Eisenhower with angel's wings descended on a waiting Nehru. The caption said, "At last."

And to complete the elevating picture of Ike in angel's wings, villagers from Mehrauli, south of Delhi, came to town—and got into the newspapers—with their belief that Eisenhower was the reincarnation of Vishnu Ka Avatar, a mighty protector in the Hindu religion.

The two major items on his agenda for the next day were visits to Delhi University and the World's Agricultural Fair. The Fair was the original pretext for his coming to India. The first announcement of the trip said he was going to New Delhi to open the Fair and the rest of the stay then grew around this single occasion. Originally, his speech to the Fair was supposed to be his major address in India, but as it turned out, his Parliament speech had more immediacy.

The University visit was colorful—and academic. Ike's scholastic robes, which he wore because he received an honorary degree, were of brilliant red and blue and his mortarboard was topped by a long white silk tassel that dropped over his eye-

glasses. Nehru, looking young for a man of seventy, was with him, in the ever-present white Gandhi cap worn over academic robes of brilliant yellow and scarlet.

Ike spoke to the students, gathered in an amphitheater walled in carpets and colored tapestries, about the contribution of exchange students to international understanding, but he was more interesting as he discussed the need for civilized nations to recognize the general principles of what he called "a reliable framework of law."

He followed this with two thoughts:

"Nations can endure and accept an adverse decision, rendered by competent and impartial tribunals," and "It is better to lose a point now and then in an international tribunal, and gain a world in which everyone lives at peace under a rule of law."

The big event of the day was the Fair. Eisenhower and Prasad arrived in style in a state carriage of gleaming black lacquer with gold trim, a scarlet umbrella against the sting of the late afternoon sun, and drawn by six brown horses. His speech captivated the Indian press as he proposed a world war on hunger under the banner of "food for peace."

The theme of the $2,500,000 American exhibit was "Food-Family-Friendship-Freedom."

"Here are four words that are mightier than arms and bombs, mightier than machines and money, mightier than any empire that ruled the past or threatens the future," he told an immediate audience of about sixty thousand, many of whom had known famine and the ugly sight of mobs rioting for pitifully small amounts of grain.

He suggested that other countries join with the United States in providing farm surpluses to meet urgent need in other nations, but here again was another field in which, because of the final control of Congress, Eisenhower could only suggest and hope.

After his speech, he toured the handsome American exhibit, which was done architecturally in gold-tinted domes suggested by ancient Mogul design. Ike was visibly cheered to learn that in the brief period since the opening of the Fair, the American exhibit with its nuclear reactor, electric milking machines, chicken incubators and modern kitchens was outdrawing by a wide margin the Russian exhibit next door with its stern display of sputniks and missiles.

Diary notes for December 11, the day of the Fair:

So much Oriental splendor, so many new sights for an American, so many thousands of people on every street corner that Ike passes, it takes a lot of effort for Hensley and me to keep from being utterly jaded.

Old men in rags sleep beneath the walls of a beautiful palace. Sacred cows tie up traffic. Hotel room keys have small silver footballs attached. Our Sikh driver with his neatly turned-under beard is a terrifying fellow to gaze upon, but one of the most gentle people I've ever met.

One never escapes completely from the musty smell of India. Not only in the air, but in the water and food. An Indian friend told us that a great many of the country people in town to see Eisenhower had only a hazy idea of his true identity.

"Many of them say he's the king of the millionaires who were over here during the war," our friend said.

Sensibly, we thought, the President scheduled nothing for the night of December 11, had a quiet dinner with John and Barbara and turned in early. He also kept his morning free the next day and did not appear in public until late afternoon, when President Prasad gave an "at home" in the Mogul Gardens.

Prasad invited about five thousand persons and over eight thousand got in before harassed Bhavan officials learned that a great deal of the overflow had come in by a remote garden gate without invitations. This left several thousand more who had been invited howling at the proper gates because gatecrashers had overloaded the party and there was no more room in the Gardens, large as they were.

The two Presidents made an effort to stroll through the crowd, but it was hopeless. Indian security agents and Secret

Service men formed a double ring around the two men and only by locking arms and bulling against the spectators could the security men keep Eisenhower and his host from being swallowed up by Indian ladies intent on touching the visitor.

Diary notes for Sunday, December 13:

Can't imagine a more varied Sabbath, starting out with Ike and Prasad before 8 A.M. to services at the Protestant Church of India Cathedral. Then by car out to Palam Airport and by plane to Agra and the Taj Mahal.

The architectural beauty of the Taj Mahal cannot be captured in words, or in few pictures. It requires a close-up. Clean, clean perfection. It doesn't show in pictures, but the lovely dome is made of thousands and thousands of very small, hand-carved stones of marble, jasper and agate, and native craftsmen work there daily, sawing out replacement parts with crude tools of wood and string dipped in pumice.

We had to be careful walking behind the President. The marble floors have been worn to ballroom slickness by the thousands of feet that padded over the place on pilgrimages for many years. Because of the holy nature of the 17th century Taj (the tomb of the builder, Emperor Shah-Jahan, and his wife occupies an ornate crypt far beneath the dome) we had to wear cloth covers over our shoes and that made the floors even more treacherous.

In the afternoon, to the huge Ramlila grounds between old and New Delhi, a civic reception for the President. Saw one million people in one spot. This is the only estimate of one million I've ever truly believed. The Indians, accustomed to crowded conditions, sat on the ground like well behaved school children as Nehru and the President spoke. The crowd stretched as far as one could see from the speaker's tower, a concrete island in the upper center of the field. Ramlila is about the width of five football fields and about a thousand yards long, possibly longer. There was not a spare inch of space and the entire area was rimmed by men and women perched on banks and ledges, or scrimmaging with the police in an effort to get inside the park.

As a crowd spectacle, the meeting at Ramlila grounds was something only possible in Asia with her tremendous populations. But even allowing for this physical fact, it was a moving sight; that many people in one clump and thousands more struggling with police in surrounding streets to join the assembly.

It was a quiet audience, too, and Eisenhower's speech suited the mood as he spoke with an almost parental air. He was not talking down to his listeners, but his phrases were more simply put together than a parliamentary address. He spoke frequently of Gandhi, who had appeared on these same grounds, but not, according to Nehru and members of his entourage and family, to as many people.

"Freedom, as Gandhi said, is the gift of God," Eisenhower said. "And God's gift cannot forever be kept from his children.

"But—immediately—we must search out with all free nations more effective and practical ways to strengthen the cause of peace and friendship in freedom; and, so doing, make our negotiations with other people more persuasive.

"One reason I came to India is to tell you that America wants to join with all free men in advancing this cause."

For many Indians, however, there could have been cause for some measure of disappointment in the Ramlila speech. Eisenhower spoke of aid, but quickly added that the best form of economic assistance was private investment.

He envisioned an era just ahead in which the rest of the world would buy increasingly from India.

"Of course, I don't think India can achieve its full potential without acquisition of more capital than you now possess," he said. "The best means for a nation, determined to maintain its independence, are private investment from outside, governmental loans from others, and where necessary, grants from other free and friendly nations."

This was regarded by some as a delicate warning that India might think again about accepting grants from Russia because the President indirectly approved this process of assistance only

when proffered by "free and friendly nations." He concluded, however:

"One thing I assure you, from now on I shall be quick to assert on every possible occasion that India is becoming one of the great investment opportunities of our time—an investment in the strengthening of freedom and in the prosperity of the world."

This concluded the public phase of Eisenhower's journey to India. He and Nehru drove back through teeming streets of cheering well-wishers to the Rashtrapati Bhavan for a private dinner. They had approved the draft of a communiqué which Hagerty issued during the evening at the press headquarters with his Indian counterparts, T. R. V. Chari and P. N. Menon, who found themselves up to their turbans in hot water because of some poorly understood press conference questions and answers. At one point, one of the Indian spokesmen said it was correct that Nehru had asked Eisenhower for assistance in coping with his problems on the northern border.

Within a short time, this drew a stern clarification from the Indian government. This was precisely the impression Nehru did not want to convey. Eisenhower would hold no press conference in India, but Nehru dropped in at the headquarters for the traveling reporters and during the course of a brief, informal chat with the journalists, the Prime Minister said he and Eisenhower had discussed the border difficulty with China, but not in any detail. The quarrel with Red China was not mentioned in the communiqué, but the document did refer to other areas of conflict in Asia and to Eisenhower's belief, after talking with the heads of the countries involved, that any current disagreements could be solved by peaceful methods of conciliation.

As communiqués go, the joint statement at New Delhi was nothing world-shaking and primarily affirmed the desire of the two leaders and their nations to go about the business of the world without the resort to or threat of force. Their private conversations, we learned from Eisenhower later, were much more fruitful than the bland language of the communiqué indicated. The visit did lead to a presidential request for increased assistance to India, but the entire foreign aid program ran into difficulty with an election year Congress.

The active schedule in India undeniably had sapped some of Eisenhower's strength and many men in the party much younger than the chief executive were downright exhausted. The President had only to keep going for another long day, and then he was scheduled to board the cruiser *Des Moines* at Athens for several days of rest at sea. At the time, to many of us, Athens and the luxury of a Navy bunk with no Asiatic hordes to contend with seemed like a million miles away. As one of our travelers said the dawn of our last day in Delhi, "Now only the armed might of Iran and Greece stand between me and Navy food."

CHAPTER 11 *A REALM OF WONDER*

Eisenhower's daily restatement of what seemed to be all-too-obvious verities may have had a dampening effect on the reader or listener subjected to them in series as he spoke of the horrors of war and the benefits of peace, the evils of prejudice and distortion, and man's basic right to freedom, justice and self-determination.

But as we flew toward Iran, a reappraisal of his reception in India and Pakistan indicated to some of the case-hardened and word-weary journalists that what seemed to them to be trite phrases were being received locally almost as new.

Eisenhower was moving across a part of the world where heads of state seldom dwelled in public on deficiencies of government; they were more inclined to boost the state of affairs at the moment. The President was hitting areas where there was little, if any, public discussion of possibly better government and certainly no widely disseminated questioning or criticism of current government policies. One of these sensitive areas was Iran; oil-rich, heavily militarized with our help, staunchly pro-Western as long as the Persian monarch, Shah Mohammed Riza Pahlevi, remained pro-Western and in power, a country urgently needing agrarian reform, both as to land holding and agricultural technique, a curious midway culture of Tommy guns and ancient Persia.

Iran was, to the West, a valuable member of CENTO (Central Treaty Organization) and Eisenhower's brief visit was intended largely as a gesture of encouragement rather than for any detailed discussion of specific problems.

This was Monday, December 14, and while on a trip of this nature there is a natural tendency to maximize one's own travail, there seemed to be more concern this day for Eisenhower than for self. Although he got to bed before midnight the night before, he had to get up before 5 A.M. in New Delhi for the long drive with Nehru to the Palam Airport.

His day did not end until shortly before midnight in the palace of King Paul of Greece, a rather long pull for a man with a heart condition.

Diary notes for a day that included New Delhi, Teheran and Athens:

This was a 26-hour day, with a total time change of three and a half hours and a long working schedule. Cold and smoky when we left Delhi before dawn. Pan American's big 707 like home. American coffee.

Cold and clear at Teheran. So much military at the field, they looked prepared for invasion. Troops almost shoulder to shoulder all the way into town. People friendly and smiling, but they seem to cheer as a cheering section.

Main street for about a mile covered with Persian rugs, an ancient ceremonial honor in the Middle East. Cars and motorcycles drive right over them. Iranian escort explains this not bad for the rugs at all; good for them. Rugs, hand-woven 500 knots per square inch, frequently very stiff when they come from the rug-maker and merchants—even without Ike—put them on sidewalks or in street to soften them. Can't help but think of the way women at home complain about a few ashes on the rug.

Watched the President and the Shah—properly called the Shahanshah—leave the ruler's Marble Palace for Parliament. They were surrounded by 11 security cars, each bristling with sub-machine guns. This Shah either likes to show off or he's truly scared of something.

Gilbert Grosvenor of *National Geographic* says we're not nearly as interested in such weighty problems as the military situation in the Middle East as in the Shah's fiancée, Farah Diba. We're told that she'll be kept out of sight with the royal

wedding scheduled in a week or so. She has another palace all to herself.

Members of the Shah's court say the lady has a cold and cannot be presented. We understand, however, that just before Eisenhower left, her cold improved sufficiently for a brief introduction.

Maybe our interest in the Queen-to-be isn't too superficial. The Shah has said that unless he produces an heir, his throne will topple, his country will sink into chaos and the Communists will take over. The Shah has divorced two beautiful queens for failure to produce a boy. As handsome as the Shah is, still a little startling in 1959 that in a country with jet aircraft, a beautiful 21-year-old girl can be transformed overnight from the daughter of a commoner to a full-fledged Queen with a gem-studded throne, a husband with an $80 million fortune but essentially, an experiment in breeding. Could an American possibly approximate or understand the thoughts of Farah Diba as she approaches marriage and motherhood? She's 21, he's 45. She'll have to produce within a few years or else. She'll never be poor, however, and in a part of the world that has known so much poverty, this could be so much more of an influence than Americans can appreciate.

The dark, handsome Shah, heavily bemedaled and in a general's khaki winter uniform, was waiting at Mehrabad Airport with Ambassador Edward T. Wales and the Iranian Cabinet on a cold runway when Air Force One landed. As "The Star-Spangled Banner" sounded in the frosty air, Iranian jet fighters roared over the field in a formation that spelled out "IKE."

Eisenhower was admittedly the wide-eyed tourist about his five hours in Iran.

"In my boyhood ancient Persia, its kings and their adventures, the nation's marvels of building, its religion," he said at the airport, "made up a fascinating realm of wonder and romance for a high school student who lived on the plains of Kansas many thousands of miles away, and a half-century ago."

The Iranian government estimated the procession crowd at 750,000, and while this may have been on the generous side, the turnout was impressive. There was no mobbing of the motorcade because of the heavy military guard, but behind the rifles, and from second and third stories of apartments, the people seemed delighted to have a chance to whoop it up.

"We Miss Mamie But Welcome Ike," one large sign said, and there were many others, spelling out greetings from various worker groups, industries and villages. In contrast with Asia, the people of Iran seemed better clothed and better fed. Of course, the Shah could have run the beggars out of town for the day, but there was no evidence of this.

On a percentage basis, Eisenhower probably spent more time talking business in Iran than at any other stop. Of his five hours in the country, he devoted two hours to private talks with the Shah, then they drove a few blocks in their heavily guarded motorcade to the handsome, modernistic new Iranian Senate with beige walls, brilliant blue carpeting and a vaulted ceiling of delicately tinted blue glass.

Addressing the serious-faced members of the Iranian Parliament, Eisenhower praised their firmness against the threats and propaganda of their sometimes menacing neighbor, Russia, and while he made no effort to minimize the importance of military strength in the East-West struggle, he accented other areas of activity—the fight against hunger, privation and disease, along with a reminder that the United States had been helping Iran in this type of endeavor.

With particular emphasis on the importance of the United Nations and CENTO, the President spoke anew of cutting down the world supply of arms to reduce man's temptation to make war.

"It could seem that, as the realities of the awful alternative to peace become clearer to all," he said to the Parliament, "significant progress in the safeguarded reduction of the arms burden can be made. To such a realistic beginning, there is no feasible alternative for the world."

Talk such as this from Eisenhower was not aimed squarely at the Iranian Parliament, but equally at the Sino-Soviet bloc, which, in truth, would be in almost complete control of when and how much the world could disarm. In fact, talk of fewer arms probably encountered a certain amount of official deafness in Iran, one of a number of nations in the area whose rulers seemed intent on building armed forces to cope with border problems rather than the lofty business of power plays between the major powers.

Over a palace lunch of Caspian Sea caviar and partridge, Eisenhower invoked the memory of the ancient Persian kings, Cyrus and Darius, in praise of Iranian resoluteness. This turned out to be standard procedure in each country; along with preaching peace, justice and freedom, praise the local people for having withstood outside efforts to take over and alter their culture. In other words: stay Persian and keep out the Communists.

A sample from the communiqué: "The President took the opportunity to express the admiration of the people of the United States for the brave stand of the Iranian people and government in the face of outside pressure."

The Shah and his government appreciated this encouragement, but they found much more satisfaction in another section of the communiqué in which Eisenhower said the United States would continue its program of assistance to Iran.

Communiqué signed, the President and the Shah sped in a white American convertible to the airport, running a trifle late for the take-off to Greece. Bill Draper made up the time in Air Force One, whipping in over Tourkolimano Harbor six minutes ahead of schedule on a mild winter afternoon.

Diary notes for Athens, December 14:

Looked like rain when we got to Hellinikon Airport, moist gray clouds rolling in over the harbor, but Ike was lucky and the moisture held off. Quite a day, breakfast in Asia, lunch in the Middle East, dinner in Europe. A total of 3,100 miles for the day and someone pointed out, we flew across the entire empire of Alexander the Great who took a couple of years for the same journey.

King Paul, a tall, dignified man, impressively regal. Brought a Rolls-Royce to the airport for Ike. Procession into town down a great dual highway, one of the best airport-to-town routes we'd ever seen, even at home. After Asia, we feel like we're back home. The Greek crowds look American in their dress and manner. Furthermore, they seemed sincerely joyous. Kids set up an awful racket yelling their version of "Ike." Only it came out "Eee-yike."

We're staying with most of the staff at the King's Palace Hotel. Understand this disturbs the Greek Foreign Minister, Constantine Karamanlis. He's afraid that if somebody gets in a fight or there's baggage swiped, the word somehow will get around that it happened in THE palace.

Police say the crowd on the way into town was about 750,000. This figure could be even a trifle low. Crowd was so anxious to see Ike that a real-life tragedy developed just two blocks from the Palace right after the procession passed. Hundreds of people were on a wall in front of an apartment building, pressing against a high iron fence. The wall collapsed, down came the fence and hundreds of spectators, first police figures say over 40 injured, some may die. Ike heard about it after he got to the Palace, quite disturbed, may go to the hospital before he leaves tomorrow.

King Paul was very sticky about letting people inside the Palace grounds. Had to peek through the fence to see Ike meet the pretty Queen Frederika, and the colorful Evzone guard with tasseled caps, fluffy black pleated skirts and their spiked red shoes. Understand these boys are tougher than tough. The Palace grounds are so sacrosanct that some of the Secret Service men, supposed to be on duty on the inside of the grounds, are standing out in the street.

Information Minister gave a mammoth party at the Palace Hotel. Most of the travel party, including Ike's staff, so tired (very few even got to bed in New Delhi last night) that not many thinking in terms of entertainment, but just a warm meal and bed. Hotel closed its dining room and the Minister's party the only immediate source of groceries. The cream of the

Greek government, the diplomatic corps and journalistic circles on hand in a lovely paneled ballroom. Never saw so many handsomely groomed women in furs. Not the coed or Fifth Avenue type of beauty regarded highly at home, but generously proportioned, luxuriant dark hair, great sense of bearing and quiet confidence.

These people must have thought we were a bunch of ill-kempt clods. Hope they've met some Americans who slept recently. Most of the Greeks speak better than passable English. Makes a phrase-book American just a bit ashamed.

The President had to attend a black tie dinner at the palace that night and he must have been as weary as most of his associates when he finally was able to turn in after a twenty-two-hour day.

Athens was frustrating in a way. Here was the seat of Western culture and civilization and much of it was impossible to see because of so little time. Driving into town with the King, the President in the early evening darkness was able to see the architectural trademark of ancient Greece, the fabled Parthenon, which was specially lighted for him, and he also passed close to the Temple of Olympian Zeus as a nearby Greek Navy band played "The Stars and Stripes Forever."

In the business sessions the next day, there were no pressing problems between the United States and Greece, a steady member of the Atlantic Alliance on the rim of the cold war and, like most of the nations that had to be helped to their feet after World War II, continuing economic problems.

In addressing the Greek Parliament, Eisenhower kept up his argument against the stupidity of "the haunting fear of global war and universal death" and he expressed confidence that the Greeks shared with Americans a determination to sustain the conditions necessary to pursue the goal of peace effectively.

At luncheon with the King and the Prime Minister, the chief executive also praised Greece for her contribution to the settlement of the troublesome Cyprus problem and he spoke, too, of the responsibilities of NATO, which he called an alliance "based upon single will to maintain human dignity."

In the streets outside Parliament, there was festive cheering as Eisenhower drove back to the palace to say good-by to the Queen; then quickly to an athletic field near the Athens Stadium, where a familiar American helicopter waited to whisk him through the late afternoon gloom to the sparkling lights of the American cruiser *Des Moines,* waiting with the carrier *Essex* in the harbor to take aboard his large party.

The joint communiqué issued in the name of Eisenhower and Prime Minister Karamanlis took note of the problems Greece faced in raising the standards of living of her people, and there was encouragement from the United States, but no new promises.

The President and the Prime Minister, the communiqué showed, devoted a good portion of their conversations to the situation in the Balkans and the eastern Mediterranean, with a promise that the two governments would take up these matters in more detail through regular diplomatic channels.

Eisenhower apparently was as happy to land aboard the *Des Moines* as we were to climb the long shipside ladders of the *Essex.* Diary notes for this late afternoon:

> Most of us turned out to be incurably American. Never was there a more welcome sight than valiant old Essex, oldest attack carrier in the Navy, our home for three nights. Smells from the galley exciting, the thought of untainted water and milk tantalizing. Very few went to the flight deck to watch the President's helicopter settle down on the stern of the cruiser. Our set unashamedly was much more interested in first things first—getting our mountains of dirty clothes into the ship's laundry. At dinner, everybody on a jag of milk and salad. The President tried to watch a Navy training movie after dinner on the Des Moines, but began to get sleepy and went to bed early.

The curative Mediterranean voyage with units of the American Sixth Fleet was a lifesaver. Diary notes for December 16:

> This morning, many people comparing notes about amount of sleep last night. People who got only 12 hours tabbed as insomniacs. President also slept much later than usual. Mediter-

ranean as calm as a lake. Barbara Eisenhower flew over from Des Moines by 'copter for lunch aboard Essex.

Barbara is an experienced helicopter passenger by now. Manages to remain very ladylike in terrific updraft generated by rotors when the whirlybirds are on the ground. Her worst moment of the trip was in India when an elephant she and John were riding backed into a tree. As Barbara, terrified and clutching at her hat, disappeared into the foliage, someone called, "There goes Lady Greystoke."

The following day, December 17, could be described as a limited success. Eisenhower's helicopter visit to Tunisia while the *Des Moines* waited offshore was simply too fast, too sketchy, and also it raised a question for the future: should presidents be quick to visit new nations? From the public relations standpoint, the idea seems appealing. New nations, however, are probably at their most sensitive stage just as they emerge from colonialism. They tend to be overly conscious of protocol, overly absorbed in their own welfare and woefully touchy about their newness.

The Tunisians had been in business on their own for roughly three years when Ike arrived. President Habib Bourguiba was a staunch friend of the West at a time when most of the other Arab states were either neutral or antagonistic. Bourguiba was playing an important role in trying to get the Algerians to accept De Gaulle's offer of self-determination. Eisenhower could have gone directly from Greece to France for the Western Summit and most of the world would have thought nothing of it. The Tunisians, in bad with the Arab League and Egypt, and under somewhat of a strain with France, would have felt it keenly, however, if Ike, representing the tiny country's biggest and best friend of the moment, had sailed by without stopping. Thus a courtesy visit was indicated.

The motive was excellent, but the execution was difficult. The visit was so speedy that many Tunisians were reported later to have been disappointed bitterly at not having an opportunity to see him.

Diary notes for Tunis:

This was the sort of a day that should have been filmed by Mack Sennett. We took off before dawn from Essex in seven helicopters. Tail lights winking like giant fireflies over the murky outline of town. Went in ahead of the President and the bulk of the party landed at an airport outside town, by bus into the city. Bus lost escort, wound up in alley blocks from destination, hoofed rest of way. Finally found spot where Ike to arrive, a freshly paved parking lot not far from Bourguiba's palace. Hard to say who was causing most trouble, excitable young men from the American embassy or Tunisian troops with Tommy guns. Absolutely no excuse for behavior of some of these Embassy people, flouncing around with arrogant high-pitched orders to stand back. They got the troops so excited that one of Ike's staff had to grab a particularly loud embassy man and tell him to leave the President's party the hell alone. By this time, troops were ramming their damned guns in the stomach of anyone in a tweed suit. A more sensible embassy man said, "This is a new country and they're sensitive." No one ever explained what they were sensitive about.

Further hue and cry from the Embassy people. Ike's helicopter blew the red rug out of place. Limited conversation at the arrival, then off to the palace. Tunisian boys and girls out in gym suits and demonstrating their various athletic skills beside the road—fencing, tumbling, balancing.

Leaving the palace after Eisenhower lunched with Bourguiba, beautiful girls draped everybody in White House party —except Ike—in flowing white woolen robes which we incorrectly identified as a burnoose. Properly called *djellapa* but can't guarantee spelling. Bourguiba's courtyard looked like meeting of Ku-Klux Klan.

Learned new English word in Tunis—ululate. That's what all the white-veiled Tunisian women did when Ike drove by. He seemed startled. Their cry sounds like a tremulous "you-you-you" uttered in a rapid soprano yowl, and coming from behind the veils, it is sort of a disembodied wail. It is a traditional form of welcome in North Africa, like the children clicking stones in Pakistan, but unearthly because an American cannot duplicate the sound.

At the airport to return to Essex, more girls presented each

member of party with large jar of dates, two large baskets of candy, a tremendous wicker hamper of books. This, with top-coat, hat, typewriter and burnoose, made quite a load for climbing into helicopter.

Don't know how things went on Des Moines, but aboard Essex, chaos. Men running under whirling rotors with burnooses flapping. Flight deck looked like a mad laundry. Flight deck officer yells, "Watch out for that next chopper. They may have a camel on it." Bill Henry of the Los Angeles *Times* fell down in escalator from flight deck, spilling his staggering load of bundles. Kind friend punched button reversing direction of escalator and poor Bill carried back up to flight deck on his stomach, enmeshed in a burnoose and a grinding mess of dates, candy and Tunisian history books.

Removed from the fun and games at La Marsa Palace, the two Presidents had two hours devoted largely to the difficulties in Algeria. They agreed that the absence of a solution was "a cause of grave concern."

More important, Eisenhower joined Bourguiba in hailing the achievement of self-determination in sections of Asia and Africa as "one of the most important events of our times."

The La Marsa communiqué also said of the two Presidents: "They welcomed the opportunity offered for the evolution of new relationships [the Congo came later] and the improvement of old ones based on a common attachment to fundamental principles of human rights and dignity."

"You have won the hearts of the men and women of Tunisia who came here as one man to acclaim you," Bourguiba told Ike before he flew back to the cruiser.

The Sixth Fleet task force picked up speed quickly and started northward across the Mediterranean to Toulon, where Secretary Herter was waiting for the President to tell him during an eight-hour train ride to Paris about the situation at the assembling Western Summit.

CHAPTER 12 *THREE WISE MEN*

In the early afternoon of Friday, December 18, the President radioed a message of thanks to the officers and men of the Sixth Fleet task force for his pleasant voyage from Greece, then he went ashore at Toulon. There was a festive crowd in the streets of the French port city as he motored from the docks, where the *Des Moines* tied up, to the railroad station.

Eisenhower seemed pleased by the crowds that cried to him during his short ride through Toulon, but the brisk manner in which he thanked the welcoming French officials and got aboard his train indicated he was thinking primarily of his long conference that night with Herter and the meeting with De Gaulle, Macmillan and Adenauer in Paris the next day.

The brief voyage through balmy weather in the Mediterranean had pushed back the threshold of the fatigue acquired in Asia, but there was something of an emotional letdown. For the most part, the drama of the big trip was over. Malcolm Moos had gone aboard the *Des Moines* with a draft of the State of the Union message and this was now something to be thought about or worked on almost daily until he delivered the message to Congress in January.

The idea of a train ride was novel to most of his party after a succession of jets, helicopters and ships. Diary notes for the 18th:

> Certainly hated to leave Essex and her supply of milk, American cigarettes and roast beef, but we should be sufficiently stuffed and stocked to last through the rest of the trip.

At Toulon, President and party went aboard a prize train of the French National Railroads. We were scarcely beyond the outskirts of Toulon before the train was doing nearly 90 miles an hour. Wonderful roadbed and track, cleverly designed and very well built rolling stock. Know of nothing approaching it in the United States. Everybody talking about the quality ride at high speed.

Aboard train for nearly nine hours, five of which spent in being served lunch (steak) and dinner (lamb chops). The considerate French went to great pains to provide the White House party with fine American bourbon. Yep—most of the people I saw were drinking either Scotch or brandy. Coaches narrower than ours but on this class of equipment, much more luxuriously appointed.

Arrived in Paris late at night. Barbara Eisenhower says the first thing she's going to do is telephone Gettysburg. Hasn't had a word with the kids since leaving. Understand we're going back to Rambouillet for at least one meeting of the principals. Also hear there's a big accumulation of official documents from Washington awaiting the President here. This'll be no rest cure.

De Gaulle at the station to meet Ike even at the late hour. Small honor guard but virtually no ceremony. The two men whisk off in a hurry, and in separate cars, Ike to the embassy residence, De Gaulle to the Élysée. If these two men are sore at each other over NATO, again it doesn't show. Both quite cordial and smiling. De Gaulle, in fact, seemed to be much cheerier than September when we saw him last. Ike knew all the time De Gaulle would be at the station to meet him, but he thanked him so enthusiastically for coming out at that time of night that he seemed to take it as a surprise.

Almost midnight checking into the Crillon Hotel. Seemed like home. Better room than three months ago, this one has a window. Party scattered in several hotels, most of Ike's staff at the Crillon. Poor White House baggage men—gear didn't arrive from the station until 2 A.M.

Despite De Gaulle's outward friendliness, his attitude toward some of the more vital questions involving NATO and France had not changed appreciably since he and the President met three months earlier. There seemed little prospect of a material change in this position at the Western Summit, but the leaders seemed more intent on developing an agreed approach to the spring meeting with Khrushchev. There was no longer any thought of getting together with the Soviets during the winter.

Adenauer wanted from the meeting a stiffer attitude by Eisenhower, Macmillan and De Gaulle on Berlin.

Eisenhower went into the conference at the Élysée Palace the next morning probably in a more powerful position than ever before. The plaudits of the crowds from Italy to India and back again rang not only in his ears, but in those of his colleagues, too.

After meetings during most of Saturday, December 19, the Western Summit on Sunday shifted to Rambouillet. Macmillan had breakfast at the American Embassy residence with Eisenhower and they drove together to De Gaulle's château. On Saturday there had been a long private talk between Eisenhower and De Gaulle, and before leaving Paris the President also met separately with Adenauer.

On Saturday afternoon, the working staffs of the principals began to leak—they had agreed to invite Khrushchev to a Summit in Paris in the spring and promised to spend the intervening months in building a solid front to present to the Russians across the conference table.

While the President was busy with the diplomats, Barbara and John Eisenhower, after checking with the children by telephone, set out for a brief, conventional tourist fling in Paris.

Barbara wanted a Parisienne hair-do and since she had become about as hot a news item as her famous father-in-law, the energetic French reporters were on her trail.

U.P.I. assigned one of its best Paris men, Robert Ahier, to trail Barbara. Bob lost the trail but by deduction he headed for the famous hairdresser, Alexander, and beat Barbara there by a few moments.

I was in the U.P.I. bureau at the time when Ahier telephoned from the beauty salon.

"I am with Barbara Eisenhower," he whispered into the telephone. "We are at Alexander's having her hair done."

"Why are you whispering, Bob?" I asked. "I can barely hear you."

"I am in the next chair to Barbara," he whispered. "What should I do?"

"Have your hair done, too."

John and Barbara went out that night with a group of young French and American couples to the Lido, as much of a tourist stop in Paris as the Eiffel Tower. The show at the Lido is superb vaudeville, with a line of stunning showgirls who waltz on stage bare to their hips.

Since the Big Four principals were working behind closed doors that night, and having seen some Lido shows on previous trips to Paris, I leaped at the opportunity to accompany Ahier to the night club in the line of duty.

When we reached the Lido, I discovered to my horror that Ahier had applied mysterious pressure on the management and had arranged for us to be seated at the same table with the young Eisenhowers. Knowing John's aversion to publicity and realizing that he probably would have been most uncomfortable with me in his lap, I congratulated Ahier but told him this was inexpedient. As Bob negotiated for a table more removed from the center of activities, he grumbled to me with deep Gallic complaint, "This is the first time I've ever tipped a headwaiter to get me a worse table."

By Monday morning, the Western Big Four were ready to report to the world on their talks. Eisenhower, De Gaulle and Macmillan sent separate but similar letters to Khrushchev, proposing an April 27 Summit in Paris. He later asked that it be set for May 16. They also envisioned a series of Summits, as Macmillan had been advocating since the previous spring when he met Eisenhower in Washington.

Eisenhower's letter to Khrushchev said, "We agreed that it would be advisable for the four heads of state or government to meet together from time to time in each other's countries to discuss the main problems affecting the attainment of peace and stability in the world."

The Western Big Four in a joint communiqué reaffirmed previously stated positions on Berlin. For Adenauer, this was progress. It meant no retreat. The Allies stood on their rights in the divided German city and this meant Allied insistence on freedom of access to West Berlin. While British and American spokesmen declined to go quite so far, Adenauer joyfully told colleagues in Paris that the Western stand on Berlin had been "extraordinarily strengthened."

The Big Four also issued a separate economic communiqué setting forth goals for closer economic co-operation in the non-Communist world, with an agreement that the industrialized part of the free world was now in a position to be of greater assistance in the development of poorer nations.

It did not show in the communiqués, but it was obvious elsewhere in Paris that Eisenhower had failed to sell De Gaulle on permitting units of the French Air Force to be integrated into the NATO command.

General Nathan F. Twining, Chairman of the American Joint Chiefs of Staff, had not helped the situation by making the statement, theoretically behind closed doors, that France was foot-dragging in her contributions to NATO. This, too, leaked and the French were furious.

Behind the scenes, Eisenhower believed he made progress with De Gaulle on NATO and French-American relations in general. The President had the delicate task of convincing the French leader that the United States did endorse his Algerian policy despite an American vote of abstention in the United Nations.

Diplomats were highly interested in the invitations to Khrushchev. Nothing was said about working out an agreed agenda in advance of April 27. This was a marked change in Western

policy. In preparing for the 1955 Geneva Summit, the problem of agreeing on an agenda required almost as much work as the main conference itself. The new attitude toward an agenda certainly marked a change in American thinking and possibly it reflected Eisenhower's efforts to try everything possible for maintaining reasonably civil relations with Russia in the hope that at least a start could be made on disarmament.

It was in Paris on the morning of Monday, December 21, that Eisenhower made one of his less immortal commentaries on foreign policy. It was a chance remark, which he possibly regretted when he saw newspaper headlines saying, "Ike's Answer to Cold War—Drink Coke."

He was at the Embassy chancery saying Merry Christmas and good-by to the staff. He had just come from the intensive meetings with the Western leaders and he was aware that the differences with France over NATO still, to many people, overshadowed the greater accomplishments of the Paris talks. He was optimistic about prospects for coping successfully with international differences.

Standing in the marble lobby of the chancery, Ike with a glowing grin said: "Now I happen to be one of those that is a born optimist, and I suppose most soldiers are, because no soldier ever won a battle if he went into it pessimistically. I make no apologies for being optimistic because I still have the faith in humans, in their individual and their collective good sense and readiness, courage to look facts in the face, that we can solve these problems."

(There was an Eisenhower sentence that sounded perfectly understandable as he said it under conversational circumstances, but in print it defies punctuation.)

"And this is between ourselves—Indians or Africans—the French—anyplace where differences occur. And one way I think we can keep them from becoming more noticeable—sometimes more irritating than anything—is when we don't help to make them worse. The criticisms we have of another people because they are different, in their background, their traditions and their prejudices, then we are—all right, let's ignore them and have a good laugh on it and drink a Coca-Cola."

There were giggles in the audience. Ambassador Houghton tried to keep from laughing. Ike, himself, realized what he had done.

"Oh-oh, I've been accused of being commercial," he said, then picking up his interrupted sentence, "—have a soft drink and in this way every one of us will be doing a job."

One of the less reverent members of the embassy staff walked out into the courtyard telling a colleague, "It's all so clear now, the more Coke we drink, the more we scare Khrushchev."

If it needs to be pointed out, what Eisenhower was saying was that tension begets tension; that it is much better to accept differences between nations in stride than it is to live constantly in long-faced apprehension.

At any rate, Eisenhower seemed to be in relatively good spirits as the Western Summit ended and he started on the home stretch of his lengthy journey. There had been no street crowds in Paris, but this seemed to have no effect on the President. This was not a parade-type visit, the weather was cold and the French people were busy preparing for Christmas. What happened in the next town, Madrid, was much more interesting from the aspect of public reaction.

There were many Americans who objected to Eisenhower visiting Generalissimo Francisco Franco, who in the preceding decade had been on the black list of just about every nation. In 1958, Spain was in dire economic trouble because of too rapid industrial expansion undertaken at Franco's behest. At the time of Eisenhower's visit, conditions were somewhat better because of a rigorous campaign of economic stabilization—and some $400 million in loans.

There were large American air and naval bases on Spanish soil and despite Franco's twenty years of dictatorship, the Western struggle with Communist expansion no longer could afford to leave Spain on the outside. She had been accepted into the United Nations and while she did not belong to NATO, her alliance with the United States was solid.

This was the largest controlled state on Eisenhower's itinerary. There was bitterness at home about the President bolstering Franco in the eyes of the world, but there was also the fact that the United States had an investment in Spain of about two billion dollars.

After a farewell luncheon at the Élysée Palace with De Gaulle, Macmillan and Adenauer, Eisenhower took a helicopter to Orly Airport, where he boarded Air Force One for a flight of less than two hours to Torrejon Air Base (USAF) outside Madrid.

The President had his special "bubble-top" limousine with its clear plastic cover sent from Paris to Madrid for the occasion.

Torrejon was under tight military control, American and Spanish, as the Generalissimo arrived a few minutes before the Eisenhower plane landed. Four carloads of security men were with the dictator, crammed eight and nine to a car, a fact which interested our agents, who wondered how the Spaniards could possibly unload in a hurry if an emergency developed.

The Generalissimo wore what seemed to be a new military uniform of a rich khaki-colored woolen fabric. Clean-shaven and hawk-faced, Franco wore no medals on his overcoat and to many of us seeing him for the first time, he was a bit shorter than we had expected, and not so old.

It was late afternoon when Air Force One roared over the field and Franco walked alone past a unit of the Spanish Civil Guard in their patent leather tricornered hats to the bottom of the landing ramp.

The President came down the steps smiling in the raw, fifty-degree windy weather and clasped Franco's outstretched hand. After military honors and presentation to a long line of Spanish dignitaries, the President and Franco were escorted to a small speaker's platform by brilliantly costumed aides carrying silver maces and dressed in purple velvet doublets with broad purple hats and towering white ostrich plumes.

"It is with deep satisfaction that I have shaken your hand for the first time," Franco said, reading from a text.

Eisenhower spoke first of the glories of ancient Spain, the

Spain of Isabella and Ferdinand, Columbus, De Soto, De Vaca and Coronado.

"But I do not come here to recall our ties of old and recent times, important though they are," Eisenhower said. "I come to this nation, one of the ancestors of the Americas, with a message from the American people to the Spanish people, looking for a brighter future in co-operative labor for the noblest of all human causes—peace and friendship in freedom."

The long parade into town, through the heart of Madrid to Moncloa Palace where Eisenhower spent the night, took more than an hour. It was the greatest crowd since India, and again an estimate of one million along the procession route was used generally, although it seemed to some of us a smaller crowd than in New Delhi.

Franco wanted his visitor to have a fine welcome and despite an intermittent cold sprinkle of rain, the streets were mobbed. Massive arches inscribed *"Hispania Saluda a Ike"* were erected over the streets. The face of one building was covered with a colored picture of the President four stories high. One five-story building was draped from top to bottom in one American flag and another building, the highest in the city, arranged window lights to spell out "Ike" vertically for over a hundred feet.

We were told that the Spanish government distributed 200,-000 flags for the occasion. There was an unusual quality to the Madrid crowd. The people laughed and shouted and called *"Viva Ike"* but their jollity seemed to drain away immediately after the President and Franco rolled by in the White House limousine. There was a rapid on-and-off quality to the enthusiasm.

It was cold, wet and dark and it seemed obvious that after paying tribute to the visitor, the Spaniards were intent on getting home as soon as possible.

Diary notes for that night in Madrid:

Spanish foreign office official who spoke beautiful English rode in the car with the press association men not far from the President and Franco. We told him that on this same day back in

Washington one of the newspapers had carried a cartoon and an editorial taking Eisenhower to task for visiting Franco. We wondered what would happen if a Spanish newspaper decided to print a cartoon and an editorial personally critical of Franco.

Man was embarrassed. Said the question was moot. It just would not happen. We persisted, what would happen if it did? Official said that such a thing was unnecessary in Spain, that if the copy for such an editorial ever reached the composing room, the printers would know someone had lost his mind and that would be the end of that.

Security around Moncloa Palace tightest ever. We were supposed to pull inside grounds and drive with President and Franco to Oriente Palace where they had dinner. But Spanish security would not hear of it. I went to gate to talk to Secret Service agent we knew, he told me to turn slowly and walk back to automobile with no more fuss, that more tommy guns than I would like to know about were trained on me. Agent returned to car with me, told us the Spaniards weren't fooling, for us to fall in behind the procession as best we could but to make no issue of it.

Newspapermen struck us as being afraid of their shadows. Spanish news agency man said he didn't understand how Marv Arrowsmith of the AP and I could go sound asleep in the car outside the courtyard of Oriente Palace. Tried to explain we were very tired, and also, if you're going to get shot, makes little difference whether one is asleep or awake. Spanish man didn't think that was very funny.

At dinner that night in the glittering Oriente Palace, relations between the two leaders were cordial but not effusive. The setting was warm but the guests seemed to be on their best behavior. Hard to define, but definitely there was a stiffness, a formality missing from a number of other similar contacts by the President during his trip.

His toast to Franco was brief and courteously friendly.

The next morning, Tuesday, December 22, the President left Moncloa before eight o'clock and drove four miles to Franco's residence, Pardo Palace, a onetime hunting lodge surrounded by delicate gardens and gravel pathways, rows of cedars and pines—and guards. To reach the dining room, Franco took the President through four gorgeously tapestried drawing rooms. The dining room was enormous, about a hundred feet long with the walls decorated with eighteenth- and nineteenth-century tapestries done from the paintings of Goya and Teniers. One forty-foot Teniers panel of a fiesta scene was so realistic and faithful in detail that it showed four celebrants retiring to relieve themselves, an art note which captivated some of the White House people as the President sat down to breakfast of steak and Sanka thoughtfully provided by the Generalissimo.

After breakfast, Eisenhower, Franco and their advisers went into the dictator's study and the meeting began with the President commenting on how much older he himself looked in black and white photographs.

Their business meeting took about an hour. Franco seemed ill at ease much of the time, while Eisenhower plunged into the discussions with his customary informal manner. The President opened with a review of his trip, an analysis of each country visited and particular reference to the Western Summit. He sought Franco's estimation of world-wide Communism and the Generalissimo responded at some length.

Eisenhower then congratulated the Spanish dictator on the evident progress in attacking Spain's economic ills. He also expressed his appreciation for co-operation of the Franco government in the matter of the American bases.

From the session came a brief communiqué which expressed the view that the forthcoming conferences with Russia would improve the climate of international relationships "although a firm defense posture should be maintained" in the meantime.

If there were señoritas with dark and flashing eyes, and the fiery crackle of flamenco music in Madrid, few of us saw them or heard the music.

I do, however, have a most vivid memory of Franco's security men. Their number and their tense trigger fingers were trademarks of a dictatorship. Even after twenty years in power,

.

Franco could take no chances, not even with the men and women traveling with the guest President. I remember, too, the uncomfortable edginess of the Spanish reporters as they listened to their American counterparts complain and criticize.

Eisenhower flew by helicopter from Pardo Palace to Torrejon Air Base in the late morning and said his farewell to Spain.

Air Force One raced toward Morocco, last stop before home. We were due late that night at Andrews Field and there were reports of heavy snow in Washington. Plans were made for a civic reception for the President and his advisers wondered how a few thousand Washingtonians on a late winter night would look beside some of the ovations Ike received abroad.

As the end of the trip neared, the speeches became blessedly shorter, but not the parades. It took only a little more than an hour to reach Nouasseur Air Force Base outside Casablanca, where King Mohammed V waited on a sun-swept runway in a long, fawn-colored burnoose with a hood and a peaked cap.

The exchange of speeches at the airport deserves recording because it was historically short. The White House transcript of the momentous occasion:

KING MOHAMMED V: Mr. President, we are very happy to welcome you and receive you among our brothers. The entire nation of Morocco is very glad to receive you, although your stay is very short.

PRESIDENT EISENHOWER: Your Majesty, it is indeed a very great honor for me to be received here on the ground of this nation which was the first nation that recognized the independence of the United States one and three-quarters centuries ago.

So it is a definite feeling of kinship with this nation that I sense as I come here to have these few hours with His Majesty and with his people. And my party and I assure you—we do so with a feeling of honor and privilege.

Within minutes, Eisenhower found himself in a rip-roaring Wild West welcome by Berber tribesmen and hundreds of thousands of Moroccans who had begun gathering before dawn beside the narrow road from the air base into the city, which had changed immensely since Franklin D. Roosevelt and Winston Churchill met there secretly during the early days of World War II.

The Moroccan welcome may have been smaller than New Delhi or Madrid, but for color and enthusiasm it matched anything on the trip. Thousands of Berber tribesmen, the sharp-faced warriors who fought the French Foreign Legion so bitterly thirty years before, came down from the foothills of the Atlas Mountains to line the highway and fire their ancient muzzle-loading rifles as Eisenhower drove by with the King in a brilliantly polished white convertible.

The crowd probably totaled more than a half-million, many of them remembering Ike from his days in North Africa and his role in forcing the Germans back across the Mediterranean. Veiled women gurgled their "you-you-you" greeting from behind their veils and children played a rattling accompaniment on countless tambourines.

The Secret Service chief, Baughman, rode ahead of the President and he found that if he waved his hat energetically, the tribesmen beside the highway fired their muzzle-loaders before Eisenhower drew abreast of them. Baughman was not so worried about a Berber shooting the President as he was concerned about the noise in Eisenhower's ears and the prospect of wadding from the blank charges spattering the open automobile. The King seemed completely unconcerned and rode almost stonelike, while Ike acknowledged the cheers with all of his well-known gestures.

The business meeting between the King and the President was brief, and over lunch at the palace Eisenhower had good news for the fiercely nationalistic Moroccans. United States forces in Morocco would be withdrawn completely by the end of 1963 and immediate steps would be taken to release one air base at Ben Slimane. The United States had announced in October, 1959, that eventually her Moroccan bases would be given up, but no date was set. Thus Eisenhower's announcement to

the King added a note of businesslike accomplishment to his brief visit.

Shortly before dark, Eisenhower drove back to Nouasseur Air Force Base and boarded Air Force One for the homeward flight. In the darkness around the ramp, it was difficult to tell whether he looked unusually tired. Most of us were so bushed that our judgments would not have been particularly valid.

After a flight of more than nine hours, Eisenhower's plane touched down at Andrews about eleven o'clock the night of Tuesday, December 22, another one of those twentieth-century days with breakfast on one continent, lunch on a second and bed on the third.

Riding across the Atlantic that night, many of us were engaged in summation and evaluation, a process also under way on Air Force One. Fatigued or not, the President was scheduled to report to the people from Washington the next night.

Hensley thought the diplomatic peaks of the trip were reached in India and at the Western Summit. As for the rest of the stops, Hensley thought that while they were highly important locally, they were largely matters of back-slapping for the West and listening to cautious explorations into the field of additional American aid. Hensley was most impressed by the President's crowd impact in Asia. He thought, too, that the announcement from Morocco about withdrawal of American forces might have a profound effect on the thinking of a number of Asian and African countries.

In the appraisal memo I wrote that night over the Atlantic, I said:

From the standpoint of foreign mass consumption, the trip was a big success. Sure, some of the crowds were manufactured but a lot of them were not. No matter how Eisenhower's motives and accomplishments may be argued, it is undeniable that millions of people on three continents turned out to cheer him.

It seems logical that when millions . . . cheer an American President in foreign lands, the United States as a whole benefits.

With this adulation, however, comes responsibility and expectation. The cheers of today can turn awfully sour if those doing the cheering are led to expect something in return—and they don't get it.

To keep some of this pro-American sentiment in flower undoubtedly will require the help of Congress. And there is reason to doubt the President will receive any unusual support from a Democratic Congress in a national election year.

The President, beneath the National Community Christmas Tree south of the White House on the night of December 23, thought the long journey had been mutually beneficial to visitor and visited.

"I wish every American, certainly every American who is recognized by his fellows as a leader, and every leader in the countries of the West could see and hear what I have seen and heard," he said. "The mutual understanding thereby created could in itself do much to dissolve the issues that divide the world."

He also said:

"I talked with Kings and Presidents, Prime Ministers and humble men and women in cottages and mud huts. Their common denominator was their faith that America will help lead the way toward a just peace."

He was impressed by the desire for self-improvement in the have-not nations and thought America's help had to continue.

Money alone, he said, could not guarantee progress in any land, but the best interests of the United States required continuation of foreign aid and investment; not alone as a single rich power but in co-operation with other nations to the extent of their ability "in a long-term program, dependable in its terms and in its duration."

On Christmas Day, 1959, the Gallup Poll informed Dwight Eisenhower that the American public regarded him as the "most admired man" in the world. Somehow, Dr. Gallup's poll-takers must have missed those who thought the President should remain at home.

CHAPTER 13 *HAIL TO THE CHIEF CHA-CHA-CHA*

Shortly after Christmas, the President began planning a trip to South America, a venture long overdue in the minds of many key State Department advisers and the President's own brother, Dr. Milton Eisenhower, President of Johns Hopkins University in Baltimore.

Milton Eisenhower, long an advocate of closer relations with Latin America, had been his brother's speaker in South and Central America on several occasions. Milton was widely respected and admired by the Southern neighbors, but he knew that in the area there was disenchantment with this country, not entirely because of Communist propaganda pouring into Latin America, but also due to economic unrest, the distention of inflation and the pinch of counteractive austerity.

The larger South American nations were beginning to feel that the otherwise friendly Western powers did not take Latin-American opinion into consideration in their summitry. This went to the roots of the Good Neighbor policy. The Latin Americans felt we were good enough neighbors, but we did not ask them over to the house when there were important guests. In essence, we took them too much for granted in a world where Soviet salesmen were beginning to stir.

Khrushchev himself was in motion, dropping new hints of recharging the Berlin crisis. Italian President Gronchi went to see the Soviet leader in Moscow, and shortly afterward the other Western Allies heard reports that Mr. K. still wanted them to get out of Berlin, he wanted recognition of the Communist East German government and he did not intend to ease up on these basic Soviet aims at the May 16 Summit in return for Allied acceptance of some of Russia's disarmament ideas. These reports of a stiffening Khrushchev were circulated authoritatively in February of 1960, long before the ill-fated May 1 downing of the American U-2.

Khrushchev also had been in Southeast Asia on a good-will tour that produced mixed results. He was not uniformly well received, largely due to his own doltish behavior. In Indonesia, for example, he waved away a gift of native handicraft, saying he was more interested in machine-made products as signposts of progress.

Nehru was complaining in India that too many people in his own country were "obsessed" with the cold war.

There had been spectacular if not deep trouble in Panama over the rights of the Panamanian Republic vis-à-vis the United States-controlled Canal Zone. Fidel Castro had Cuba in turmoil and spores of his anti-Yankee doctrines were finding fertile cultures in some Latin-American areas, particularly in normally left-wing labor and student groups.

At the peak of the Panamanian difficulty and with Castro's actions beginning to match his invective against this country, I heard one of the ranking career men of the State Department argue with vehemence unusual for a professional diplomat that Eisenhower's personality was needed in Latin America more than any other part of the world.

"How do we expect those people down there to feel about their good neighbor to the north when the President visits places like Afghanistan and Iran and doesn't give his good friends of South America so much as a howdy-do?" this official said.

"I've been urging a presidential good-will trip to South America for two years without getting anywhere. We better start paying some attention to Kubitschek as well as Chiang Kai-shek."

(The author is not being coy about this man's identity, but

he still is a ranking American diplomat in a sensitive post where he might be embarrassed if he were named.)

Against such a background of international developments, regional feelings and urgent recommendations, the President gave the go-ahead for a fast aerial tour of over fifteen thousand miles to Puerto Rico, Brazil, Argentina, Chile and Uruguay. He called it a tour of the "southern tier" of South America. Presidents Hoover, Roosevelt and Truman had been to Brazil and/or Argentina, but it was the first time an American chief executive had visited Chile or Uruguay. There were strong feelings in Washington and elsewhere that he should have gone to Peru and Venezuela, the country where Vice President Nixon was stoned, but the four-country itinerary stood.

Departure from Washington was set for Monday, February 22, with Eisenhower's return planned for about March 6.

Jim Hagerty, per custom, made an advance tour of the route and came back to Washington with a doleful report. He called some of us into his office as soon as he returned from the survey flight.

"This is going to be the toughest one yet," Jim said. "It's summer down there and we'll be in hot or rainy weather most of the time. To get to some of these places, we'll be switching from jet to prop planes and back to jet. The baggage will never catch up with us. The schedule is faster and tighter than Asia and there are all sorts of possibilities of trouble in Argentina and Uruguay with the Peronistas and student groups but the police say they can handle it. They're small groups and they don't represent the feelings of the countries, but you'll have to play heads-up ball all the way."

Diary notes for February 22:

Hagerty was right—right at the start of this trip. We had to be at the White House at 4:30 A.M. Hensley and I teamed together again on this one. He called about 2 A.M. to say it was snowing and we'd better allow extra time for getting to 1600. Cabs in Washington hard to get even in a heavy dew.

Same old system. We took off from Friendship near Baltimore, DDE from Andrews. Press party over 70, Pan Am 707 jet again. Hauling White House personnel, Secret Service and State Department people, too, we have to leave in time to put them on the ground an hour ahead of the President. This can become so irritating on a trip like this that it becomes obsessive and one begins to think of Ike as plotting against sleep for all other people.

Capt. Aurand out ahead of us with his covey of helicopters. We hear he flew one over the Andes. The choppers and the White House cars—the big bubble-top Lincoln and the enormous SS follow-up phaeton—were shipped down ahead by cargo plane or naval vessel.

Barely time for breakfast before we landed in San Juan. Winter clothing very scratchy in Puerto Rican sun. Eisenhower shifted to a lightweight suit by the time he arrived.

On to Ramey Air Force Base about 75 miles from San Juan for the night. Eisenhower went to a party at the Officer's Club and seldom seen him so tappy-toe. What got him in such a swinging mood was a group of Navy musicians playing Caribbean music on steel oil drums. He climbed up on the bandstand to get out of the rain and kept vigorous time to the music by tapping his foot. Someone says the band is playing the "Hail to the Chief Cha-cha-cha."

The brief stop at the San Juan Airport was primarily a matter of courtesy. With Secret Service memories of the Puerto Rican Nationalists who shot up Blair House and the Congress, the crowd at the airport was tightly controlled. On the highway leading to the field, there were demonstrating advocates of Puerto Rican independence but Eisenhower did not see their placards saying "Go to Hell and Leave Us Alone." The short time he had with Governor Luis Muñoz Marín was devoted largely to discussing the Cuban situation.

Muñoz Marín concurred in Eisenhower's attitude of forbearance toward Castro. Both men felt that, for the time being, moderation had to be the Washington policy.

Traveling with Eisenhower on the trip, in addition to his

regular staff, were Secretary Herter; the President's brother, Milton; five members of the President's National Advisory Committee on Inter-American Affairs; Robert Cutler, U.S. director of the new Inter-American Development Bank; plus Roy Rubottom, Assistant Secretary of State for Inter-American Affairs, and Wiley Buchanan.

Winter clothing deposited for safekeeping with the Air Force at Ramey, Eisenhower and company left early next morning for a flight of nearly six hours to what in many ways was the most interesting stop of the trip.

His destination: Brasilia, the amazing new capital of Brazil, a still unfinished metropolis being driven to completion as the pet project of President Juscelino Kubitschek, a Czech immigrant's son who gave up a flourishing surgery practice to enter politics in the mid-thirties, a man inflamed with the idea of hastening Brazil out of the jungle into the mainstream of industrialized expansion.

Estimates of the cost of Brasilia ran as high as a half-billion dollars, many Brazilians called it "Kubitschek's Folly," the diplomatic corps was grumbling about having to leave the urbane comforts of Rio de Janeiro for a raw outpost six hundred airline miles inland, but Kubitschek was determined to force the attention and energies of his countrymen from the coastline which they had hugged for centuries to the vast natural riches of the interior.

Brasilia was designed for an eventual population of about 500,000, but at the time of Eisenhower's visit, there were only about seventy thousand people on hand, most of them construction workers and a few of their families plus a vanguard of Brazilian officialdom. There were only two restaurants open, an overcrowded dining room of the only hotel, and a grubby bar and grill. Most of the workers ate and lived in a frontier camp town on the edge of the capital or in muddy cantonments of crude lumber shacks around the foundations of the buildings on which they were working.

Diary notes for February 23 in Brasilia:

From the air, the world's most modern capital looks like an enormous housing development not quite ready for the tenants; on the ground, more like a half-finished movie set than a city where government servants will report for work in two months. Most of the buildings and roads still under some form of construction except Kubitschek's palace, a modernistic establishment of reflecting pools, great expanse of glass, free form concrete gables and the only lawn in town.

Such red, red faces at the airport. Someone passed the word to Kubitschek back at his palace that Air Force One would be 20 minutes late. It wasn't. No host, so Ike remained aboard the plane chatting with Herter. Protocol men wore ruts in the runway pacing up and down in their anxiety. This just doesn't happen in their world. Ike sends word down to them: don't worry.

Their worries were only beginning. Kubitschek arrived in a cloud of dust of which Brasilia has more than her share. Functionaries rolled out the required red carpet, but to their livid embarrassment they had about 60 feet of carpet left over when they got to the ramp. The left-over made a sizable roll, so big Ike couldn't get over it. One has never heard consternation expressed to its fullest until it's done in Portuguese. Crowd of dignitaries at far end of rug made it impossible to cinch it up in that direction. Ike stood leaning against the door of AF 1 smiling. Kubitschek standing helplessly down below.

Dreadful stage wait of several minutes before intelligent USAF sergeant in his overalls slipped in among the mustache-biting diplomats and solved the problem so simply with his pocket knife. Cut the rug neatly at the foot of the ramp and removed offending surplus. Band played "Star-Spangled Banner," guns sounded 21-shot salute and Eisenhower came off the plane to begin his visit to South America.

There was a tumultuous ride to the heart of the city. More than a procession, it was a rag-taggle chariot race with ambulances, clay-covered construction trucks, careening mobile platforms for photographers and dauntless Brazilians on motor scooters, some with wives clutching babies in their arms on the

rear fenders—all competing to ride abreast of the two Presidents.

It was safe to say that the entire present population of seventy thousand turned out, many of them piled atop earth-movers, dump trucks and tractors. The elaborate highway system was only months old, but the presidential car had to veer around large potholes punched into the pavement by heavy construction vehicles.

The President's first stop was an open-air cellar beneath a massive traffic cloverleaf. At this stage of development in Brasilia, it was the best place for a civic reception and several thousand workers gathered to greet the visitor. The government also installed an escalator to transport the President from ground level to the rostrum about a hundred feet below.

After greeting the pioneers of Brasilia and comparing their activity to the boom spirit of the American Western frontier, Eisenhower visited the site of the future American Embassy, occupied at the time only by a green house trailer and the ever-present White House telephone.

Then the two Presidents went to a grassy woodland to unveil a monument commemorating the visit. In this sylvan setting not far from the towering skyscraper offices and apartments of the new capital, Eisenhower joined with Kubitschek in a Declaration of Brasilia which called for a "hemispheric crusade for economic development." This was the keynote of Eisenhower's entire South American trip, the need for co-ordinated action by the Americas to combat underdevelopment and the realization that economic advancement was an integral part of preserving the peace.

The document was prepared in advance by the two governments and read in behalf of two chief executives by Herter and Foreign Minister Horacio Lafer. Many South Americans had felt that the United States was so preoccupied with self-security and the problems of Europe and Asia that she had neglected co-operation and progress within the Western Hemisphere. The Declaration of Brasilia and subsequent statements by Eisenhower in South America were designed to ease these fears.

With his public duties for the day at an end, the President then motored between columns of chuffing construction equipment, much of it imported from West Germany, to Kubitschek's stunning Alvorada Palace. Diary notes on his arrival there:

The President was stopped a bit cold by the modernistic magnificence of Alvorada. He had just come from the towering center of the city, yet when he walked through the enormous glass doors of the main entrance to the palace, Eisenhower saw the Brasilia skyline stretched out before him through what seemed to be a giant picture window.

"I'm all turned around," he said to Kubitschek. "I thought we just came from there." Then he discovered he was looking into a vast mirror, an incredible mirror running across the full length of an enormous room. The colors were startling—the silver sheen of the mirror with no perceptible seams, a broad white wall at one end and at the other a two-story wall of gleaming gold bricks.

DDE had a second floor suite, ceiling-to-floor plate glass on two sides of his dining room, bedroom overlooking a crescent-shaped artificial lake. Tired as he was, the President was like a boy with a new toy, kept exclaiming that no head of state in the world had a place like this. Dr. Milton, John, Gen. Goodpaster and Ann Whitman also installed in Alvorada, but the rest of the party split up between the small hotel and a nearly finished apartment house.

Our apartment, with a lovely approach through several acres of adhesive red mud, was a gem. Ultra modern. Much smaller scale than Alvorada, but similar room design. All rooms solid glass at one end (except bathroom). No curtains. Women in party had to undress in the dark. What an incredible effort Kubitschek undertook to have the President begin his visit here. The apartment house was not ready for occupancy and had to be furnished just for this overnight stop. Living room chairs, couches and tables shipped from Rio by air and overland by truck, 850 miles by road. Beds were built here out of two-by-fours.

One member of the party had to switch apartments—the

electric light socket over his bed was leaking water. Hagerty had no sheets on his bed, slept on hard felt mattress. Not a trace of clothing hooks or hangers. Left clothes on living room couch.

Communications problem from Brasilia terrible. Radioteletypes out for about three hours. Telephones, too. We were cut off from the world as far as I could tell, but the White House maintained communications with Rio through their own radio facilities.

Lights burning in almost all government buildings during the night from skyscraper offices to the soaring, modernistic cathedral. Periodically, much whistle-blowing and sirens, signaling change of construction gang shifts. At the bar and grill, the people talk about reinforcing some of the concrete with wooden timbers instead of steel, wondering how Brasilia will look 10 years from now. Within a maximum of two years, all of the diplomats will have to vacate Copacabana Beach in Rio and head for these hills. The grass should be growing by then.

On February 24, the scene shifted to Rio, one of the more beautiful cities of the world. Kubitschek flew out of Brasilia ahead of Eisenhower, who arrived at midday in the old capital for an enthusiastic but slightly curious metropolitan reception. It was just a few days before the annual pre-Lenten carnival season, Rio's traditional time for celebration, and many Brazilians were preoccupied with their preparations for the holidays. By delightful coincidence, the top carnival song, always composed and exploited some weeks in advance, for 1960 was "Hey You, Give Me Money," which was used waggishly by cartoonists and editorial writers in Rio to sum up Ike's visit.

Brazilian officials estimated the crowd that greeted Eisenhower on the streets of Rio at one million or better, insisting that it exceeded any reception accorded a foreign visitor in Brazil's history. (I thought Truman did better in 1947.) White House officials openly went along with the million estimate, but privately they said the turnout had not lived up to their expectations. It was midsummer, many Brazilians were away and not planning to return until, or after, the three days of carnival. It was like trying to drum up a crowd in midtown New York on the Saturday afternoon before Labor Day.

There were clouds of confetti and carnival serpentine. Samba bands serenaded him as he drove through the howling heart of Rio with Kubitschek at his side. On Rio Branco, the broad avenue beside Guanabara Bay, Eisenhower saw his first evidence of Castro's just-beginning impact on South America. Young Brazilians leaned from the windows of a building and roared "Fidel, Fidel." From another building, a crude fifty-foot portrait of the Cuban fluttered beside Ike's procession. If there were other evidences of this sentiment, they could not be detected from the motorcade to the American Embassy residence.

Eisenhower was off to another strong personal triumph and his speeches were marked by much more substance than many of his remarks on the December Asian trip. On his first day in Rio, he made two important talks. In the classic old Tiradentes Palace, he told the Brazilian Congress the United States would take a stern attitude toward any outside efforts to meddle in the internal affairs of any of the Americas.

"We would consider it intervention in the internal affairs of an American state if any power, whether by invasion, coercion or subversion, succeeded in denying freedom of choice to the people of any of our sister republics," he told the cheering joint session of senators and deputies.

This was obviously a warning intended for Communism, a modernized and flexible restatement of the Monroe Doctrine. It remained debatable as to how this would apply to Cuba, where the Castro regime sought out contacts with Russia.

A driving rain swept Rio as Eisenhower left Tiradentes Palace and headed for the Brazilian Supreme Court. This was something new in his travels, a special call on the judicial branch of government in each country. The President was embarrassingly late at the court because of the rain and an unexpected social reception after the appearance before the Congress.

The justices, sitting calmly behind banks of flowers around their U-shaped bench, did not seem to mind. They listened attentively as he paid tribute to the rule of law over rule of the sword, then he swirled off in the rain again, running over an hour late for a date with the ambassadors of the other Latin-American nations to whom he wanted to explain why he could not visit their countries. He said his schedule back in Washington would not permit more than the four countries and he urged them to convey his explanation and regrets to their presidents.

Rain continued to harass Eisenhower in Rio. Not only the President but members of his party. One man sent his baggage on to the plane and then decided during the night before departure to rinse out his theoretically drip-dry shirt, underwear and socks. It rained all that night and in the humidity the laundry was even wetter the next morning. The thrifty traveler had to make his way aboard Air Force One thoroughly sodden.

Rain also caused difficulty for the Brazilian Foreign Office on Ike's first night in Rio. He went to dinner with Kubitschek at Itamarati Palace, a gracious, handsome structure around a beautiful courtyard with a palm-guarded pool and garden walkways. Diary notes for that night:

> Because of the rain, the Foreign Office during the afternoon tried to cancel an after-dinner reception for 3,000 guests, but the women of Rio were not to be denied. They showed up in the rain, presented their invitations and marched in beneath husband-held umbrellas. Foreign office man said many of the ladies had spent a thousand or more dollars for their dresses just for the one evening. They looked it, too, except for the wet weather cases of drooping hair-do. Poor gals barely got a look at Ike and Kubitschek. Everybody had to stay under shelter and the palace, a succession of fairly small rooms, made it too much of a job for Eisenhower to plow his way through several thousand people. He saw a few and headed for home while hundreds were clamoring for entrance. Is this man's weather luck running out?

The rain stayed with him the next day, Thursday, February 25, when he switched from his jet to the old prop-powered *Columbine III* for a side trip to São Paulo, the booming industrial heart of Brazil with a population of 3,500,000, about the size of Rio. In a predominantly agricultural country with its industry heavily dependent upon foreign sources for basic industrial raw materials and machinery, the industrialization of São Paulo had been painful but the results were a great source of national pride.

The people of São Paulo, the Paulistas, were not at all modest as they referred to themselves as "the locomotive pulling twenty cars." The Paulistas, makers of automobiles, trucks and farm machines, were a much different people compared with the pleasurable *cariocas* of Rio. They were brisk, energetic, let's-get-moving types on a continent where this attitude of hustle seemed rare.

Diary notes for that day with the Paulistas:

> The booming factory prosperity makes one think of Pittsburgh or Detroit; the boastful pride recalls Texas. The locals started telling Ike's party at Congonhas Airport that their city was the biggest and best. "This is Brazil," they said, "not those samba dancers in Rio." One thing for sure: they outdid Rio by a lot in turning out for Eisenhower, even in a heavy rain that plastered his bald head with wet confetti; looked like a man with Technicolor freckles. Ike got soaked in the parade and changed clothes at the governor's palace. Got wet again at the memorial to the Brazilian war dead of World War II. Buzz in White House walkie-talkie radios disclosed a live electric wire dangling from a loudspeaker post at the memorial. Gave it careful distance.
>
> This is the automobile capital of Brazil, our driver an employee of the local Ford assembly plant, can't understand the diplomacy of Ike importing the bubble-top limousine from Washington. Neither could we. This is a security measure and in many foreign countries without big automobiles, a parade practicality. But it didn't sit well in São Paulo.

Crowds didn't seem to care, however. Scads of "Welcome Ike" signs. When they yell his name down here, it comes out "Eeek," like a woman in a comic strip seeing a mouse. There were at least a half million people and quite probably more out in the heavy rain. Ike standing and bare-headed most of the drive. Gov. Carlos Alberto Carvalho Pinto was smart and stayed under the bubble-top.

Even in the downpour, São Paulo—they pronounce it "Sown Pow-lo"—a most attractive city with towering, ultra-modern skyscrapers that disgorged tons of colored paper as Ike drove by. A blizzard of color—confetti dotting the robes of priests and nuns as they scampered through the downpour, center of the city a vast mushroom bed of red, blue and yellow umbrellas. Hardest worker in São Paulo—Tico Tico, a combination Lowell Thomas and Mel Allen of Brazilian radio, rode in a mobile unit beside Eisenhower and never once stopped talking during entire one-hour procession. There were wild bursts of applause and shouts of "Tico Tico" to Ike's right rear and he couldn't understand it. Col. Vernon Walters, along again as interpreter, explained. Poor Tico Tico in the rain. He came to inglorious end. Tried to go in the governor's palace with Ike. Police bounced him but good.

At lunch given by an industrial association, Eisenhower made one of the more effective speeches of the trip, a speech which went almost unnoticed back in the United States because of a tragedy that occurred that afternoon over the Rio Harbor.

For one thing, Eisenhower promised that "within our financial and economic capacity, we shall continue to support Brazilian development." To the Brazilians, this seemed like a hard promise with no qualifications because of Congress. Eisenhower, however, was speaking as much, if not more, of private investment as of federal funds.

He also said something else that was popular with the Brazilian workers:

"I wish that all the world could see what I have seen today in this city—a demonstration that a dynamic economy, based on private enterprise and free labor, redounds to the benefit of the worker, the consumer, the public at large and the state which embodies their sovereign will.

"I am sure that your workers, as ours in the United States, have attained positions of influence, honor and prestige. Surely the old concept of 'the exploited masses' deserves to be discarded, along with the idea of State Omnipotence and the divine right of kings."

At the airport leaving São Paulo, Eisenhower left a reminder with the Paulistas, who produce and ship much of Brazil's famous coffee.

"We of the United States are the most insatiable coffee drinkers in the world," he said. "Indeed, we buy nearly 60 per cent of your coffee exports. And I doubt that you would have a surplus here if you drank as much coffee as we do."

We were making wisecracks in the plane about how Ike told the French to drink Coke, now the Brazilians to drink coffee. The bantering stopped abruptly—there had been an air collision over Rio killing over sixty persons, including nineteen members of the Navy band which was to have played that night at Eisenhower's dinner for Kubitschek.

Diary notes for that afternoon and evening in Rio:

> Not only was this an awful tragedy to the families of these men, many of whom we knew personally, but it cast a pall of sadness over the entire Ike visit to Brazil. The President was gray-faced at the Rio airport, waited for no one as he raced from the Columbine to a helicopter that soared off immediately beneath the same leaden rain clouds that caused the collision. Ike went right to the hospital and looked in on the two Americans who survived miraculously by riding down with the severed tail of the Navy plane.
>
> Ike's after-dinner reception tonight canceled and only a small private dinner with Kubitschek and ranking advisers.

Unfortunate events seemed to haunt the party. Diary notes on the next morning:

Waiting to leave the Copacabana Palace Hotel in Rio for the airport and Buenos Aires early today, there was a bloody auto wreck a few feet away from where the White House staff and travel party were loading automobiles. Three people pinned moaning in the wreckage. Col. Walter Tkach, the assistant White House doctor, freed one of the trapped victims and cut himself about the hands on broken glass. Another rainy miserable day.

The Brazilian visit may not have produced the crowd pyrotechnics normally associated with a triumphal Eisenhower personal appearance, but there seemed to be more solid accomplishments. Eisenhower talked to Kubitschek about Castro, and about the Summit, where he promised to tell the other major nations how Latin-American nations felt individually about world tensions. It was important that Eisenhower spoke in terms of individual Latin-American nations rather than a geographic and ethnic region because one of the principal Latin complaints against Uncle Sam was his tendency to lump everybody together south of the Rio Grande.

CHAPTER 14 *"WE ARE NOT SAINTS"*

Since this was Eisenhower's third trip barnstorming by jet, it was only natural that he and those traveling with him adopted or drifted into a peculiar pattern of airborne life.

We have referred to Air Force One as a Boeing 707. That was the commercial designation. The Air Force knew the President's plane as a VC137A. Eisenhower's compartment was in the center of the plane, arranged as a combination office, lounge and bedroom. There was comfortable seating for six people in the chief executive's space, but only on short hops did he ever have that much company. By using the couch and working space, as many as twelve could have been put in the compartment but this was out of the question with a ranking V.I.P aboard.

Using every seat, the huge plane had space for only forty-eight passengers plus a crew of never less than eight, usually more. The forward passenger compartment held eight passengers, usually Secret Service men and plane guards; the aft compartment had seating for twenty-eight with sixteen of the seats arranged around four work tables. Some of the table space always was occupied by the electric typewriters of Ann Whitman and Mary Caffrey, Jim Hagerty's secretary.

Leaving one country and headed for another, Eisenhower and his staff usually were grateful for the interlude of enforced idleness while AF 1 took off and climbed to her cruising altitude of 30,000 to 35,000 feet. Once the aircraft commander, Bill Draper, flicked off the seat belt sign, the interior of the plane became a strange workshop of varied endeavor.

Secret Service men, their eyes frequently glazed with the fatigue of working double shifts, pulled off their coats and fell asleep within minutes in the foam-rubber comfort of the plane's large reclining chairs. Frequently the men were too tired to pull off their shoulder holsters.

Goodpaster, the pivot man of Eisenhower's staff, quickly got to work on reams of messages, schedules and correspondence concerning the next stop. State Department men went into conference with Hagerty around another table. The electric typewriters chattered out a departing message of thanks to the head of state just visited and this was taken forward to the radio compartment and dispatched back to the last capital.

On the longer hops, drinks were available before dinner but they were seldom in much evidence. The ranking staff members could ask for a highball and get it. If the President was going to nap, he would have a light Scotch and water.

His compartment was something like a bedroom connecting the living room and kitchen in a small family home. Crew members went through as unobtrusively as possible, but the passengers generally avoided his area unless summoned.

Actually there was little need for passengers to move out of their assigned compartments. Meals were brought to their seats and there were ample bathroom facilities at either end of the ship. Eisenhower had his own bath.

There were anguished moments for the staff at times when they were thoroughly convinced that Ike had gone to sleep and would so remain for at least an hour. Then, just as Hagerty or Tom Stephens or Kevin McCann decided to attempt a nap, there would be a steward, shaking gently and saying, "The President would like to see you when it is convenient." This meant any time in the next minute.

Eisenhower visited the aft cabin usually once or twice during a flight, depending on the length of a hop. A favorite form of hazing aboard AF 1 was to tell a member of the staff after he or she awoke from a deep sleep that the President had come back to the cabin, tried to carry on a conversation with the person involved and returned to his own quarters muttering about people who came on these trips for their health.

There may have been many actual cases of this, but the only one I know of involved Mary Caffrey, a most attractive asset to Hagerty's staff, whose almost madonna-like placidity frequently counterbalanced Jim's fiery Irish emotionalism. Mary had worked virtually all night on speech texts in one of the South American capitals and gone to the plane in the morning with nothing but a shower and coffee in lieu of sleep.

She settled down in her work space across the table from Ann Whitman and a ton of paper work descended on both women. Their typewriters began a drumming duet, but Mary's machine soon fell silent. She was sitting perfectly erect, hands on keyboard, but sound asleep.

Ike picked that moment to stroll back in the cabin to chat with Goodpaster, and hand the draft of a letter to Mrs. Whitman. He finished his business with his own secretary, then spoke quite amiably to Mary and walked on to his space.

When Mary finally shook herself out of the upright nap and resumed typing, the staff gave her a frightful few moments telling her the President had tried yelling in her ear, then given up in disgust and stumped back to his quarters.

The staff was most impressive in the few minutes before a landing in a foreign capital. By the time they tackled the South American trip, it was a well-oiled team operation. The word would pass that Draper expected to have the plane on the ground in ten minutes at the ramp, door open.

One of the assistant supervising agents of the Secret Service, Campion or Jerry Behn, would come through the compartment with a last-minute schedule.

"The boss is going off the front end. Who has the walkie-talkies? O.K. Kellerman will meet you at the bottom of the rear ramp. You men who're going straight to the palace will have to hustle. Two blue station wagons waiting about fifty feet from the rear ramp."

Dick Flohr, the ever-present S.S. driver for Ike, would gather

up the presidential and American flags to be bolted quickly to the procession car immediately after landing. Signal Corps men eased down the aisle with their tape-recorders.

"They promised 220 A.C. on the ground, but the last place it was D.C. Don't forget that converter."

Then Goodpaster, never ruffled, usually soft-spoken: "One of the President's old friends, a retired colonel, lives in this town. Here's his name and address. We can't spare the time for a separate appointment, but be sure he and his wife are invited to the embassy reception tomorrow afternoon."

Dr. Snyder's secretary, Captain Olive Marsh, checked the location of two medical bags—one went straight to the palace or embassy, the other in the trunk of the car in which the doctor would ride.

"That Signal Corps man wouldn't have been sick if he'd taken those dysentery pills. Tell him to see me as soon as we get to the palace."

. . . Who has the Tommy gun? O.K., you Morgan? We just got a revised chopper list by radio. Major John [the President's son], you'll be in helicopter two instead of three. Jeez, don't forget the boss's raincoat this time. I know you won't have time to type this now, Ann, but the boss has decided to change those last four paragraphs of the Congress speech.

Joe, be damned sure the speech typewriter gets into town right away. He's decided to expand the toast for the dinner tonight. Mr. Stephens, there's been a change—you won't be staying at the palace, you'll be at the Grand. Yes, Mr. President, I have it in your brief case. I'm a press secretary, not a magician: how can I be at the palace and downtown issuing the communiqué at the same time? Get me out of the dinner, will you?

Man, will you look at that crowd down there? Hey, I just heard up front it's snowing again in Washington. Somebody wake up Elmer. Nah, let him get every minute. The poor guy hasn't been to bed for two nights. Woodie, could I have a glass of water for this aspirin? Oh, never mind, there's the seat belt sign. Don't think about tonight, think about next week. We'll

be home. You will. I'll probably draw Gettysburg. My wife'll
kill me. The President wants to know what? It's in his brief
case. . . .

Such was the cabin buzz on Air Force One as she nosed down
to a landing at Ezeiza Airport outside Buenos Aires at 10:44 A.M.,
Friday, February 26.

There had been warnings of possible trouble in Argentina.
The White House would not concede it, but the decision to
airlift Ike from Ezeiza direct to the American Embassy by
helicopter was made after outbreaks of bombing. Supporters
of the ousted Juan Perón had painted his name all along the
highway leading into town, on the pavement, across bridges
and underpasses.

The Peronistas were more of an annoyance than a threat to
Eisenhower. In Moscow, *Pravda* used the helicopter lift as proof
that Eisenhower was unwanted in Argentina. The Russian
publication also called attention to pamphlets being distributed
in Buenos Aires saying "Eisenhower, clear out." The Argentine
Socialist party had issued a statement saying the visit was not
welcome because of Eisenhower's "close ties with the capitalists
of Wall Street." Moscow, in fact, tried to give the impression
Buenos Aires was a welter of bombs and pamphlets.

What Moscow failed to report, however, was that the dissidents
of Argentina were aiming primarily for the embarrassment of
Arturo Frondizi, the tough-minded President, who had forced
his country into a program of economic austerity to try and
tame the vicious inflation that sapped the vitality of his nation
in the wake of Perón. Many of the Peronistas had voted for
Frondizi two years earlier, but with another election coming
up, they were displeased with his austerity program and using
Eisenhower as an alternate punching bag.

The night before the President arrived in Argentina, several
hundred demonstrators tore down American flags and banners
hung in the center of Buenos Aires for the Eisenhower procession from the embassy to the Congress, where Ike was to speak.
There had been three bomb explosions and the situation

called for extra security precautions, which Frondizi ordered during the night.

With an 86 per cent literate population of about twenty million persons, Argentina was fighting the economic hang-over of Perón, who left the country in a financial shambles. The skyrocketing cost of living had moderated somewhat, but it still was so inflationary that workers of many political convictions were pressing Frondizi for wage increases. And without too much reason, blame for Argentina's economic woes was placed largely on Uncle Sam.

The United States was involved at the time to the extent of $254 million in economic assistance to Argentina (since 1958), and Eisenhower's gambit was to encourage Frondizi's continued battle for economic stability.

Diary notes for February 26, and the arrival in Buenos Aires:

Blessedly sunny weather in B.A. Had no difficulty in switching from Portuguese to Spanish language since virtually speechless in both. Got into the airport ahead of AF 1 and raced into town by car to be on hand at the embassy for the chopper landings. Argentine troops at airport difficult. Had to move within precisely marked corridors or gaze into business end of loaded carbine. So many guns have been poked at us now that they no longer seem a threat. Hard to believe any of these fellows ever shoot, but decide not to test it.

Perón's name splashed all over the highway into town. Particularly noticeable around housing developments for workers. The embassy fronts on a large park. Steel cable strung through trees to prevent spectators from getting any closer than about 200 yards. Only reporters and dignitaries around when helicopter landed within a few feet of Ambassador Willard L. Beaulac. U.S. certainly could do with a new house for Beaulac. This one is large enough but still sort of shabby looking from the outside.

Police are like coiled springs. I was standing on the first step of a photographer's platform watching Ike get out of helicopter when B.A. detective said I'd have to move to Step Two. His orders were that no one stood on Step One. Ike spoke to several of us as he walked into embassy grounds, but detective kept complaining about Step One. Followed me out to car still jawing over a difference in altitude of six inches.

Just time enough to run down to the hotel, send a story and get back to embassy before Ike's big public procession. Hotel like a political convention—girls giving away Pepsi.

Procession from embassy to Congress with Ike in the middle of mounted Grenadier Guards. Horses caused more trouble than the Peronistas. Kicking automobiles, people, anything in sight Ike plainly disgusted. At one time, he quit waving, rammed his hat on his head, put hands on hips and just stared glaring at the horsemen whaling away at people with flat of their sabers.

Finally Ike could take no more of it. He motioned to the horsemen to either go ahead or move out to either side. Crowd terrific, dense, friendly between embassy and Casa Rosada where Ike called on Frondizi. But from the Casa to Congress, a different story. Peronistas ganged up on corners and chanted "Pay-rone, Pay-rone, Pay-rone." How many of them hard to figure, but many were running from intersection to intersection. At Congress, police called up reinforcements, chased them away. Also used first tear gas of the trip, but nowhere near Ike. We didn't hear about it until later.

The performance of the Peronistas was a flashy but minute part of Eisenhower's over-all reception in Buenos Aires, where again the figure of one million was used widely as a crowd estimate. This was a local estimate, too, and apparently where the total population of a city could possibly support such figures, one million was going to be the minimum crowd wherever Ike went.

In his speech that afternoon to the Congress, Eisenhower lavished praise on Frondizi and delicately reminded the lawmakers that Argentina had been the prime beneficiary of dollar credits from private and government sources in the United States and from international institutions to which the U.S.A. made substantial contributions. He used a total of about one

billion dollars and said, "This is the most intensive program of financial co-operation to have been carried out in the history of this hemisphere."

There was little opportunity for extended discussions in Buenos Aires. These awaited the weekend in San Carlos de Bariloche, the lovely Alpine-like resort on the Argentine slope of the Andes. We left next morning for Bariloche with a side stop at Mar del Plata, on the Atlantic. Diary notes for Saturday, February 27:

Received a very ornate invitation to Frondizi's dinner for Eisenhower in Buenos Aires last night. Somewhat of a surprise, but valiantly burrowed into baggage for wrinkled white dinner jacket. Had a delightful time until the dinner started. Argentine protocol man looked at my invitation, shot up his eyebrows and said, "A journalist? Heavens, no!" Asked what the hell the invitation was for. Said it was dreadful mistake, that I was to be admitted only at the end to hear the two Presidents exchange toasts. Told him already had copies of both. Headed for hotel dining room. Sorry, we're closed. Grand dinner of malted milk tablets from Higger's Drug Store in Washington. Third time this week.

Today—Saturday—full of pleasant surprises. First to Mar del Plata, Argentina's big summer resort on the ocean. Tremendous place. Looks bigger than Coney Island, Jones Beach and Atlantic City put together. Eisenhower exhilarated by the crowd and the salt air. Perfectly amazing crowd, up in the hundreds of thousands and most of them in bathing suits. Ike missed a lot of them. So many people in the ocean that they were standing in line to get out.

Ike flew to Mar del Plata over the *pampa*, the fertile heart of Argentina farmland. He kept remarking about the "native richness" of the country.

It was during his brief visit to Mar del Plata that the President reacted frankly to the type of traveling he had done since he started out the previous summer in Europe.

He told the mayor: "I seem to travel so often, so fast and so furiously, that I am given little opportunity to see any real estate (from the ground) but I do see people."

We continued on to Bariloche. Diary notes:

> At the small airport, the Secret Service was up in arms but couldn't do anything about the dozen or so soldiers from Argentina mountain units who strolled around through the White House staff with Tommy guns at the ready—activators pulled back and set on full automatic. One tap of the trigger and gunfire at the rate of 600 slugs in the time it takes to snap your fingers. When Ike landed and made his little speech about the beauties of flying over Patagonia, the agents had no recourse. They just drifted in front of the men with the guns, trying to keep between the Tommy boys and the President. Damned glad to get out of there.
>
> Bariloche itself looks like a village in Switzerland. Behind us, the towering, snow-capped Andes. Most of us stay in the Llao Llao Hotel. Ike has a second floor suite overlooking the incredibly blue lake. Water looks dyed. Name of hotel pronounced "Zhyow Zhyow." We've seen most of the better resorts of this hemisphere with one President or another, but nothing to surpass the physical charm of this place; until you went to bed, four to a room, and the beds side by side. Two snorers in our room. A night in the lion house.

The President got in about four holes of golf after he arrived, but there was no electric golf cart available and he decided against too much walking at that altitude. He played only the flatter holes, then loafed until time for dinner with Frondizi.

At dinner that night in a large rustic hall of beautifully polished logs, Eisenhower continued his "we're all for you, but count your blessings from the United States" theme:

"When freedom, democracy and national sovereignty are in jeopardy in any country, they are to some degree in jeopardy in all free countries of the world.

"This is one strong reason why the United States is vitally interested in the development and general well-being of all free nations. It is why the United States—despite unmatched levels of taxation, heavy economic and military problems—continues to make sacrifices in helping other free nations with their problems of national development."

The next day, Sunday, Eisenhower flew over to Frondizi's *estancia* on the other side of the lake for trout fishing and private conversation. When Ike returned to the Llao Llao that afternoon, many people at the hotel were alarmed. He looked suddenly drained of vitality. He had fished, stream-wading, for trout and salmon for two and a half hours with virtually no luck. It was too hot and native fishermen had warned him of poor prospects.

He stepped from his helicopter and started for the hotel. He had to walk up an inclined driveway and a small flight of stairs. At the bottom of the stairs, Eisenhower looked physically whipped. His face was haggard, a picture of weariness, and his ruddiness suddenly vanished. It seemed to be the cumulative effects of a harshly rapid schedule, the South American summer and the exertion of that Sunday.

Dr. Snyder followed him upstairs to the suite, where Moaney was waiting with a hot bath ready. The news stories that left Bariloche that night almost overshadowed the joint declaration of the two leaders, which was largely a to-be-expected statement of mutual desire for improved living standards and economic progress, plus a sentence that seemed to be a gentle reminder to Castro and his new-found Soviet friends:

"Experience within the inter-American system has taught that non-intervention is the keystone of international harmony and friendship and that its corollary is mutual respect among nations, however large or small."

The American stories from Bariloche, however, dealt largely with Eisenhower's apparent fatigue. My diary notes for Sunday night showed:

Everybody talking about how bushed the President looked when he came in from fishing. Several people claim he had to hold on to Jim Rowley's arm to get up the stairs. Jim says no. Two hours later, Ike looked like a different man when I saw him in the hall. He knows a lot of stories were filed tonight about his health and we hear he's burned up. Says this'll get Mamie all upset and he'll hear from her. Understand he griped to one of his staff, "They didn't look so hot to me, either," meaning the press.

Can't blame him much, although I'll still write what I see. If this man had not gone through three severe illnesses, nobody would pay the slightest attention to his fatigue. Also he doesn't have to sleep four in a room and listen to the snoring.

Monday, February 29: Bariloche: We should know better by now than to send stories about Ike looking poorly. Someone saw him this morning and said, "I'm only 40 and I wish I looked that good." Hagerty, of course, in an acid mood. He's gotten a playback on the health stories in the States. He issues a statement by Doc Snyder saying Ike is in "fine physical condition and . . . good health."

My pet theory again: when the White House writes a schedule so brutally fast and tiring that most of the travel party gets bushed, they begin to think the President must be in the same shape. I feel sorry for him, but not nearly as sorry as I feel for myself after two nights in beautiful Bariloche-by-the-Snore.

All manner of hell at the hotel office this morning. We were there two nights, everybody charged for from four to six nights. U. E. Baughman clipped for six nights. He put down $10 American and stalked off. Kevin McCann says, "They've taken foreign aid into their own hands." Embassy man tries to explain this is the custom in Argentine hotels. Rate on my room was $120 for two nights for four. Meals extra. Management also wanted to be paid in dollars instead of pesos. Asked the manager, "What's wrong with your own money?" His reply, "Why shouldn't an American pay his bill in American money?"

Things had quieted down to only mutters and snarls—Ike was coming down the hall—when an embassy man, trying to be helpful, whispered that meals were included in the rate. Fortunately for him, Ike walked out on porch instead of coming by

hotel desk. "Son of a bitch" and "thieving bastard" were among the politer terms used. Most everyone had paid cash for meals. Hotel men stood ground beautifully, knowing that in two minutes we'd have to leave. We did. Chalk one up for the Llao Llao and I hope to go back some day when things are not quite as hectic.

During the short hop from Bariloche to the next stop, Santiago, Chile, we heard that over on Air Force One the people were shocked, even flustered, by the intimate detail on Ike's life printed in the Buenos Aires papers.

La Prensa of Buenos Aires is one of the great newspapers of the world and when they decide to cover a story, it gets covered. U.P.I.—the Smith and Hensley part of U.P.I— was happy to have *La Prensa* on our side that Sunday. Their men gave us a blow-by-blow account of what went on inside Ike's suite that morning, obviously from hotel servants on the presidential assignment. And the *La Prensa* men also graciously provided us with a copy of the joint communiqué two hours before it was released by Hagerty's staff.

As the Chilean phase of Eisenhower's South American venture began, the late Henry N. Taylor, the highly capable roving foreign correspondent for the Scripps-Howard Newspaper Alliance, wrote an interesting story; interesting because, for one thing, I knew Henry personally and he could not be classed as pro-Eisenhower. Taylor's dispatch opened by saying:

It's easy for a Washington reporter to become cynical about President Eisenhower's smile. But travel along with it for weeks through foreign lands and you begin to realize what a national asset we will be losing next January.

Taylor closed by noting:

It's easy to argue that Ike hasn't delivered one public sentence on this trip which would stand up as news, once the fluffing had been peeled away. As one Ike follower summed up: "Here we go again, around the world in 80 platitudes."

But any appraisal of reporters means absolutely nothing to people who stand beside these streets [of South America], patient in the summer sun, waiting to see the last active leader from World War II pass thru their city, a general of the army who has managed to convince the world he stands for peace, not war.

In Chile, a nation about 10 per cent larger geographically than Texas with a population of close to eight million, Eisenhower faced no political problems with his host, President Jorge Alessandri, a staunch friend of the United States and another South American who left a professional career (he'd been a mathematics professor) relatively late in life to enter politics. Chile, however, was suffering from about the most painful case of inflation in Latin America.

Chile wanted to sell more copper and iron ore to help raise wages and combat the mounting cost of living. The United States had a number of economic and social advancement programs operating in Chile, but these had not calmed the dissatisfaction with Uncle Sam in some areas of the population; usually to the Left where such feelings could be expected, but on occasion this dissatisfaction was on a broader plane, partly because of heavy U.S. ownership of units of the copper industry.

Eisenhower reached the Los Cerrillos Airport outside Santiago at noon the twenty-ninth, where he was met by Alessandri, who wanted to talk more than most South American Presidents about the cold war and Russia, particularly because he had a pet plan for disarmament which was directed primarily at nations of his own area, but which, if it were to be successful, had to follow the lead of the major powers.

Diary notes for Santiago on the 29th:

Seems like a wonderful town, full of spirit and the joy of living with little evidence of the economic pressure on working people. Chileans seem absolutely nuts about band music. Navy

band been playing here for audiences of 40,000 and up. They played in the square just below our hotel and the exuberant Chileans saluted Ike and the band by covering the front of a five-story building with a portrait of the President in fireworks.

Secret Service says this is one of the finest police forces in the hemisphere. A national organization, no city police. Almost everywhere, we found ordinary police privates speaking English. They are specially selected and trained for duty around the hotels and embassies, also paid extra. They have an academy like West Point. Quite an honor to go there. Operating with a national organization that extends into even the smallest village, easy to see, however, where the cops also could be trouble in certain political situations.

Shopkeepers around the hotel are adjusting their prices for the visiting Norteamericanos. One of the girls on Ike's staff priced a leather bag before lunch: $11. Three hours later: $15. Local friend told her, "If you want the bag, I'll get it for you after you leave for about $8 and ship it to you."

Everywhere Ike goes, people throw flowers at him. He's deeply impressed. People aren't boisterous like they were in Argentina, but there seems to be a sense of warmth that projects up to Ike's car from the crowds. Back home in staid old Washington, a President of the United States attracts virtually no attention and it is downright embarrassing to the State Department when a visiting dignitary comes to town. Only way State Department can build a crowd is bring the visitor down 14th Street at lunch hour and trap the government workers at the intersections.

On this third country of his tour, Eisenhower seemed to receive the most enthusiastic welcome of the journey. Chief Baughman thought the parade crowd ran as high as 700,000, which would be close to one-tenth of the national population.

One group—police said they were Communist union workers, an always easy label under such circumstances—shouted "Down with Eisenhower" outside a union building. The demonstrators pressed into the crowd with a large picture of Castro, but as soon as the two Presidents passed, other spectators grabbed stones and began to chase the picture-carrying objectors. Police had to step in and stop the stoning.

That night at dinner in the La Moneda Palace, a stark monster of a structure dominating midtown Santiago, while joyous red, white and blue fireworks showered overhead, the two Presidents talked more of peace, the cold war and the forthcoming Summit.

Eisenhower pleased Alessandri and the Chileans by saying for publication what he had been telling his opposite numbers privately in the other South American countries: that their views on world peace and disarmament were highly important; that "I wish to go to Paris with a clear understanding of the views of our friends in this region."

Of the Summit, Ike said: "While I am too realistic to expect miracles, I do hope that in Paris we may reach some agreements which will lessen the tensions that divide and vex the world."

Somehow, it seemed possible at the time.

The following day, Tuesday, March 1, probably was the most important day of the entire tour for the President, and the implications went far beyond Chile as he answered complaints from Chilean students about the United States, spoke to the National Congress and visited the San Gregorio housing project outside Santiago.

That morning, the President received a lengthy letter from a group of officials representing the Chilean Students Union, an organization claiming 25,000 members, and with a counterpart in almost every South American country, where the students take current affairs, national and international, much more personally than some of their neighbor students to the north.

Sitting in an upstairs drawing room of Ambassador Howe's residence, Eisenhower was perturbed by the cynical attitude of the students toward not only the United States, but the Organization of American States, both of which the letter signers said were instruments of the rich, inconsiderate of the weak.

A speech prepared earlier for delivery to the American

Society of Chile in a mid-town movie house was torn up, a new one drafted. Then, facing his audience, the visiting President advised his student critics to seek out better sources of information.

"We are not saints," he said. "We know we make mistakes, but our heart is in the right place, and we believe that aid given by the United States to the people who want to work, who welcome some help, who are energetically working for themselves to raise their standards of living, not merely for themselves as individuals but for every single individual in the nation, these are the people from which we get great satisfaction in helping."

He seemed to be almost in a combative mood, but the time had arrived, in a particularly friendly nation, to start unloading on some of the basic points of anti-Americanism. He said, for example, that "nothing could be more erroneous" than the serious misunderstandings in South America of the United States' purpose in helping other areas of the world.

He pointed out that money spent in the construction of a common defense perimeter was an expenditure for all free nations, including Latin America. And he also reminded his listeners that with U.S. investments and loans in Latin America, then totaling more than eleven billion dollars, new private and public credits were being made available at the rate of about one billion dollars a year.

He also hit as ridiculous the idea in some areas of Latin America that "the United States supports dictators." But he didn't press this point. At the time, the U.S. still recognized Trujillo.

Later in the morning, before a joint session of the National Congress, he seemed a trifle edgy when his host, Senate President Herman Videla, in introducing him, said nearer neighbors of Ike's country deserved preferential treatment. The Senator said the United States must settle on an attitude, "that of preferring your nearest neighbors, your truest friends, when the need arises for support and help.

"The reality of an America (all of the Americas) organically united already exists," Videla said to the President. "Your nation should ratify it with the full intensity of its power."

Eisenhower looked at the Senator questioningly as Colonel Walters whispered the translation into his ear. The President, however, stuck to the theory voiced earlier in the day, that the quest for peace and all of its expensive involvements had to be a multilateral approach. He praised Alessandri for trying to reduce armaments in Latin America and he also promised solemnly in the quiet chamber of deputies: "Should any American republic be the victim of aggression, the United States is ready to fulfill its treaty [Rio treaty of 1947, a mutual defense pact] obligations with strength, promptness and firmness."

And as for monetary assistance, he had a word that was directed at the nations toying with expropriation of American holdings:

"Investment capital is limited. Competition for it is keen in the United States and in many other countries. It will flow only to those areas where it is actively sought, welcomed and treated fairly. More and more it seeks the partnership of local capital and local experience."

Diary notes for that night of March 1, Santiago:

Ike said more in two speeches today than he has the whole trip. Some of it could not have been too popularly received, although all the local newspapers are drumming on the idea of growing U.S. investment and other forms of economic assistance.

Fatigue is beginning to show itself in the travel party. The President seems untouched, but some of his traveling companions are beginning to come down with dysentery which is sadly odd since this is one place where the water is good.

The abomination of this trip is having to turn in your luggage the night before, always by 11 P.M., while some of us are still covering Ike at a banquet. We won't see our big bags after tonight until we get into Puerto Rico two days from now. Live out of brief cases in the meantime. Sent eight shirts to the laundry, got two back clean, six dirtier than before. Maid says

we're all too mucho dirty for them to handle in so short a time. Very fine hotel, the Carrera. Drink the tap water without worrying. First place like it this trip. Peculiar restaurant prices. Fish costs three times as much as steak.

The next morning leaving Santiago, the President was chatting with the Chilean officials who saw him off.

"Technology has indeed shrunk the world," he said. "Today all men are close neighbors."

There were numerous neighbors waiting for him at the next stop in Montevideo, Uruguay. Neighbors and tear gas.

CHAPTER 15 *IKE WEEPS—*
THOUSANDS CHEER

Eisenhower's overnight stop in Uruguay provided a classic example of one of the sadder truisms of a complicated business, public relations. His few hours in Montevideo proved, as any editor could have told him and as Hagerty most certainly knew, that bad news is good news.

Montevideo was the scene of one of the more jubilant receptions accorded Eisenhower on any of his tours. But what dominated world attention? Tear gas, fired into a crowd of rowdy students by itchy Montevideo police. The whole incident took up only a few minutes and of that time, Eisenhower was involved for perhaps twenty or thirty seconds. But this was the story:

"IKE TEAR GASSED."

"IKE GOES THROUGH RIOTS."

"Ladies and gentlemen, we interrupt this broadcast to bring you a bulletin from Montevideo: Police were forced to use tear gas today as President Eisenhower . . ."

It is accurate and possibly a bit understated to say that Eisenhower was angry in Montevideo, not at the students but at the inevitability of the headlines and broadcasts which would drown out the preponderantly positive side of his visit to Uruguay, last scheduled stop of his tour.

The President might better have directed his anger at human nature. If it had been a pleasant day with just another sunny

parade through Montevideo, public interest outside the area would have been minimal, considering that the tour was at an end. But a few whiffs of tear gas and interest was intensified around the world.

Even after nearly eight years in the White House, and, for that matter, much of his adulthood spent in the eyes of the public, Eisenhower still had difficulty fathoming the reaction of all media to some of the circumstances in which he occasionally found himself. The publicity attending a noticeable cough or cold puzzled and irritated him. He seemed to forget at times that the unnoticed travail of the average human becomes world news when it involves the President.

Uruguay, the smallest of the South American countries, for many years had been liberal and even experimental in new democratic political forms. One result of this was the existence of highly vocal minorities, of which the Communist and Socialist parties were participants. It was in Montevideo that Vice President Nixon ran into the first violence of his South American trip two years earlier.

The government was somewhat difficult to understand for many North Americans. In 1951, after a plebiscite, the presidential form of government was dropped in favor of a nine-member National Council of Government. The Council is composed of six representatives of the majority political party, three from the minority.

The presidency of the Council is rotated annually among the first four members of the majority party on the national ballot in elections held every four years, and for protocol purposes the member serving his one-year term as head of the council also serves as President of Uruguay.

Benito Nardone, a fifty-four-year-old former journalist with an Italian background common to many Uruguayans, was serving as President at the time of Eisenhower's visit on Wednesday, March 2. Nardone, sweating with an inflation problem like most of his fellow South American chief executives, and his eight council members met Eisenhower at the airport and drove into the city beside Montevideo's beautiful beaches.

Diary notes for March 2 in Montevideo:

Nothing seems to match the intensity of a Uruguayan college boy. Some of them quite anti-U.S.A. and pro-Castro. Fidel is rapidly becoming a symbol all through this part of the world. Quite aside from the issues, the justice or injustice of his revolution, Castro symbolizes the little man against the big man and the Communists love a situation like this. Could it be that the only way to ever eliminate anti-Americanism completely is for the United States to go broke?

Traveling the world with Ike, one wonders about pride in our accomplishments. Would a hard-luck Mississippi sharecropper look at an oil-rich Texan in an air-conditioned Cadillac and say "There goes a swell guy"?

Not quite sure of the attitude of several hundred students in Montevideo. The police were energetically embarrassed to the point of using sabers, tear gas and specially designed turret-type engines to chase students waving banners denouncing *Yanqui imperialismo*. Police tore banners down, students didn't like it and the fun began.

Police used fire hoses at one point, just as Eisenhower reached the center of town. Procession stopped for Ike to greet some troops. Decided to get out of car for a stretch. Surrounded by soldiers with Tommy guns which, for a change, were pointed at the people, not at Ike or his procession.

When we reached the Law University in town, second fight between police and students who were throwing tin cans and leaflets from upper stories. Police fired a string of tear gas shells against the breeze, gas drifted right across procession just as Ike arrived. He plopped down in the seat for a few seconds, then got back on his feet with eyes streaming. Rest of the ride, he waved weepily at the cheering Uruguayans.

Most of these boys looked like anything but law students. I saw several of these kindly pupils who must have been well over 40 years old. Local people say, however, that they're really students doing graduate work; some spend their lifetime in and around the universities. They also explain these grizzled kids are

not Communists, but Trotzkyite Socialists (there is a difference), who tend to anarchist beliefs, in that there doesn't seem to be any form of government around these days of which they approve.

Ike went to dinner tonight at Nardone's official residence, a pleasant old chalet behind high walls. With today's violence downtown, we decided to stick with him; spent the evening sitting in Nardone's courtyard eating enormous meat sandwiches from a *cantina* down the street; photographers call it "José's Carryout Shoppe." Police got word students were going to march either on the embassy residence or the hotel where the White House staff is staying.

Great uproar outside Nardone's as carloads of police reinforcements quickly assembled outside courtyard gates and sped off to town. Night was turning windy, cold and wet and the students decided to stay indoors and yell about the Yanquis instead of marching. First sensible decision today.

At the embassy residence and also at Nardone's, Ike visibly angry re: what he knows will be scarey stories about today's parade. Says at Nardone's he wishes there was some way he could get us to realize the gas incident was a very minor aspect of the day compared with the overwhelming reception which he thinks, for the size of the town, matches anything he has seen.

Hell, we know that. But what do we do about the pictures— one of three policemen with drawn revolvers and night sticks whaling the daylights out of one demonstrator; of Ike with tears running down his face; of Dick Flohr with his eyes so full of tears he could scarcely see to drive; of a student stretched out on the ground, his leg bleeding where he was hit by exploding fragments of a tear gas canister and a cop with the barrel of his .38 at the man's head?

There are times when Ike expects too much of the men traveling with him. Suppose every one of us played down the tear gas story? There still are a couple of hundred other reporters here who would send stories all over the world and the American press would look frightfully shady. No, the very strength of the press on a trip like this is that we don't play a house game; the readers, viewers and listeners get as honest a count as possible. I really don't believe Ike expects a house game. He's sore at the inevitable. Things will look a lot better tomorrow night in Puerto Rico.

From the long-range viewpoint, Eisenhower's appearance at Montevideo was a plus in public relations. Publicized pockets of anti-Americanism certainly made the ovations he received elsewhere more believable and avoided having the chronicle of his travels become a one-way story of crunchy goodness.

As it was, responsible Uruguayans said no foreign visitor to Montevideo had ever received such a reception. The procession crowd was estimated from a quarter-million to upward of 400,000, out of which there may have been as many as three or four hundred overt objectors. And the news stories from Montevideo reflected this.

The procession route in town covered about three miles. The first trouble developed at the School of Architecture of the National University. Pictures of the incident show about twenty-five students on top of the building, waving two big banners denouncing U.S. imperialism: "Viva the Cuban Revolution."

Eisenhower was riding in an open car with U.S. Ambassador Robert F. Woodward and General Enrique Magnani, chief of staff of the Uruguayan Army, who was something less than popular with the left-wing students. In the front seat were Flohr, Rowley and Walters, the interpreter.

The architecture school roof on which the students were scampering and waving their banners was a good hundred yards from the President. If the demonstrators had thrown hand grenades, they could not have reached Ike. The police, however, wanted no negative demonstrations and brought up their turret-top fire wagons to shoot high-pressure jets of water at the roof. Some of the spray drifted back over Ike who was standing, waving and smiling.

Then, as the President neared Government House to confer with the National Council, police in front of the University Law School building were disturbed by student antics in the upper stories. There were cries in Spanish of "Death to Yankee

imperialism," and a few empty tin cans rattled to the sidewalk. Some of the students raced out of the building and headed for the line of march and the police let go with a string of tear gas shells.

Eisenhower reached Government House a few minutes later and Dr. Snyder took a quick look at his eyes. The tears had stopped and aside from being a trifle red-eyed, Ike seemed to have suffered none for the incident. He quickly assured the apologetic Nardone, "It was a small thing."

And Hagerty came into the street in front of the government building to tell reporters, "The President asked me to say that the two very small demonstrations should not impair one iota the magnificent and very warm reception he received."

Joseph Newman, the able South American specialist of the *Herald Tribune*, cast what might have been a much more realistic light on the Montevideo troubles after Ike left. Newman wrote from Uruguay:

A group of about forty agents who arrived in Montevideo recently from Cuba were primarily responsible for the organizing of the anti-Eisenhower demonstration by students here yesterday, according to a report today from Uruguayan intelligence sources.

The presence of these agents at Montevideo has given rise to speculation that they may have had a hand also in the abortive anti-Eisenhower and pro-Castro demonstrations which went almost unnoticed at Rio de Janeiro and at Santiago, Chile.

Part of the trouble stemmed, too, from South American student opposition to the execution of convicted California sex criminal Caryl Chessman. There was considerable sympathy, too, in the United States for Chessman because of the many times he had neared the gas chamber and won delays in his sentence. North Americans, however, better understood that Eisenhower could not halt the execution, which was for a state offense. Many foreigners could not comprehend a national chief executive being without the power to intervene.

If the Uruguayan intelligence reports cited by Newman were relatively correct, another interesting point was raised in the minds of people around Eisenhower, and possibly with the chief executive himself: With Cuba suffering a shortage of operating government funds, how was Castro financing the movement of large groups of agents over South America? The broader extent of Communist activity and influence in Havana did not manifest itself until months later.

While the demonstrations dominated the news from Montevideo, there were other more far-reaching developments in progress. Nardone was worried that the Communist program of economic penetration might make headway in Latin America if the United States did not step up her purchases of raw materials in the area.

Henry Taylor of Scripps-Howard got into Montevideo two days ahead of us and saw Nardone, who pointed out, "We'd prefer to buy United States oil, but already the gasoline in those cars outside this window has come from Russia."

For a country with a gross national product in 1957 of about $1.3 billion, Uruguay's trade deficit that year reached a staggering $98 million. The government brought this figure down in 1958, but with catastrophic floods in 1959 and falling wool (Uruguay's principal export) prices in the world market, the imbalance of trade shot upward again in 1959.

"The United States stands ready to help in any way it soundly can, within the framework of our world responsibilities and the limits of our resources," Eisenhower told the Uruguayan Congress.

But he also used his last major appearance in South America to attack once again the feeling that his country, "while giving bounteously for postwar reconstruction and mutual security, has been less generous with our good neighbors of this hemisphere.

"I am the first to acknowledge the fallibility of nations and leaders, even those with the best intentions," he said. "But I ask you and all our good friends of the Americas to consider this:

"The aid we gave to Europe after the Great War helped re-

store that area as a producer and buyer, to the benefit of Latin America as well as to ourselves. During the war, the trade of Latin America with the United States increased sixfold, and has been sustained at a higher level since then.

"The resources we have exported for the construction of a defense perimeter have been for the benefit of all those who desire freedom, independence and the right to be unmolested as they work for the improved well-being of their own people."

Leaving Montevideo the next morning, Thursday, March 3, Ike seemed to be in better spirits than the night before. He walked out into the garden of the embassy to greet the employees. Spying a public address system microphone installed by the Signal Corps, the President sighed and said, "It's getting so that when I see one of these, I can't let go."

He made a quick flight aboard the trusty *Columbine III* back to the airport at Buenos Aires, where he switched to his jet for the long flight northward to Ramey Air Field base, where he planned to spend several days in the sun before plunging back into the work piling up in Washington where Congress was in full swing.

Diary notes for March 3:

Can't wait until we run into a town-dropping travel snob. Breakfast at the hotel in Montevideo, thence by helicopter to the airport. Coffee in Buenos Aires; lunch aboard Ike's plane (Marv Arrowsmith and I traveling in style today as pool reporters for the rest of the gang), fruit juice in Surinam and dinner tonight at the Ramey Officers' Club.

The stop in Surinam was funny. One engine on AF 1 developed oil trouble and had to be switched off two hours out of Paramaribo where we were scheduled for re-fueling. We didn't know about it until we had been in Surinam 20 minutes. Disturbing thing about jet travel: fellow can't tell when he's in danger any more now that planes don't have propellers.

Bill Draper told Gen. Goodpaster when he cut out the engine and air rescue units in the area were notified (we were over the worst part of the Brazilian jungle at the time) but they didn't worry Ike until 15 minutes before landing. We then waited at Paramaribo airport for arrival of the back-up plane, a duplicate of AF 1.

Never saw a more colorful crowd than the gaily dressed natives who greeted Ike at the airport in Surinam. People here very proud of their varied national origins and showed up in many different homeland costumes. One lady from the jungle took her place in the receiving line, pretty damned proud of her lineage, too. She didn't have a stitch on from the waist up. If Elizabeth Taylor is proud of her endowments, advise her to stay out of Surinam. She'd look like a spindly boy beside our lady of the jungle.

Other Surinamese quite perturbed. Scowled at bare-breasted woman. Local photographers gave her a wide berth. Tried to urge local photo stringer (part time representative) for UPI to get pix of Ike with lady in background. He refused on grounds of local pride. When Ike about 10 feet from woman, someone threw a shawl over her. She didn't like this at all and walked away from the whole affair. Couldn't blame her. A girl dresses up in her best skirt and comes to the party and some social climber ruins everything.

Bill Draper did one of the finest reporting jobs I've ever heard as he told Marv and me about the engine. Because of our pool positions, Arrowsmith and I had to file, too, for our associates on the press charter plane, particularly for John Heffernan of Reuter and Jean LaGrange of France Presse, two of the finest guys in the world, who certainly saved my hide repeatedly by their ability to speak foreign languages all over the world while I scrambled around in shouted pidgin.

Arrowsmith, Heffernan, LaGrange and I have spent so much time together in cars behind Ike that we've made a solemn pact—to meet at midnight every December 9 at the Inn of the Seventh Happiness in Samarkand, but with separate checks, please.

Ike spent nearly two hours in the Paramaribo Airport lounge chatting with Surinam officials. Called Marv and me over to see one of his gifts, an American flag (48 stars) made of salad. He looks tired, but not as tired as Marv and I feel after sweating out the pool story through a single Dutch cable circuit which

was busy carrying Paramaribo social notes filed in longhand Flemish. Ike says, "I suppose you fellows have scared the day-lights out of everybody about our engine." Tell him we're thinking instead of those lucky fellows on the charter who by this time are in the swimming pool at Ramey.

As Ike switched planes, sure felt sorry for the hard-working AF 1 crew. Had to transfer all the luggage in less than 45 min-utes in a blistering hot sun and jungle humidity about the con-sistency of peanut butter. Inside the new AF 1, a bargain day jumble of papers, brief cases, overnight bags, walkie-talkies.

Back on American soil tonight in Puerto Rico to hear Wash-ington had another heavy snow. President looks like a man who'd like to be snowed out for a few days.

With the travel party back together in Puerto Rico, Eisen-hower spent about ten hours in bed and flew sixty miles by helicopter the next day to the delightful Dorado Beach Club to speak to the American Assembly, a group of experts he helped organize back at Columbia University to improve hemispheric understanding.

He was pleased with the over-all results of his trip, but he thought there were still too many South Americans who knew little of the United States record of assistance to the area and who misunderstood the purposes of this nation in a cold war world.

While U.S. assistance should continue at a high level, he re-ported a strong feeling in the countries he visited that any idea of developing "a so-called U.S.A. master plan for raising of living standards throughout the hemisphere" was foredoomed to failure. He was much more pointed than he was in South America in his firm belief that while there had to be outside help, most of the work in attacking economic ills had to be done within the countries themselves.

We got the first clue to the extent of Ike's fatigue as he spoke in the panoramic dining room of the Dorado overlooking the sea. His voice began to crack and he stopped to cough.

"If I have to apologize for my voice, I can do so by saying I left most of it in South America," he said, stopping to gulp water before going on with his speech.

Hagerty and Dr. Snyder told us quickly that his trouble seemed to stem from the dust he inhaled in his open-car processions. The physician was not disturbed and the condition might have escaped notice—Ike went right out and played eighteen holes of golf on the hotel course—if the President himself had not called attention to his throat.

Eisenhower returned to Washington Monday, March 7, apparently recovered from his dust irritation. If the stay in Puerto Rico helped him, it restored life to most of us. Flying up the southeastern coast of the United States, we traded notes on the real but little-known benefits of Ike's South American tour.

In Latin America and elsewhere, he had been responsible for vast highway and street improvements. A Brazilian diplomat had said, "The President's visit was more beneficial than he'll ever know—he was responsible for filling up most of the potholes in the roads of Rio."

Seriously, however, the most vivid lesson Eisenhower brought back was the fact that Latin America wanted aid but not direction from the United States. He also got a firsthand look at the spread of dissatisfaction or unrest as represented by the splinter groups seizing upon Castro as a cause.

Back in Washington, Eisenhower went on television almost immediately, the night of March 8, to report on his trip, but he still was sensitive about the publicity from Buenos Aires and Montevideo.

"There is a vast reservoir of respect, admiration and affection for the United States of America," he said. "The expressions of this attitude by Latin-American peoples and their leaders were so enthusiastic and so often repeated as to admit no possibility of mistake. Two or three insignificant exceptions to this may have made a headline, but they were only minor incidents, lost in the massed welcome."

He acknowledged the existence of pronounced misunderstandings between North and South but he saw signs of im-

provement. In balance, he thought the trip was a success in that it produced voluminous evidence of basic friendship between the Americas despite the misunderstandings.

The President did not call particular attention to it in his report and this may have been a tactical error from the diplomatic standpoint, but some of the more valuable work on the trip was done quietly and with little or no publicity by Herter and members of the Inter-American advisory group. Theirs were the working contacts that promised later, specific development. Hidden largely from public view by the parades and ceremonies focused on the President, Herter was gathering the material required for later implementation of any negotiative results that were to come from the trip.

Speech over and the television crews packing up their gear in his office, Eisenhower turned to a host of problems—Cuba, the increasingly disturbing antics of Trujillo in the Dominican Republic and the larger challenge, Khrushchev at the Summit. Despite indications of difficult dealings with the Soviet Premier, Eisenhower gave orders to go ahead with plans for his Russian trip and the tour of the Far East.

He was convinced of the rightness of his travels and criticism in Congress of permitting himself to be hooted by the students of Montevideo was brushed aside.

CHAPTER 16 *A SHUDDERING THING*

Down they came with a crash—the U-2, the Paris Summit and for a time, it seemed, all hope of improving relations between East and West.

The crash was a shuddering thing. Months, even years, of painfully, patiently trying to keep the diplomatic door open. And then—SLAM! This was the immediate reaction to the one meeting of the Paris Summit on Monday, May 16, 1960.

The event itself took only about as long as a New York advertising agency man would devote to lunch with a promising client. Khrushchev stormed into the Élysée Palace, hit Eisenhower in the teeth with the U-2 and that ended the meeting. De Gaulle and Macmillan both tried to lure the Soviet leader back to the conference table, but he went off in the country for a drive and ignored them.

Leading up to the Summit and even before the U-2 incident, which took place on May 1, there were straws in the wind indicating that Khrushchev was considerably less than happy with the East-West situation, particularly as it involved the United States. There was the winter trip to Moscow by Gronchi of Italy, the difficulty that dogged the disarmament and nuclear test ban negotiations in Geneva, Russia's open encouragement of Castro. And, always, the space race.

Khrushchev in February grew expansive over Lunik I, the missile shot which Russia claimed hit the moon.

"Our flag is flying on the moon," he said. "This means something. Is this not enough to prove the superiority of Communism over capitalism?"

Eisenhower was asked at a press conference what he thought of such remarks.

"I think it's crazy," he shot back.

Most of the correspondents near his desk understood him accurately, but there were many others who thought he said, "I think *he's* crazy." Furthermore, it showed up this way in the unofficial conference transcript used by most news organizations in Washington as a reliable reference to the President's remarks.

Hagerty began to receive telephone calls: had the President really meant to say Khrushchev was a crazy man? A check of the tape recording of the conference and later the sound track of movie film made for television proved beyond any doubt that Eisenhower had said *it's* and not *he's*. The major press associations carried the story accurately from the start, but a sufficient number of people heard it the wrong way so Washington that February afternoon was buzzing with the latest—Eisenhower openly called Khrushchev a maniac.

This was the sort of human error highly difficult to avoid in a press conference. The Washington diplomats and correspondents probably were among the few who saw much difference between calling a man crazy and saying something he said was crazy. There was, however, a delicate shading of difference and quite possibly the fleeting remark mirrored the tension between Moscow and Washington; tension reflected more in secret diplomatic cables than in public affairs.

De Gaulle arrived in April and Ike gave him the ceremonial works, including a brief trip to his Gettysburg farm, where the big Frenchman seemed bored stiff while the President showed him his finest Aberdeen Angus cattle. De Gaulle was extremely well received in Washington, although the street crowds he attracted could not approach the receptions for Eisenhower in Paris. Washington is not a demonstrative town, but the French were pleased and said De Gaulle was, too.

He and Eisenhower discussed the Summit (De Gaulle had recently played host to Khrushchev) and for a short time there was a slight air of hope for better relations with the Kremlin.

Herter, however, was arguing publicly against expecting too much from the meeting. Eisenhower was saying the same thing to conferees in his office, stating the situation more reservedly than the Secretary of State.

De Gaulle left Washington on April 26 and a few days later, the President went to Pennsylvania for the weekend. On Saturday, April 30, he played golf at the Gettysburg Country Club, and the next day, a quiet, beautiful spring Sunday, he drove with Mamie to Camp David, twenty-five miles away just over the Maryland border. It was on this same Sunday that Francis Gary Powers lost jet power in his American U-2 spy plane and was brought down in the heart of the Soviet Union.

Washington and Moscow for several days played a cat-and-mouse game. Moscow said only that an American plane was shot down inside Russia. On May 5, the National Aeronautics and Space Administration said the missing aircraft—still not specifically identified by the Russians—was one of its weather research planes, probably down in Soviet territory because of an oxygen equipment failure.

Lincoln White, the State Department spokesman, followed N.A.S.A. by saying the United States had never voluntarily sent a plane across the Soviet borders.

In the week of May 1, Eisenhower flew down to Fort Benning, Georgia, to watch a display of the latest Army infantry weapons and spoke of the need for armed strength in the quest for peace. On May 5, he flew away for part of the day with the National Security Council to a Civil Defense relocation center outside Washington as part of a nationwide drill. On Friday, May 6, he went back to Gettysburg for the weekend, the weekend in which Khrushchev lowered the boom.

On Saturday, March 7, the Soviet Premier tossed Powers, the plane and its equipment at the world, complete with pictures and a detailed description of the intelligence mission. Khrushchev was either baiting Eisenhower or trying to leave him an escape hatch, for in announcing details of the flight, he said, "I fully admit that the President did not know that a plane was

sent beyond the Soviet frontiers and did not return. But this should make us even more watchful."

The State Department (the White House had been silent except to say Eisenhower had ordered a full report made to him on the plane) followed Khrushchev by saying, "As a result of the inquiry ordered by the President, it has been established that insofar as the authorities are concerned, there was no authorization for any such flights as described by Mr. Khrushchev."

The Department conceded that the plane involved "probably" was on an intelligence flight and admitted for the first time that such flights had been made for the preceding four years "along the frontiers of the free world."

James Reston wrote for the *New York Times* on May 8 from Washington:

> This was a sad and perplexed capital tonight caught in a swirl of charges of clumsy administration, bad judgment and bad faith.
>
> It was depressed and humiliated by the United States having been caught spying over the Soviet Union and trying to cover up its activities in a series of misleading official announcements.

Eisenhower was on the telephone from the book-lined study of his farmhouse in Gettysburg, sitting at the desk made for him by White House carpenters from wood of the original Executive Mansion and looking out at the rain making puddles in the gravel of his circular driveway. He arranged for Herter to meet him at the White House in the late afternoon.

From that meeting came a statement by the Secretary, who said yes, the United States had been conducting this sort of intelligence for some time because the Russians had open access to the free nations of the world, while keeping their own society tightly controlled and in secret preparation of armed might with which "to face the free world with the choice of abject surrender or nuclear destruction."

"Specific missions of these unarmed civilian aircraft have not been subject to presidential authorization," Herter said.

Herter concluded with a monument to diplomatic blanditude: "Far from being damaging to the forthcoming meeting in Paris, this incident should serve to underline the importance to the world of an earnest attempt there to achieve agreed and effective safeguards against surprise attack and aggression."

On May 11, Eisenhower had to cope with the mounting crisis in a press conference. He called intelligence activity of the government "a distasteful but vital necessity" in dealing with a nation where there was "a fetish of secrecy and concealment."

"No one wants another Pearl Harbor," he said.

Soviet Foreign Minister Andrei Gromyko that morning, before Eisenhower's press conference, had accused the United States of deliberate provocation.

"With statements like this," I asked Eisenhower, "do you still maintain a hopeful attitude toward the Summit?"

He answered with a shaky affirmative, pointing out the Russians had been saying things like this for years.

"We are looking to our own security and our defense and we have no idea of promoting any kind of conflict or war," he added. "This is just—" and he threw up both hands—"It's absolutely ridiculous and they know it."

This chapter is not intended as a definitive history or analysis of the U-2 incident and the Summit, but the foregoing recollection of events is necessary to appreciate the situation and the atmosphere as Eisenhower prepared to depart within a few days for what he knew would be an unsuccessful mission. His statement of hope at the press conference was halfhearted. He knew there was little or no basis for expecting Khrushchev to discuss disarmament, Germany or Berlin. But what could he say? Certainly not that the Summit was foredoomed as he knew it was. He couldn't stand up and say publicly, "Frankly, I know it's a waste of time but I have to go anyway."

There were some speculative cables from Ambassador Llewellyn Thompson, who had left Moscow some days earlier, but even

Thompson offered no real ray of hope. Actually, these men were talking only in terms of how bad the ruckus would be.

Members of the staff watched the President closely during these tense few days leading up to the Summit. One of them who had been close to Ike for years told me: "He's a most unusual man when he's in the middle of a crisis. The tougher things really are, the more soft-spoken and considerate of others he becomes. He's been so polite and kindly around here today that I need nothing else to tell me that we're in a heap of trouble. Not that he's the opposite when things are going well. But today, he seems to be going out of his way to think of others."

The bluest people around the White House were the men who had slaved over plans for the Russian trip. Hagerty, Stephens and the other advance men had made their survey trip and come back with an amazing itinerary in Russia, scheduled to begin June 10 and continue within the Soviet Union for nine days.

Eisenhower planned to visit five major cities—Moscow, Leningrad, Kiev, Irkutsk and Khabarovsk, deep in Siberia. Also on the schedule were Russia-wide radio and television speeches from Moscow, Kiev and Leningrad, plus a full-scale press conference in Moscow, a no-holds-barred question-and-answer affair at which he was prepared to deal with the sharpest questions Russian reporters could throw at him.

All this quite obviously went down the diplomatic drain because a few hours after Eisenhower's May 11 press conference, at which he said hesitatingly that he still expected to go to Russia, Khrushchev in Moscow burst out, "I would be mad to say to the Russian people to welcome . . . a man who sends espionage planes here."

As insulting as Khrushchev was, this spurred some hope in the State Department that having said his piece in Moscow, Mr. K. might not be so frontal in his abuse at Paris and thus permit the Summit to make at least a start.

This, of course, turned out to be so much wishful thinking,

which Eisenhower quickly determined for himself shortly after he reached Paris on the afternoon of Saturday, May 14. Khrushchev followed him into town and in separate Sunday conferences with De Gaulle and Macmillan he told them almost entirely what he intended to do—publicly rub Eisenhower's face in the mud.

The details of the May 16 meeting have been amply recorded: Khrushchev's demand that Eisenhower apologize publicly for the U-2 flights, punishment for all those responsible, promise not to do it again and, above all, for Ike not to come to Russia.

Eisenhower, noted in the past for a sulphurous temper, knew this was not the time to cut loose with invective. Sitting across the table from the Russian in a classically decorated conference room on the second floor of the Élysée Palace, Eisenhower with studied, determined calmness told Khrushchev that the flights had been halted and would not be resumed, that they were conducted only because of Russia's refusal to join the free world in exposing armaments to full view and that for the sake of keeping the Summit going he would be willing to negotiate separately with Russia on the question of the flights.

Khrushchev would have none of it and when the meeting ended in the early afternoon, the principals left De Gaulle's heavily guarded courtyard one at a time. Khrushchev smiled in the cocky manner of a man who had just drubbed an offensive neighbor. Macmillan seemed wan and droopy. Eisenhower smiled thinly on the palace steps as he said good-by to De Gaulle.

While the meeting was in progress, the Russian attitude toward the West manifested itself in the courtyard of the palace as we watched through the curtains of the tiny office of M. Perlou, personal press attaché to De Gaulle, who had become a highly helpful friend in our recently frequent trips to Paris, the Élysée and Rambouillet.

Automobiles of the principals were drawn up on the shady side of the courtyard. The Russian security men and drivers remained entirely to themselves, refusing to have anything to do

with the American, British and French security men who gossiped with each other during the long meeting.

Khrushchev's chauffeur looked like the classic villain in an American wrestling show except for his bright green felt hat.

On the day before the meeting, when Khrushchev visited the Élysée to call on De Gaulle, the driver was tieless and wore a light gray shirt open at the throat.

A French reporter gave his office a colorful description of the driver, but an editor misunderstood and put together a story about how Khrushchev himself arrived at the palace for a formal call on the French President with no tie, but wearing a bright green hat.

The story spread through Paris quickly and the Russian Embassy must have taken note, because when the man drove Khrushchev to the Élysée for the Monday meeting, he had on the same gray shirt and green hat, but this time a tie.

The Russians were so jittery during the Monday meeting that the Soviet security agents brushed aside the fact that they were within the jurisdiction of the French President and forcibly prevented French cameramen from photographing Khrushchev's empty automobile.

The one and only full session of the Summit was an hour behind schedule in beginning, the delay requested by the Russians without explanation. Ike was informed and came late. The Soviet, British and French delegations were seated when he arrived.

The French chief of protocol showed the President to his seat. Before he took his chair, Eisenhower greeted his fellow conferees individually. When he came to Khrushchev, the President bobbed his head in a quick bow and said, "Good morning, Mister Chairman."

Khrushchev glared back, grunted and turned to look at the Soviet advisers beside him.

Later, we found out that Khrushchev on Sunday told De Gaulle virtually everything about the planned denunciation of Eisenhower except one major item. He neglected to tell De

Gaulle in advance that he planned to withdraw his invitation for Eisenhower to visit Russia.

When the President drove back to the embassy residence and his big Cadillac bumped softly into the walled entrance yard, his jaw was sternly set. There were patches of red above his cheekbones. He seemed to be clamping down on himself until he could get inside and blow up, which, incidentally, he never did.

One of the Americans who sat behind Ike during the Élysée meeting said it was a most curious session, obviously charged with drama and excitement without the participants seeming to be excited, themselves.

"They looked like heavy-stakes poker players late at night," this man said. "It was the coldest gathering of human beings I believe I've ever seen. They were almost antiseptic in their dealings. Not once during the three hours was there a smile or even a colloquial aside to relieve the tension.

"I thought the President would choke when Khrushchev threw his hands toward the ceiling and said 'as God is my judge' the Russians were without aggressive intent.

"Khrushchev looked menacing enough, but the picture of dominating evility was Malinovsky, the Soviet Defense Minister, who sat beside K. in full-dress uniform and thirty-four medals, including two Orders of Lenin. Maybe it was the uniform and chestful of medals, but Marshal Malinovsky seemed to be vastly more dominating and stern than Khrushchev."

Marvin Arrowsmith and I had arranged with Hagerty to meet him in front of the Crillon Hotel thirty minutes after the meeting broke up, then ride with him to the Palais de Chaillot, press headquarters for the four powers, to get some sort of advance idea of what would be said in the first public briefings on the Summit.

The press secretary failed to show up, however, and Marv and I began tracing him by telephone. He was at the embassy residence with the President and there we sped. There were no reporters or photographers outside when we sent word to Jim that we had arrived. He sent for us immediately and Secret

Service men directed us to a small office, normally a library and reference room where we had spent many hours in Paris eating the Ambassador's *croissants* and awaiting news developments.

After about thirty minutes, Hagerty burst into the room with a handful of notes. He had just come from the President and Herter, who were talking in an upstairs study. Jim did not want to violate a general agreement for all of the Four Power spokesmen to brief at the Palais simultaneously, but neither did he want the Russians to beat the rest of the world with their version of what had taken place there.

He began to read from his notes. A Secret Service man standing by the coffee bar whistled in amazement as we rapidly filled our notebooks with the raw ore of history. Within seconds, Marv and I were on telephones to our conference bureaus and between the two of us, we gave the world the first news of what had happened. I have the copy of my story as it rolled out of Paris:

PARIS, MAY 16 (UPI)—Soviet Premier Nikita Khrushchev today angrily withdrew his invitation to President Eisenhower to visit Russia and Western sources said his "insulting" attack on Eisenhower and the United States had wrecked the Summit meeting at the outset.

Khrushchev said he would walk out of the conference unless the United States punished those responsible for the U-2 spy flights and promised not to conduct any such flights in the future.

He demanded a public apology from the President.

The Western sources said Eisenhower replied to Khrushchev in equally blunt language. Eisenhower rejected Khrushchev's demand and said Russia's warlike preparations made it necessary for the free world to keep track of what was going on inside Russia.

The emphasis in this particular story admittedly was misplaced, but the few paragraphs quoted here are just as they were dictated over the telephone from the little library in the embassy; dictated from raw notes and with the knowledge, too, that we were saying some kind of requiem over the remains of what might have been a positive moment in history.

The Western leaders gathered at the Élysée the next day and again on Wednesday, but their efforts to keep the conference alive were fruitless. On Wednesday, however, Khrushchev put on one of the more amazing public displays of violent anger known, at least, to modern history.

He held a press conference at the Palais de Chaillot that may have played well to the homefolks back in Russia, but to the rest of the world it was a frightening demonstration.

Pudgy arms flailing and the greasy sheen of angry excitement over his ovoid face, the Russian became almost incoherent with rage in the long second-floor hall of the Palais where more than two thousand reporters and demijournalists crowded to hear him. West Germans, Hungarians and others from Central Europe booed K. as he came in. He also had been booed on the streets of Paris earlier in the day.

He roared that his detractors were "German riffraff" and he pounded the table in front of him so harshly with his stubby, meaty fists that mineral water bottles beside his public address system microphone rocked and toppled over.

For two and a half hours, the Russian stormed. Much of what he said was from his published statement of two days earlier, but he embroidered it with new invective against Eisenhower, whom he likened to "a thief caught red-handed in his theft." The journalistic situation called for all possible detachment, which was difficult in the surroundings.

It was amazing to the Americans in the audience to hear a head of state roundly booed. The derogatory sounds began as Khrushchev entered the hall, the boos piercing through the boisterous applause of Soviet employees, diplomats and others from the Iron Curtain countries who came early to jam the rows immediately adjacent to the platform.

Khrushchev started to read a prepared statement in Russian and the booing broke out again. He pointed to his head with

the universal, finger-twirling sign for "crazy." Some European reporters leaped from their seats and shook their fists. Khrushchev's face reddened, he shouted back in a raucous voice and at times he became so infuriated the veins stood out in his temples to the point where they were noticeable on television.

Watching the occasional knots of Europeans who rose from their folding chairs to shout angrily at Khrushchev, one thought of the scene in an American football stadium when a fist fight breaks out and the crowd rises and falls in waves to see the action. Except here there were no pretty girls with plaid lap-robes, laughing through their State U. banners. This was ugly sight and angry sound. At one point, Khrushchev said something that produced laughter from those who understood Russian.

An American standing near me started to laugh, too, but stopped quickly in self-disgust.

"What the hell am I laughing for?" he said. "This man could fly out of Paris tomorrow and start World War III in two or three hours."

Khrushchev during the day motored about Paris paying his farewell calls on De Gaulle and Macmillan. Eisenhower also was on the move. He visited Notre Dame, one of Christianity's ancient cathedrals, and the exquisite Sainte Chapelle.

As he walked out of the darkened aisles of the towering cathedral with one of the priests, an impassioned Frenchwoman broke through the security men around the President to clasp both of his hands and sob, "Be firm—stand firm above all."

Eisenhower nodded gravely, thanked the woman and returned to his car. As he drove back to the embassy, people along the streets held up their fingers in the World War II "V" signal popularized by Churchill.

Back home, the newspapers and magazines told of Eisenhower having suffered the greatest disappointment of his life. He was disappointed, of course, but as to how Paris related to other low moments of his career was a matter of conjecture.

Several of us had an opportunity to chat quietly with him twice during those three tense days in Paris. If he suffered a severe emotional jolt, it started before he left Washington. He had known he was in for a storm, that Khrushchev's smile of Camp David had disappeared some time before. Eisenhower, no stranger to crisis in his military days and having learned to accommodate his life to the zooming peaks and slumping valleys of everyday life in the White House, had gone to the Summit prepared for the bombast that came.

Several of us—Arrowsmith, Heffernan, LaGrange and I— saw him on at least three occasions the second day of the meeting, the day when De Gaulle and Macmillan were attempting to salvage the conference.

Eisenhower was subdued, but he seemed to be in easygoing, affable spirits. He gave me the impression of having detached himself from the immediate crisis. There was nothing more to be done for the moment.

He took Macmillan for a drive in the country and seemed almost elated when we stopped to surprise the Mayor of Marnes-la-Coquette, a village about ten miles from Paris where Eisenhower lived during the early fifties when he was the European defense commander.

The two leaders drove first to the quiet estate and white-walled villa Eisenhower once occupied. Then they motored to the tiny *hôtel de ville*. The Mayor, a grizzled patriarch named Jean Minot, was home preparing for his midday meal when the President and the Prime Minister descended on his placid village. The Mayor came running down the street, clucking with joy at seeing his old friend, Le Génerale, again.

Later in the afternoon, during the painful session at the Élysée Palace where Macmillan and De Gaulle tried in a series of telephone calls to get Khrushchev back to the conference table, Eisenhower relieved the tedium by recounting the surprise of Mayor Minot and laughing at how the Prime Minister of Great Britain had to serve as his interpreter.

That night, in the American Embassy residence and later at the Élysée where he went for an after-dinner visit with De Gaulle and Macmillan, the President seemed calm and relaxed.

His face turned flinty, however, when he thought back to some
of the things Khrushchev had said to him, and, for the most
part, he avoided reliving the Monday meeting.

There were a few new lines around his eyes and even when
he was talking amiably about his disappointment at not being
able to revisit the cathedral at Chartres because of poor helicopter weather, he seemed to be thinking of something else.
We talked with him in the center hallway of the embassy that
night as he prepared to join Macmillan and De Gaulle for
another look at the plainly hopeless situation.

Eisenhower spoke of the beauties of Chartres, the most beautiful blue glass windows in the world. He seemed to me to be
avoiding any mention of Khrushchev. One of us asked how he,
Ike, was holding up.

He seemed almost surprised.

"Oh, me?" he said. "These things are not very pleasant, but
otherwise I feel fine, perfectly fine."

After talking with him at the embassy, I wrote a story that
night which concluded with these lines:

> While he may be smiling on the outside, he cannot help but
> feel a deep disappointment that at what in all probability was
> his last major appearance at a meeting of Summit proportions,
> the results had to be completely negative.
>
> He feels quite encouraged by press reaction to the stand taken
> by the West against Khrushchev's attacks and continuing
> truculence. Eisenhower finds particular satisfaction in the edi-
> torial response of the press outside the United States. He has
> watched Congressional reaction closely and feels the support
> there also is gratifying.
>
> But he knows, despite the encouraging remarks and editorials
> from his side, that the Summit smashed on the rocks of Russian
> opposition and he is deeply disappointed that he has to go
> home this week without being able to say that things are better.

As Eisenhower said in his only public statement at Paris:
"Mr. Khrushchev brushed aside all arguments of reasons, and

not only insisted upon this ultimatum, but also insisted that he was going to publish his statement in full at the time of his own choosing.

"It was thus made apparent that he was determined to wreck the Paris conference.

"In fact, the only conclusion that can be drawn from his behavior . . . was that he came all the way from Moscow to Paris with the sole intention of sabotaging this meeting on which so much of the hopes of the world have rested.

"In spite of this serious and adverse development, I have no intention whatsoever to diminish my continuing efforts to promote progress toward a peace with justice."

Eisenhower had promised to make an overnight visit to Portugal on the way back to Washington after the Summit and the Lisbon stop had to be advanced when the Big Four meeting ended so abruptly. Tom Stephens rushed to Portugal to determine whether the officials possibly could change their plans. They were happy to do so, and after saying good-by to De Gaulle and Macmillan, Eisenhower left Paris on Thursday, May 19, for Lisbon and a visit with President Americo Thomaz and the real boss of Portugal, Premier António de Oliveira Salazar, the seventy-one-year-old autocrat who for thirty-one years had dictated the policies of his small country.

Eisenhower was again criticized at home for consorting with dictators, but Portugal, a small but steady part of the Atlantic Alliance, felt overlooked the previous December when Eisenhower visited neighboring Spain.

The Portugal visit was a brightly colorful twenty-four-hour succession of castles and formalities for Eisenhower. But even diplomatic civility and Salazar's success in promoting an enthusiastic welcome could not shake the shadow of Khrushchev. When the President settled briefly in historic Queluz Palace outside Lisbon, Eisenhower learned there had been a sharp rise in concern over international tension among the Portuguese people due to the Summit collapse.

Once the palace of Portuguese royalty in the eighteenth and

nineteenth centuries, Queluz was designed in the manner of Versailles with beautiful formal gardens through which Eisenhower strolled during the late afternoon. I had left the press center in downtown Lisbon to go to the palace on some other business with the White House staff and happened to be standing in the red-floored diplomatic reception hall when Ike walked by on the way to the gardens.

I fell in with the aides behind the President, who was talking earnestly with Ambassador Elbrick and General Goodpaster. Hagerty was right when he described Ike as "disgusted and fed up" with Khrushchev's tactics.

Eisenhower had expressed disappointment at Orly Field in Paris as he departed, and during the brief flight to Portugal, he talked with Livingston T. Merchant, Undersecretary of State for Political Affairs, on his approach to the subject of the Summit in his upcoming report to the American people.

And by the time Eisenhower reached Lisbon and could walk off some of his pent-up feelings in the gardens of Queluz, he seemed to be feeling the effects of Paris.

Sensing his mood and not wanting to get caught in the crossfire as an eavesdropper, I stayed well removed from him in the gardens while he talked with his staff. I walked over to one of the eighteenth-century French fountains and was idly tossing leftover French coins into the water when Eisenhower walked by.

"That how you're keeping busy?" he asked impassively.

"No, sir, this is just for luck."

"Then you'd better throw some in for us all," he said with a wry chuckle and walked on back to the castle with his hands clasped behind his back.

Later that afternoon, the American Embassy families came to call and Eisenhower, speaking extemporaneously and with an informality much more expressive than the manner of a larger public appearance, gave perhaps his best summation of Paris.

The slanting just-before-twilight sun streamed in through the tall windows of the ornate palace reception hall and the massive chandelier over the President's head cast crystal droplets of reflected rainbow light around the mirrored walls.

The President spoke slowly, deliberately, with his hands rammed in his trouser pockets.

"While none of the free world thought that there would be any revolutionary gains at the Summit conference, they did feel there was a good chance of some amelioration of some of the tensions in the world," he said.

He paused for a few seconds and looked down at the three-hundred-year-old dull-red tile floor.

"You deserve to know that the representatives of the United States, the United Kingdom and France did our very best to bring about that condition. We answered abuse with dignity and logic. We answered accusations with facts.

"There is no reason to be dismayed or disheartened. We have had these conditions before in dealing with the Soviets.

"Rather than being dismayed, we must tighten our belts, keep our chins up, and each of us work a little harder for the great cause of peace with justice and freedom. . . .

"Whenever these situations occur, we have to work ever stronger to strengthen our own camp and to bring it ever closer together."

The next morning, Friday, May 20, Eisenhower's last crusade to Europe ended in a manner befitting the broken Summit. Air Force One developed mechanical trouble and Colonel Draper had to switch again to the back-up plane, but fortunately, before the President reached the field.

The President traveled from Queluz to the airport by helicopter, which was to pick him up in a picturesque old-world cobblestone plaza between the palace and an ancient cathedral. The plaza was powdered with heavy dust and Portuguese officials had promised to water down the area before the choppers came in for landing.

The water wagons failed to arrive, but the helicopters came in on schedule. Their swirling rotors raised a biting dust storm

and the air was filled with fine gravel. Eisenhower had to clutch his hat and close his eyes tightly as aides led him through the turbulent street dirt to the first helicopter.

Members of his party assigned to subsequent helicopters took an abrasive beating as they raced across the plaza to the waiting aircraft. Women in the group were dotted with tiny bruises on their arms and legs and their stockings were shredded by the miniature cyclones.

And to complicate matters further, there were three more passengers than space available aboard the choppers. This meant quickly assembling a motorcycle escort and speeding the left-overs through Lisbon to the airport within the time required for Ike's helicopter flight and the airport farewell ceremonies.

Back at Andrews Field outside Washington late that after-noon, Mamie rushed up to Ike with tear-filled eyes. He looked away for a fleeting moment and, as he put his arms around his wife, his eyes seemed near tears, too.

Senator Everett M. Dirksen, the GOP leader of the Senate, was in the throng of officials who gathered around the President and Mamie with words of encouragement.

"I don't see any scars," Dirksen quipped, trying to be light.

Tiredly, he looked at Dirksen with a shake of the head and said, "Boy, I've got them all right."

There were, the police said, 200,000 people out in Washing-ton to cheer Ike and Mamie as they drove to the White House. Beneath the slump of his shoulders and the fatigue lines in his face, Eisenhower seemed genuinely pleased as he waved his thanks to the crowd.

As Ike sat down to prepare his report to the country, the returns from Paris flowed in, many of them discouraging, some reflecting a deep concern for his own welfare in the period of reaction to being reviled by Khrushchev. Marquis Childs wrote from Paris of the Big Four principals, "They are all without exception reduced in stature."

Eisenhower was under particularly heavy criticism for having failed to take a way out of the U-2 debacle offered by Khrushchev when he assumed the President did not know about the plane being sent into Russian territory.

C. Wright Mills, professor of sociology at Columbia University, wrote in *The Nation* of the opportunity for Eisenhower:

> He did not take it; he did not disclaim knowledge of the adventure in the normal diplomatic manner expected. For the first time in modern history, the head of a state declared his personal responsibility for an act of espionage.

There were similar arguments in other quarters, but Eisenhower thought they were dead wrong. It was a matter of conjecture as to what the Russians might have done if Eisenhower had tried to lie his way out of the U-2. Some of the British thought Eisenhower might have been a bit more sophisticated and their feeling was that, having stretched morality to the point of sending the spy flights over Russia, an additional bit of stretch would not have compromised the chief executive's principles.

The President thought his information and his conjecture possibly were better founded than the suggestions of his critics. He had reason to believe, with Francis Powers in their possession and apparently talking, the Russians would spot a diplomatic lie for what it was and this would give Khrushchev still another propaganda weapon if he chose to use it.

Eisenhower decided to follow his line of open admission and on the night of May 25, speaking from his office cluttered with television cables and camera tripods, he unveiled a frightening photograph to illustrate the effectiveness of the U-2 flights and why they were indispensable to world security.

His Exhibit A was a large picture of an American naval installation made from a U-2 at an altitude of about thirteen miles. The resolving power of the high-altitude camera was so fine that pedestrian cross walks, parking lot stripes and home plate on a baseball diamond were clearly visible.

This, he said, was proof of what could be accomplished through United Nations aerial surveillance, his "open skies" proposal. But his message with the picture was deeper. It was intended to show the type of material the planes had brought back from Russia before May 1. As to the timing of the flight with the imminence of the Summit, Eisenhower said:

"The plain truth is this: when a nation needs intelligence activity, there is no time when vigilance can be relaxed. Incidentally, from Pearl Harbor we learned that even negotiation can be used to conceal preparations for surprise attack."

The world grew no easier as the result of Eisenhower's speech. Khrushchev's anger seemed to mount. He called Russian and foreign newsmen together in Moscow to picture Eisenhower as a spineless boob.

"When he is no longer President, and if he chooses to work in our country, we could give him a job as a director of a children's home—I am sure he would not harm the children," Mr. K. said. "But it is dangerous for a man like this to run a nation."

Malinovsky ordered his rocket forces to be ready to fire at the bases from which any foreign planes might take off to fly over Russia.

"We do not trust the imperialists," thundered the Soviet defense chief. "We are convinced that they are only waiting for an opportunity to attack."

With nine days of slack left in his Far Eastern tour due to the canceled Russian visit, Eisenhower ordered this itinerary enlarged. Riots against the government of Premier Nobusuke Kishi and the impending presidential visit began to torment the police in Tokyo. There were cries in Congress that Paris was enough, Eisenhower should not go to the Far East and risk being humbled a second time in little more than one month.

Eisenhower's attitude toward such reasoning was, to hell with it, we're going. Because of Paris, Khrushchev's continuing vilification and the rowdyism in Japan, Eisenhower felt it was more necessary than ever to go through with his travel plans.

Also, his time was running out. Time for the political conventions was nearing and he said frankly that once the two nominees were selected, his activities would cease to attract much attention abroad.

Whereupon, he prepared for the Orient, the first President ever to venture into an area where we had such an investment of pain, people and substance.

CHAPTER 17 *STAY OUT OF JAPAN*

Looking back on the mass of evidence that was available at the time, it becomes all the more unbelievable that Eisenhower thought he could go to Japan in June, 1960.

Even at the time of the disastrous Paris Summit, he must have known there was a distinct possibility that the long-awaited trip to Tokyo would have to be abandoned. His personal safety did not concern him greatly because he had long ago reached the philosophical conclusion that this matter would be taken care of by the proper authorities. In this he was right because a President to lead any sort of intelligent life cannot move in personal fear. If he is emotionally capable of it, he should dismiss security from his mind, but this is no license for foolhardiness.

This is not to say Eisenhower was foolhardy about Japan. It was painfully evident to many close to him, however, that a month of violence in Tokyo would not subside simply because he rode through the streets with the Emperor. The feelings of these associates largely were pushed aside by optimistic prognoses from the American Embassy in Tokyo, estimates that turned out to be shockingly wrong.

Aside from the situation in Japan, Eisenhower was determined to go through with the announced Far Eastern trip. While there were ever-present differences with the other countries on his schedule, the Philippines, Formosa and Korea, his purpose was what he believed to be a badly needed good-will trip through an area under the daily prodding of anti-American propaganda from Communist China.

The degree of Communist responsibility for disenchantment with America in sections of the Orient was highly debatable. It was easier to blame it all on the Communists and thus conveniently chalk off the emergent nationalism, which was complicated, hard for the Occidental to understand and difficult for many Americans to accept from those they thought should have been scrapingly grateful for postwar beneficences.

Khrushchev, however, was keeping the fires well stoked. It seemed self-evident that he was doing his best to destroy the image of Eisenhower before he reached the Far East. Leading up to the trip, the Soviet boss fired shot after shot at Eisenhower and the United States. He said Americans needed generally to be "taken down a peg or two." He ridiculed Eisenhower for regarding golf as more important than the presidency. He said that when and if summitry was resumed, he wanted Communist China and the Asian nations included. He also forecast that "Eisenhower's presidency will come to be known as a dark period in the history of the United States and the world."

In China itself, leaders of the 2,500,000-member army called for full war readiness "ultimately to wipe out entirely the imperialist system."

Tokyo was the focal point of trouble for Eisenhower. He was scheduled to arrive there June 19, effective date of a defense treaty with the United States. The mutual security pact gave the U.S.A. the right to Japanese land for military, air and naval bases. The original treaty was signed in 1951, later denounced as one-sidedly favoring the United States and revised extensively at the behest of Nobusuke Kishi after he became Prime Minister.

The new treaty was rushed through the Diet by Kishi May 19 after 107 days of deliberation so heated that at one point the opposition Socialists held the house speaker as a prisoner.

A conglomeration of anti-Kishi forces, including virtually all of the left-wing elements of Japan, protested the parliamentary tactics bitterly. They argued that the treaty would involve Japan in the cold war. The agreement was to become effective one

month after passage, provided Parliament was in session, and Eisenhower's arrival was timed for the effective date.

In this one-month period, there were daily demonstrations against the treaty, Kishi and finally Eisenhower. Kishi's residence and the American Embassy were stoned. The hard core of the demonstrators seemed to be the Zengakuren, a down-with-everything anarchist faction which this government maintained was Communist-directed. This rather flat position, however, was not shared by many Westerners on the scene because it indicated Communist totality, which was not true.

The situation in late May and early June became progressively worse. Injuries in street fighting went higher with each riot. The big labor union, Sohyo, believed to be at least Communist-tainted, was paying for demonstrators. There was no hatred for Eisenhower expressed. They were after Kishi, through Ike if necessary, because the Kishi government was doomed to fall if the visit had to be postponed.

Jim Hagerty flew into Tokyo about a week ahead of Eisenhower and several thousand demonstrators ganged his car outside the International Airport with such obstinate and carefully directed force that he had to be extricated by an American helicopter and whisked out of danger. Secret Service advance agents in Tokyo angrily called Washington and, contrary to the estimates of Ambassador Douglas MacArthur II, told their executives the President would be endangered unless plans for the visit were changed radically and Eisenhower virtually kept off the streets.

A restrained U.P.I. dispatch from Tokyo two weeks before Eisenhower's scheduled arrival said many Asians were having second thoughts about the wisdom of his coming because of bad timing in the wake of the Summit collapse. The story went into detail about the "Ike Stay Home" signs, the daily angry demonstrations and the certainty of these riots while Eisenhower was in Japan.

The Secret Service men called again from Tokyo. Japanese police officials, themselves, were beginning to doubt whether they could control the mobs over a thirteen-mile route Eisenhower and the Emperor were to parade by car on the arrival day.

Eisenhower persisted. He was going to the Far East and if the Tokyo stop had to be dropped—he was supposed to be there three days—that would be up to the Japanese government.

Public attention was so diverted by the continuing Tokyo riots that the full scope of the trip received scant notice until Eisenhower himself explained his mission to the public as he departed on Sunday, June 12.

He acknowledged the warnings against his trip, but he said he decided to go because the continued promotion of "a better understanding of America abroad, which, particularly in the circumstances of the moment, is a compelling responsibility of me as President of the United States."

His statement translated a bit more practically to this: Eisenhower hoped to rally support for American policies in the face of a stepped-up campaign of Chinese Communist infiltration, subversion and threat in Asia.

Somehow I had the feeling I had left Stew Hensley in Paris only a few moments before, but there we were again, a Sunday dawn aboard a creaky bus heading for Friendship Airport, another Pan Am jet and what seemed to be several million miles of travel ahead of us. Eisenhower had added America's newest states, Alaska and Hawaii, to his itinerary and our first stop was Anchorage, a flight of seven hours from Washington.

Diary notes on the first leg of the trip:

Flight to Alaska smooth as glass at 33,000 feet, but hard to sleep. Everybody jabbering about the outlook for Tokyo. We're learning to live together. Snore consecutively.

Jim Hagerty waiting for us at Anchorage, still full of his harrowing experience at the Tokyo airport. Waiting for Ike to land at Elmendorf AFB, we asked Jim why he didn't take a helicopter in the first place, why ride right into those babies? He growled, "I don't bluff."

When Ike spotted Jim, he hailed him with a big laugh. The President looked fine, but he seemed flat and listless in delivering his arrival remarks. Maybe he's thinking about Tokyo like the rest of us.

Went to the Jonas Bros. Fur Store with Ike. Barbara Eisenhower along again as a sub for Mamie who's in the hospital. Barbara looked at the fur parkas for children but didn't buy. Furs look marvelous here, but how would they seem in Gettysburg?

One of the lady clerks came outside and did some Eskimo dances for Ike. He looked puzzled and the lady looked like she was about to melt in her parka. Alaskan cost of living item: bread, 50 cents a loaf.

Diary for June 14 (we crossed the international date line, thus doing away with the thirteenth):

Spent 13 hours in the air getting from Alaska to the Philippines. Up in Anchorage at 4 A.M. and learned why they call it land of the midnight sun. Broad daylight and cold. Ike took off about 7 A.M. looking fussy and sleepy.

We took off right behind him and settled down for a day aloft. Weird way to live—all day in the air. Coats and shoes shucked, making luxury airliner resemble a bus hauling class D ball team between mill towns.

Ike flew to Manila via Wake Island but we took shorter route and refueled at Tokyo. To be on safe side we had our one Japanese correspondent aboard, Omori of the Mainichi papers, print a sign in Japanese which we stuck in one window, saying, "Hagerty is not on this airplane." Airport could not have been quieter. Arnold Dibble of the UPI Tokyo bureau came to talk with Hensley and me. Showed us an underpass where the Zengakuren will hit Ike. We order more walkie-talkies.

Manila: Beat Ike in by two unnecessary hours. Airport so hot shoes sink in the asphalt. Found an air conditioned room but so many people made same discovery that we went back out into the sun. Cooler. Welcome face: Ambassador Carlos Romulo, one of our favorites; great man, never heard anybody knock him.

Procession into town almost like India again. Screaming thousands, flags, confetti, cries of "*Mabuhay*" which means in New Delhi "*Zindabad.*" How can we do justice to another crowd story? People now talk about crowds of a million before they've gone five blocks. Ike and President Carlos P. Garcia hitting it off well, laughing and joking with each other.

Eisenhower was certain to be well received in the Philippines, not only as President, but sentimentally as a former Army officer who was stationed there for four years. The Philippines became independent of the United States in 1946, but years as a U.S. territory had firmly implanted American culture in the islands. Since independence, differences had arisen between the two countries over war damage claims, civil aviation rights, the sovereignty of American bases, but these were not deeply divisive matters. This was friendship territory for Ike and his reception proved it.

With a population of slightly more than 1,500,000, Manila went wild in the crushing summer heat and humidity. The national population is about 25,000,000 and police officials tried to tell us there were 4,000,000 on the streets that afternoon. We settled for about 2,000,000, which was another way of saying the reception seemed larger than New Delhi, which I never would have believed without riding through it myself.

Battalions of police used brute strength to hold back mobs that surged through the streets around the car bearing Ike and Garcia. Many spectators were injured, trampled or shoved into moving procession cars during the humid fog of confetti that poured down from upper stories of midtown buildings. Near the end of the parade, our press association car became hopelessly bogged in humanity and Eisenhower was inside Garcia's Malacañang Palace by the time we bruised up to the gates. Eisenhower adjourned quickly to his apartment in one wing of the palace, while we sped to the air conditioning of the Manila Hotel to recuperate from another twenty-five-hour day.

His second day there, Wednesday, June 15, followed a stand-

ard pattern for his journeys—breakfast at the palace with the host President and then a morning business conference in which Eisenhower was flanked by his son, Goodpaster, Ambassador John D. Hickerson and J. Graham Parsons, Assistant Secretary of State for Far Eastern Affairs.

That afternoon Eisenhower went before the Philippine Congress and promised steadfast American support of her friends against any incursions by third parties. That night, Garcia entertained at the biggest social event of the trip, a formal dinner at Malacañang. Diary notes:

> The President showed up in a native barong tagalog, looking very sheepish about wearing his shirttails out at a banquet where ordinarily he would be spiffy in a white dinner jacket.
>
> Filipino men wear a barong, a filmy thin, embroidered shirt of fiber made from pineapples, as conventional business or formal evening attire. No coats. Just the shirt and dark trousers. Younger men wear the collar open. Older or more conservative men wear collars buttoned, frequently with jeweled studs, but no tie.
>
> Eisenhower has an aversion to any sort of "funny" attire; won't pose for pictures in ten-gallon hats, blushes when Asians put flowers around his neck. But Garcia gave him the barong, told him he planned to wear one, himself, and Ike had no choice.
>
> Most of the men traveling with Ike planned to wear summer dinner jackets, but word passed during the late afternoon that the President was going native. Men's shop in the Manila Hotel never had it so good. Sold almost all of their barongs in the space of two hours. Bob Montgomery paid $45 for his by mistake, right price: 45 pesos.
>
> At the banquet, Eisenhower's advisers eyed each other like boys at dancing school as they walked self-consciously into the red velvet and paneled reception room to await the two Presidents. Dr. George Kistiakowsky, Ike's science adviser, looked like a nervous druggist in his barong; Jim Hagerty, a barber without a chair; Kevin McCann, a clergyman puttering around the house.

The people around Ike remain on pins and needles about Tokyo. More rioting tonight. Hagerty's temper wearing thin under the pressure. There are reports of deaths in a riot before the Japanese Diet tonight and Jim wants to know what the hell he's expected to do about it when we ask him for a comment.

The White House telephone circuit to Tokyo has been busy all afternoon and evening. Hagerty can say nothing more than the trip still is on. While Ike was dining at the palace, we stood in the next room bulling with the Secret Service. One of them said, "What can ten men around a car in a foreign country do with a mob of several thousand if the local police can't keep them under control?"

Hagerty is holding up a revised Tokyo schedule. They're going to drop the long auto ride with the Emperor or at least shorten it.

Back at the Manila Hotel, Chief Baughman openly concerned. He's leaving Manila pronto to have a look at the Tokyo situation himself. (He didn't make it—situation moved too rapidly.) Never have seen Baughman this worried. My impression from him is that the situation is impossible. Sent story to this effect. Also, stories from American sources in Tokyo say the situation is expected to calm. If this is coming from Ambassador MacArthur, his neck is out about ten miles. There are men in his own Embassy who don't believe Ike should risk it.

The next morning, Thursday, June 16, I left the hotel before seven o'clock to have breakfast with Romulo at his handsome home on the outskirts of town. Parsons was there and he seemed utterly shocked when he heard Marv Arrowsmith and me discussing the worst riot yet in Tokyo, fighting of the night before when a college girl was crushed to death at the Diet. Parsons, the ranking State Department officer on the tour and Eisenhower's chief adviser on Far Eastern affairs, had not been told of the most serious outbreak of violence since the anti-Kishi disturbances began. We felt embarrassed for him in front of Romulo. Of course, it could have been that Parsons *had* been informed and he was playing a cautious game with two reporters

at the breakfast table. If so, this was a little odd. What did he have to lose or gain?

Later in the morning, the President went by helicopter to the University of the Philippines to receive an honorary degree. Police picked up a young man with a hidden gun waiting beside the President's route on the campus.

Eisenhower, in responding after the degree ceremony, predicted that someday millions "chained in the dictates of a tyrannic master plan" would break their bonds in "increasing resentment that finally ignites revolt." This obviously referred to the Soviet satellite nations and Red China.

"Tens of millions cannot forever be denied their freedom to venture on their own," he said. "They will not eternally remain chained to the mastery of other men."

While the President was having lunch with the Chamber of Commerce at the Manila Hotel later in the day, we ran into Baughman again. He said the situation in Tokyo was so bad that he wanted to be identified publicly with a statement of deep concern for the President's welfare if he went through with his planned visit.

Baughman, becoming angry at this point, was getting his own reports out of Tokyo and not relying entirely on the embassy, which still was trying to keep the trip alive. Not that it meant anything, but the Washington reporters traveling with Ike took an informal poll in the press room: the vote, twenty-nine to five against the advisability of the President going. The men wanted to go themselves, and some of them did even after Ike canceled, but they thought news reports from Japan were far more powerful and convincing than anything coming through diplomatic channels, which tended to accent the positive possibilities.

Right after lunch, U.P.I. Tokyo carried a story quoting Japanese government sources as saying the invitation to visit Japan was being withdrawn because of danger to the President's personal safety. Hensley called Hagerty immediately and Jim said he found it hard to believe. He said that although the situation was subject to change, our story from Tokyo was contrary to his information.

Jim later repeated this denial to some of the men in the hotel lobby, but Hensley and I thought then that Hagerty was fencing for time. He did not have much of it, either.

Inside Malacañang, the situation was tense. The telephone circuit to Tokyo was busy constantly. Eisenhower returned from lunch at the hotel, where things had gone less than perfectly. Power circuits had failed just before he spoke and if the vast Fiesta Pavilion had not been open on two sides facing Manila Bay, the room would have been plunged into darkness. The microphone system failed and was not restored until after he started speaking. The luncheon guests were in three different rooms and that made for a poor audience.

A crisis was building in Tokyo. The State Department forwarded two different versions of a statement the President might make when and if Kishi announced the inevitable, but still the embassy tried to keep open a last chance.

Eisenhower had two more important dates on his public schedule before sailing that night on the cruiser *St. Paul* for Formosa. At four-fifteen he had to leave with Garcia for the Luneta, the huge park beside the bay where a freshening wind was kicking up whitecaps in the hot afternoon sun. There was his dinner that night, too, for Garcia at the embassy.

The President had to keep a good public face on the rest of the schedule despite what was happening in Tokyo. This was most important in the Far East.

The situation still was up in the air as the two chief executives left for the park.

I went to the Luneta early because of the thousands packed in the park before the reviewing stand, which was blessedly shielded from the burning sun. I climbed high in the stands to the immediate right of the speaking platform so I could keep an eye on Eisenhower and his staff and still watch an ivory White House telephone sitting in the dirt beside the structure. I had a walkie-talkie radio with me and Hensley was on the

other end of the circuit back at the hotel where he could maintain telephone contact with our Manila bureau and the all-important news wires from Tokyo.

Just after Eisenhower arrived and Filipino troops began to march in review, Hensley crackled over the radio, "Smitty, this looks like it. The Japanese Cabinet is in emergency session and Kishi is preparing a public statement in which he will ask the President to delay his trip."

At the moment, Eisenhower and Garcia were standing far downstage on the edge of the platform, reviewing the troops while a tense drama began to unfold behind their backs. I caught the attention of Jim Rowley and motioned for him to come my way. I couldn't move because of two friendly but firm Filipino sentries and I also did not want to lose a vantage point from which the short-wave radio was working perfectly.

With my message from Tokyo, Rowley shook his head woefully and said he was going to talk to his own men in the Japanese capital. Rowley returned to the telephone, squatted down on the ground and talked earnestly for several minutes. Then he walked up a side stairway onto the platform section reserved for dignitaries and motioned to Goodpaster. The White House staff secretary, who managed somehow to look blissfully cool while the rest of us sweated unmercifully, crawled over several Filipino generals and admirals, climbed down to the telephone and began talking first to the White House offices back at the palace and then to Tokyo.

While Goodpaster, a scholarly, crisply efficient West Pointer, was conferring by telephone, the review band across from the platform boomed out martial marches and the President was frozen at attention, his shoulders erect and his hands tensely at his sides as the colors of the Filipino Army units strode by.

Hensley relayed more details from Tokyo and I scribbled them down on a notepad and sent the message over to the White House officials seated behind the President's chair. Eisenhower, the review over, returned to his seat while Garcia spoke. Hagerty and Goodpaster put their heads together in serious consultation and I could see Arrowsmith on the other side of the platform, feeding AP dispatches across the knees of the Filipino V.I.P.'s to the White House staff.

Hensley's voice crackled over the radio again, "Smitty, the trip is off. The official Japanese announcement is out. Tokyo has gotten a copy of it ahead of the official release. I suppose they want time to get it to Ike."

"Stew, this is a one-way street. We're giving 'em a lot of information I don't believe they have and we're getting nothing in return. Send two men down to the press room because I know damn well Hagerty will go busting out of here. Better tell the bureau to make sure the palace is covered, too, until you and I can get disconnected and get to the press room through these crowds."

The President rose to speak, to speak of the enduring friendship between the two nations and their resolute togetherness against the encroachments of controlled societies.

As he read from a prepared text, Jack Lynch, one of the top State Department security agents who had gone out ahead to the cruiser St. Paul with some secret files for which he was responsible, arrived on the run at the edge of the crowd around the stand. He had a long, sealed white envelope in his hands. He passed it up to a Secret Service man, who relayed it to Goodpaster. Lynch came in my direction as he tried to get out of the crowd. He shrugged his shoulders and said, "Don't ask me 'cause I don't know. They hauled me back from the cruiser and said to get those papers from the embassy to Goodpaster as fast as I could."

Goodpaster ripped open the envelope and scowled as he read the contents. The President finished his speech, bowed perfunctorily to the applause that broke like a typhoon from across the broad park. Several men applauding from a tree fell onto the heads of the crowd below, but picked themselves up smiling and still applauding.

When Eisenhower took his seat again, a male chorus walked to center stage while a Filipino official gleamingly explained

they were to sing a song written specially for the visitor, "The Eisenhower March." Eisenhower tried to pay attention, but possibly because I knew what was coming over the radio from Tokyo, I thought the expression on his face said, "Let's get this the hell over with."

The filmy barongs of the singers eddied in the breeze from the bay as Goodpaster leaned over the President's shoulder to talk into his ear. The choristers proclaimed in song the glories of the visiting chief executive, who looked at them vacantly while he tried to listen to Goodpaster. Suddenly, the President turned and gave Goodpaster a long look, eyebrows raised and lips pursed.

The song ended and Eisenhower moved as swiftly as possible from the hand-shakers on the platform. He jumped into a waiting green convertible, gave the crowd a parting wave and sped back to Malacañang to examine official dispatches that had started to arrive from Ambassador MacArthur and, from what we could observe, long after the story had been told on the press association circuits. This fact is not so critical as it may seem, because government communications invariably are slower than commercial channels since diplomatic reports, when they deal with something as important as Ike's visit to Japan, have to be based on official fact with supporting documents in hand.

Hagerty pushed through the Luneta crowd with the fixed determination of a late commuter, rushing for his car to tail the President back to the palace. Jim was grim-faced as he shouted to us over the heads of cheering Filipinos that he would return to the hotel press headquarters as soon as possible.

While thousands cheered, Eisenhower had suffered a second serious diplomatic setback. While Garcia draped a medal around his neck and choristers sang the glories of Eisenhower, the President was being told to stay out of Japan. The friendly government of our defense bastion in the Far East was toppling while he had to stand and bow to crescendo applause.

Back at the palace, Eisenhower, once he had thanked Garcia for the enthusiastic demonstration at the Luneta and told him briefly what he was up against in Japan, went into seclusion with the staff. Those who saw him in Paris said he seemed to be a little less placid in Manila, perhaps because there had to be rapid improvisation. The Tokyo collapse came as no surprise to him. He was prepared for it before leaving Washington, but not to the extent that he knew what to expect as in Paris.

The scene around the President at the palace was more hurried than excited. A number of people were talking at once in the converted parlor that served for a White House office, and the President strolled out of the jabber into the calm of his own sitting room with John. Hagerty wanted to move as rapidly as possible, knowing the tension that was building up downtown. Parsons wanted to be sure MacArthur knew what the White House was saying. At one point, the State Department expert was yelling into a telephone that was disconnected.

Down at the hotel, we sat around for more than an hour hunched over our typewriters and telephones, waiting for Hagerty. Suddenly Jim swept into the smoky room and plopped down behind a battery of public address and newsreel microphones. Cleve Ryan, our traveling light technician, switched on a battery of floodlights and Jim was in business. He'd not had time to get the President's statement copied, but he read to us slowly: ". . . fully accepts the decision of the Japanese authorities and therefore will not visit Japan at this time.

"In so doing," Jim continued, "the President wishes to express his full and sympathetic understanding of the decision taken by the Japanese government. He would like also to express his regrets that a small organized minority, led by professional Communist agitators acting under external direction and control, have been able by resort to force and violence to prevent his good-will visit and to mar the celebration of this centennial of Japanese-American relations."

Hagerty thought this was not overplaying the Communist involvement. He said privately that, from the photographs of the airport riot in which he was involved in Tokyo, Japanese police were able to pick out at least ten known Communist

leaders who controlled the mob expertly with staccato whistle signals. A few days later, Eisenhower was to see this sort of thing for himself in Okinawa.

There still was business to be done in Manila. The two Presidents issued the expected communiqué in which they warned that any armed attack against the Philippines would be regarded as an attack against the United States and "would instantly be repelled." These were welcome words in Manila, although for the moment no one seemed to envision any threat of attack. More than that, it was a warning to the expansion of Chinese Communism which Radio Peiping largely ignored because the Chicoms, as the American Navy called them, had a much better thing going—a factual report from Tokyo.

Light rain squalls began to blow over Manila Bay as Eisenhower, this time in his own native dress of a dinner jacket, toasted his friend Garcia and headed by launch out to the waiting *St. Paul*. Down the line a bit, the Chicoms were having their own kind of celebration by plastering artillery fire on Quemoy, the offshore punching bag held by the Chinese Nationalists, Eisenhower's next hosts.

CHAPTER 18 *END OF AN ODYSSEY*

Most of two nights and a day aboard the *St. Paul* gave the President an opportunity for a look at the Far Eastern situation post-Tokyo and to draft necessary changes in his itinerary.

Korea was quickly expanded into an overnight visit instead of the originally planned one-day affair, and the cruise to Taipei took up most of the additional slack left by the Japanese cancellation.

The cruiser bearing the President and his immediate staff was heavily protected by a task force from the Seventh Fleet, the largest ship of which was the antisubmarine aircraft carrier *Yorktown* on which we traveled.

The *Yorktown*'s commanding officer, Captain Charles E. Gibson, considerately warned his officers that we were coming aboard late that night in Manila probably exhausted by the Philippine heat. Consequently we were treated with sympathy ordinarily reserved for casualties as we climbed aboard and headed for the bunks. Captain John H. Maurer, skipper of the *St. Paul*, was following the same strategy with Ike and showed him to the flag cabin with a minimum of naval ceremony.

The President's course took him during the early morning hours of June 17 off the east coast of Luzon, main island of the Philippine group, then across the Luzon Straits and the Bashi Channel up the east coast of Taiwan (or Formosa, as it was called before it was returned to China as a province after World War II). His destination was Keelung Harbor, well removed from the Formosa Straits and the Chicom artillery batteries on the mainland a little over a hundred miles away.

During the night, Chicom shore batteries raked the Nationalist Islands and Radio Peiping shrilled that Eisenhower was a "god of plague" with evil intentions for the Far East. Peiping broadcast the mainland version of the shelling, saying her troops roared anti-Eisenhower epithets—"Eisenhower go back" and "Get out of Asia"—as they jerked the lanyards of their cannon. In Taipei, the Nationalist Defense Ministry said the shelling lasted an hour and fifty minutes, one of the heaviest artillery attacks on Quemoy in years.

During the night and early the next morning, the Seventh Fleet put out a heavy air and sea antisubmarine screen around Ike, who slept late as did most of his party.

Vice Admiral Charles D. Griffin, Seventh Fleet commander, had his flag aboard the *Yorktown* on June 17 and he dropped down to the wardroom to explain that the heavy screen was to guard against possible "adventurisms" by the Chicoms. In the task force or supporting it were other American carriers, cruisers and submarines, whipping along at speeds of better than thirty knots, the pace being another protective measure against submarines.

The Navy should not be faulted for taking all possible precautions with a President in semi-enemy waters, but all admirals, when playing host to a chief executive, invariably show the Navy at its best, carefully slipping in at the same time bits of information on how the Navy could use additional strength. This is as much Navy tradition as the annual football game with Army.

Diary notes from that morning with the President's host afloat:

Admiral Griffin says naval intelligence reports over 20 outmoded subs in Chicom fleet; about 100 Soviet subs operating in Pacific area. Visions of pink periscopes all around us until, in response to a question, the admiral said in his four months as 7th Fleet commander, there had been no contacts with Chicom subs.

Griffin says that for practical purposes entire 7th operating directly or indirectly in support of Ike task force and fleet consists of about 125 ships and over 500 aircraft. Walter Winchell, making his first trip of this type and an amazing dynamo of journalistic energy even if he does have to learn some of our idiosyncrasies, leaped to his feet in alarm, crying, "Admiral, you know these men will print that, don't you?" Walter thought the figures might be classified. Admiral assured him he was not telling everything.

While antisub helicopters buzzed around St. Paul, dipping sonar gear in the sea to listen for Chicoms, Hagerty got on the ship-to-ship radio to tell us Ike got up late, breakfasted leisurely, then in conference on rejiggering Korean schedule.

Critical heat on Eisenhower was building up back in the U.S., once the first reaction of "our President, right or wrong," simmered down. The critics were after him for letting himself in for two successive flops, Paris and Tokyo. Hagerty said he did not believe U.S. prestige had suffered because of Tokyo. Some of our set sneered at this, but my feeling was that Jim was trapped. The day a press secretary to a President says yes, the prestige of the country suffered as result of an event in which the chief executive was involved, immediate preparations for the Second Coming are indicated.

After lunch, Eisenhower took a nap unusually long for him. It meant he was genuinely tired, but in the late afternoon several of us took a helicopter ride over to the *St. Paul* and he seemed to be in good physical shape but subdued spirits.

He came out on a forward level to watch the screening helicopters dipping their sonar buoys off the starboard bow. Barbara was peeking out from the bridge above as Skipper Maurer explained the operation to Eisenhower, who kept glancing over at our small group. We were standing respectfully distant, but still trying to listen. He obviously wanted to talk, but we were waiting for something more indicative than facial expression because Ike could be a most abused man at times when reporters sought to chat with him informally when he thought the cir-

cumstances were improper. We saw Hagerty's thumb waggle toward the President and moved in. Because so many of our colleagues were back on the *Yorktown* and would be mortally wounded by such an artificial scoop, we agreed not to quote him, and also, to report to our fellows before filing.

Eisenhower felt solidly that the Communists, largely under control of Peiping, seized on his Tokyo visit and the left-wing protest against Kishi to make propaganda capital in the same way Khrushchev seized on the U-2 to wreck the Summit. He gave no indication of being particularly depressed as he stood by the rail, casually dressed in a raw silk jacket and gray slacks with a white shirt and dark blue tie. The Tokyo situation was nothing he could control; it was up to Kishi. He thought the magnitude of his reception in Manila to some extent offset negative aspects of the Tokyo cancellation.

We were somewhat amazed when he expressed keen curiosity about the world reaction to Tokyo. He said he had asked Washington to send him a detailed summary for delivery in Taiwan. What caused our amazement was his statement that up until that afternoon he had received no information whatever on world reaction. We had seen some opinion roundups on *Yorktown*, where our transmitters were so busy with outgoing news copy that they had little time for incoming material. *Yorktown* had sent a helicopter over to the cruiser *Canberra* and ferried back some incoming reports from a few world capitals.

Eisenhower still was intrigued, as he had been in Paris, by what he regarded as tangible evidence of trouble between Moscow and Peiping. He did not regard it as a major split in the making, but he thought increasingly measurable differences over ideology boded well for the West.

As for his own well-being or lack thereof, he could not recall being more weary than he was after the long flight from Alaska and the Manila arrival parade, but the rest at sea was a wonderful healer.

Before flying ashore the next morning, Eisenhower saluted the men of the Seventh Fleet by radio.

"The American people know you are doing your job well," he said. "They and the people of the free world are not deceived by the false propaganda of the Communists."

There were no outstanding differences between the United States and Generalissimo Chiang Kai-shek, so Ike's interlude on Taiwan was bound to be friendly. In his position, there was little Chiang could demand of anyone, and he also was buttressed by America's treaty commitment to defend Formosa.

On Saturday, June 18, Eisenhower flew ashore in Nationalist China to receive not the largest, but certainly one of the more colorful and enthusiastic receptions of his travels. Chiang met him at the airport, trim, amazingly well preserved for his seventy-two years and dressed in uniform.

Diary notes for the 18th in Taipei:

As we rolled into town behind the car of "Geemo" and Ike, somebody says, "By God, we're really in the Orient." Massive but orderly crowd. Every block or two, dancing dragons, clashing cymbals, banners in the brilliant red that only the Chinese can achieve. They're pitifully short of many things here, but not paper. As a consequence, clouds of American flags. These people must be excellent parents. Children better dressed than adults and bouncingly happy or a reasonable facsimile thereof. Suppose all kids like parades and this one is a dilly, but the children are most impressive.

With Ike installed and resting for a bit in his suite at the hillside Grand Hotel, dashed into town to UPI bureau-and-home-for-the-night, Friends of China Club. Ogling pedicabs (bike-drawn rickshas to the Charlie Chan age group) and porters staggering under enormous loads on their backs.

After unloading assorted news on Al Kaff, one of the smartest UPI men Hensley and I encountered in Ike's travels, marched to club dining room, intent on monster Chinese meal since am nuts about their chow. Darkest moment of gustatory life: first item on menu: hot roast beef sandwich; second item: veal chop and spaghetti; third item: cheeseburger. Finally wangled a

dish of chicken and walnuts. Awful.

Back to Grand, with Ike to Chiang's massive presidential office building in center of city. No elevators. Up three long flights of crimson carpeted stairs with walkie-talkie.

Chiang's office simply decorated, high ceilings, brilliantly yellow upholstered chairs and couches. Chiang's cigarettes excellent.

Later in the afternoon, upwards of 300,000 Chinese jammed the square in front of Chiang's office while Ike thanked them for their welcome. He seemed more emotional about the crowd than usual. After finishing his fixed speech, he walked back to the mike and ad libbed a crackle-voiced message of extra thanks. Skyrockets filled the air with tiny parachutes bearing strings of U.S. and Nationalist flags.

That night, thousands of Chinese waited for hours in the darkened square just to glimpse Ike as he arrived for dinner about 8 and departed at 11. White House staff reports Ike, walking through the corridors of the Grand before dinner, admitted that with each new country, he found himself saying he'd never seen anything like the reception.

While he banqueted, I drove back to the Grand and by God, I got a Chinese meal with a capital C. Pretty damned wonderful cooking.

(If the diary entries quoted in this book are grammatically irritating as they switch between present and past tenses, forbearance is requested. The entry for a single day may have been written at several different times and places, in a palace, during a motorcade, aboard a helicopter. Not even E. B. White could keep his tenses straight in a helicopter.)

Sunday, June 19:

To church with Ike, the Generalissimo and the Madame in their small private chapel on Chiang's estate. Physically, she's more amazing than Geemo. Excellent figure, jet black hair (many Chinese never seem to turn gray), soft but authoritative voice, accent-less English. I must be getting tired. Felt truly

throat-catchy and misty in chapel listening to children sing the
Doxology in Chinese. Madame gave Ike a fan. He won't use it.
No collection taken.

After church, walked through gardens to Chiang's house. I've
known Madame to be gloves-off rough some years back, but she
couldn't have been nicer to Marv and me. She started showing
Ike some of her delicate water colors and he wandered off, but
she continued with us, explaining the furniture. Living room
immense with a mixture of modern and classic Chinese furniture. Overstuffed chairs have straw mats over the upholstery
to make them cooler. We were still in the room when Chiang,
Ike and their advisers settled down around a beautiful lac-
quered table for their concluding business meeting. Went out in
driveway and pondered the tragedy of Taiwan. When Chiang
goes, what happens to these people? When will the statesmen of
the world meet in some distant palace or historic hall and trade
off the whole island, people and all?

One, at least this one, found it a slippery problem to avoid
thinking of the trip as being over as Arrowsmith and I flew
aboard Air Force One as pool men again from Taipei to Seoul
via Okinawa. Instead of being anticipatory, I felt like I was
doing time. I had been in Korea with Ike in 1952 and while
I was interested in seeing a peacetime Seoul, Korea was going
to be another mob scene of the New Delhi-Manila variety with
a police force still shaky from the deadly riots that forced old
Syngman Rhee out of the presidency.

Okinawa was just a quick stop—a landing, a drive into town,
no speech and back to the plane. Okinawa, won by U.S. forces
in 1945 in one of the bloodiest battles of the Pacific war, was
now our biggest base in the Far East—the jump-off spot for
trouble over a frontier of thousands of miles.

Okinawa was the seat of the Ryukyu Islands group, Chinese-
controlled until 1874, then under Japanese rule until the end
of World War II. The United States now was an occupying
power with a local government operating under an American
civil administration.

The Parliament, a small body empowered to legislate on local matters, was controlled by the anti-leftists, but there were left-wing extremists cut from or allied with the Zengakuren pattern, and battling for return of the Ryukyus to Japan. And as long as they were demanding, the extremists also wanted the U.S. to close her bases and get off Okinawa, where thirty thousand American servicemen provided a sizable payroll.

The dissidents had been frank in their announced intention to stage a token demonstration against Eisenhower. That was before the Tokyo cancellation. Encouraged by what the Zeng-akuren had been able to do to Eisenhower in Japan, their Ryukyun brethren decided to do some of the same. It was too late to stop Ike, but not too late to let him have a taste of Japan.

His arrival at the big American air base was uneventful and he drove into the capital city of Naha to greet federal and native officials. There was a tremendous crowd along the highway, tremendous for the island, and the usual "I Like Ike" signs and banners.

A British reporter whose name escapes me—and for this I'm ashamed because this man was a wonderful help—rode with Marv and me behind the President. In the center of Naha, he pointed ahead and said that was the spot where the left-wing unions planned to demonstrate. As Eisenhower drew abreast of them, the demonstrators on his left side waved their "Reunion with Japan" banners and surged against the police, but suddenly, on the right side, hell really did break loose.

We settled later on a considered figure of a thousand or fifteen hundred people, but at the moment they seemed many more as they hurled themselves at the police, their faces distorted with anger and the air ugly with hoarse cries of "Ike go home."

We saw what a small civilian police force could do, properly placed and instructed. The squat Ryukyun cops bent their backs, shoulder to shoulder, to keep the whirling and shouting leftists from breaking through. In the peak of the demonstration, we came to a stretch where standing behind the police with bayonets pointed at the crowd were U.S. Marines in battle dress. It could well have been the bayonets over the shoulders of the police that stayed the crowd, but still we saw no Americans in physical contact with the maelstrom.

Eisenhower stopped at the assembly, met the members and continued on to the Federal Civil Administration Building. On the second floor, we stood at an office window for about thirty minutes and watched the demonstrators, who quickly followed Ike and began trying to break through the police again to over-run the yard and auto-parking area beneath the elevated building.

From an elevation, we could see that the working group of demonstrators consisted of possibly five hundred people, mostly young men in dark trousers and white shirts. They were under the co-ordinated control of about a half-dozen leaders, who wore distinctively lettered headbands and carried megaphones and police-type whistles.

Their technique was a twisting, prancing snake dance that circled at a rapid clip, usually a short distance from a small fence separating the grounds of the government compound from a small park. Hundreds of friendly Ryukyuns gathered on one side of the fence, the police on the other, backed up by Marines. On a signal from the leaders, the demonstrators lunged suddenly at a weak point in the security guard, but each time the police bunched up with sufficient strength to push back the invasion, while the theoretically friendly Ryukyun spectators stood by and watched impassively.

The Marines, aided by short-wave radios, moved squads of reinforcements from place to place along the fence and around the entrances to the compound to prevent the shouting leftists from breaking through.

While Eisenhower talked with the Ryukyun officials, the windows of the building shook with the strident chant of "Go home, go home" from the demonstrators, who grew in number as reinforcements for their group scuttled through sentries

along the main street to join the snake dancers in the park.

The Secret Service conferred with Marine officers and there seemed a strong possibility of injuries if the President attempted to retrace his original route through the center of the city. He had intended all along to fly back to the air base by helicopter from a nearby field. The security men were not fearful of their ability to keep the President from harm, but he did not want to be the excuse for injuries in the crowd, so we departed by a completely unguarded rear entrance and drove a dozen or so blocks through equally unguarded and empty back streets to the helicopter pad. A few minutes later we were on the way to Korea.

In the high-altitude security of Air Force One, Eisenhower did not seem to be at all shaken by the demonstration. He shifted to his travel sweater and snoozed in his cabin. In reexamining the incident back in the main compartment of AF 1, we were impressed by two aspects: the effective discipline maintained by the demonstration leaders, plus the fact that, as far as we could tell, no one was hurt. Eisenhower rode through the "go home" shouters in an open car and there simply were not enough Marines or Secret Service men to keep him from possibly serious injury if the Okinawa affiliates of the Zengakuren had decided to throw rocks. It was, as the leaders had said in advance, a token demonstration. The Ryukyuns, on an island with thirty thousand American servicemen, must have known, too, that one rock against Eisenhower's head and they would have been in for painful trouble. The Zengakuren in Tokyo had been more than willing to have casualties with resultant martyrdom for the victims, but not on Okinawa. They would have suffered first from their own well-armed police and behind them, in full battle dress, stood three companies of Marines with leveled bayonets.

The Okinawa demonstration dominated only three or four city blocks of a crowded, friendly procession of more than twelve miles. The snake dancers were well organized and their pattern followed the general plan of the Tokyo disorders, with the milling, circling columns of young men four or five abreast with arms interlocked, then the sudden lunge into the police lines. There the similarity to Tokyo stopped. The Okinawans did not break through, they threw no stones, overturned no cars, caused no apparent injuries.

Eisenhower, while at the Ryukyun office building, had considered making a statement at the airport dealing with Tokyo and Okinawa, but he decided against it. Naha was a situation somewhat similar to Montevideo, a predominantly friendly crowd, but the headlines would focus on the relatively small display of unfriendliness. Eisenhower may have groused about the situation privately, but he said nothing about it to us en route to Seoul.

In Korea awaiting the President was a staunchly friendly nation of 22,000,000, a perpetually poor country then in grave difficulty due to political chaos that followed the end of President Syngman Rhee's twelve-year regime. The American-trained Republic of Korea (ROK) Army was in sad spirit. Many of the Army's most capable leaders had been driven out by rebellious younger officers in the upsurge that chased Rhee from the country. Rhee had been held responsible for a scandalous election and many of the top military men were involved.

Acting President Kwak Sang Hoon shortly before Ike arrived admonished his uneasy people to turn out for the visitor as "a symbol of the freedom crusade." The Korean government decided that Prime Minister Huh Chung, formerly the acting President, would serve as Eisenhower's host because Kwak frankly did not want the chore. Korea, called "Chosen" and "the land of the morning calm," also ordered mobilization of ten thousand police for Ike's visit.

Although Ambassador Walter P. McConaughy had been specific about the good-will, nonnegotiative nature of Eisenhower's travels, the Koreans wanted to seek his influence for their increased assistance needs. Their aid from America amounted to $188 million for 1960, but the ROK's wanted a 15 per cent increase, plus more modern, more powerful weapons.

There were many other problems which the ROK government wanted solved—reunification of the Korean peninsula, admission to the U.N. and the long-pending status of forces agreement covering American troops stationed there. The ROK government had been so recently—and violently—reorganized that there was little chance, however, of substantive discussion or solution while Ike was in town overnight.

He landed at Kimpo Airport and flew by helicopter to the Tongsan Golf Club, which served as the staging area for his motorcade with Huh through the city to McConaughy's residence.

If there were political difficulties or anti-Ikeism present, they were swallowed up in a frenzied crowd of more than a half-million, a crowd that became so carried away that Ike had to abandon his parade route and reach the embassy through a series of winding, narrow back alleys.

Diary notes for the next day in Seoul, Monday, June 20:

> Standing in McConaughy's kitchen this morning with Tom Hansen, an old S.S. friend from the F.D.R. days, we were cribbing ham sandwiches off the cook while we waited for Ike to drive through the streets of Seoul again. An agent laden with walkie-talkies came through and summed it for all of us, "I feel just like a soldier who's been told the Armistice will be signed tomorrow, but there'll be a helluva battle tonight."
>
> He was referring to yesterday's struggle to get Ike through the crowd. Hundreds were hurt in the massive crush in front of the railroad station. This was the point where the Korean police decided the motorcade could not follow the planned route and Ike's car bumped over sidewalks and traffic islands to reach the safety of back alleys.
>
> I knew we were in a hellish mess at the railroad station. Tried to get out of the car, got door half open and crowd closed in. Door nearly sawed me in half. Jabbed walkie-talkie aerial into screaming women to get door closed.
>
> We weren't genuinely alarmed, however, until this morning when we saw an aerial photograph of the crowd when Ike had

to turn off. His car never could have made it. Conservatively, there were 50,000 people jammed in the street in front of him, building to building, and bulldozers couldn't have moved them.

Americans had a helicopter over Ike's head with escape harness [referred to in an earlier chapter] but it would have been difficult to use because of overhead electric wires. Couldn't have landed the chopper without killing scores.

Today, the tough Korean national police seem to have the situation under much better control. Ike drove through the city from the embassy to the national assembly and the presidential palace. Americans infuriated at the assembly. Korean cops frisked everybody before allowing entrance. This was so typical of over-security. While the row was raging over a physical armpits-to-toe frisk of Harrison Salisbury of the *Times* and Wayne Hawks of Ike's staff, Arrowsmith and I were able to move around with freedom. Once *that* fuss simmered down, the Koreans began to give us the fishy eye so we headed back for the follow-up car. American colonel—God, there's always one—rushed up to say, "You men will have to get out of this car." Somebody told him, "Colonel, we can't, our clothes are in here." Seemed to satisfy him.

Driving from assembly to presidential palace, young girls in flowing white robes rushed by police into the street, dodging the police jeeps, to throw flower blossoms at Ike.

Crowds by now are old stuff to most of us but the Seoul mobs seemed somehow to be more frightening than the immense crowds of Delhi or Manila. Perhaps it is because here we saw people being hurt, clubbed with rifle butts, whacked by split bamboo police whips and literally run over or hit by police jeeps.

In front of the national assembly there was a big sign in red, white and blue, "Welcome Ike, God Will Protect You." Agent looked at the mob across the street battling with thin line of police and said, "Hope the message gets through."

Secret Service studying pictures of yesterday's mob scene at every opportunity. They point out if the same condition had developed in Japan with Eisenhower in the center of an unfriendly mob, there would have been no earthly way of saving

him. Gunfire, except possibly a concentration of murderous machinegun fire, would not have dented the Seoul crowd. Ten agents with revolvers could not have protected Ike effectively in a concentrated jam of 50,000.

Everyone glad to see the trip ending tonight. Been vastly interesting, but terribly tiring and a constant battle with crowds, heat that makes mid-summer Washington seem inviting. For all of our many years of experience, am not so sure we become better travelers from the standpoint of international relations. We complain about balky elevators, lousy telephones, screwy plumbing. Constantly tired and nagged by impossible schedules, we tend to forget that the local people would like things better, too.

The hotel in Seoul urged us to change dollars into local currency, set up special desk for this purpose. Then when we went to check out they refused to accept Korean money, only dollars. This was one time I thought ugly Americanism was justified and as ugly as possible, told hotel manager he should be ashamed of himself for openly subverting the currency of his own country. Several more of our party unloaded on him, too, and halfway through checkout crowd, hotel management met and changed policy.

As Far East phase of trip concludes, seems utterly amazing Ike came through unharmed. Friendly people frequently worse than sullen crowds. Eisenhower more endangered in Seoul by enthusiasts than by "go home" shouters in Okinawa. We hear there are reports all over the world, but particularly in Far East, that Okinawa demonstrators did break through the Ryukyun police and had to be driven back by Marine bayonets. This represents a small but important difference from the truth. If there was a break-through, it did not happen while Ike was nearby. Secret Service and Marines did think it would happen any second, but Ryukyun cops, the best we've seen since Chile, kept control, even by a narrow margin.

All night flight to Hawaii and a few days rest before going home. Ike wouldn't land on Japanese soil to refuel. Returned to Wake. We went to Japan, all quiet at the airport, ate four ice-cream suckers, slept.

While Eisenhower golfed and slept at Kanehoe Marine Air Station in Hawaii, we settled gratefully in Henry Kaiser's new Hawaiian Village Hotel across Oahu from the President. The Japanese security treaty was ratified by the U.S. Senate and went into effect. Ike was preparing the customary report to the people on his trip and scanning reports on editorial opinion, which was not good.

The storm was building and Hagerty knew it.

"Editorial and press reports around the world do not make any difference as far as his views are concerned, particularly when written by editorial writers who were not there," Jim said, possibly forgetting how anxious Ike was aboard the *St. Paul* for a roundup of world reaction to Tokyo.

Herter had testified back in Washington before Congressional committees and conceded mistakes of judgment in evaluating the Japanese situation. Dispatches from Washington attributed to Herter a statement that Eisenhower had abandoned personal diplomacy. Hagerty checked the Herter testimony and came back with his version, that Herter had been asked if Ike planned more trips abroad and the Secretary had replied that none were contemplated at the time and the more conventional avenues of diplomacy would be relied upon. Of this I am certain personally—if Herter thought or meant to suggest that Eisenhower had abandoned the idea of personal diplomacy, the Secretary was woefully mistaken. Herter may have felt that way himself, but not Ike.

Eisenhower was nettled by some of the Democrats on Capitol Hill who said he should not have planned the Japanese trip when he did. Hagerty said Ike was "somewhat puzzled and somewhat amused by the fact that some of these gentlemen eight or ten days ago said it would be a catastrophe if he did *not* visit Japan."

As the President worked on his speech in Hawaii, he didn't make the critical situation in Washington any better for himself by letting it be known he also was planning a summer vacation in Newport, Rhode Island. This seemed to be pro-

viding more fuel for Khrushchev, who was sniping at his golf.

As the speech took shape on Oahu, the St. Louis *Post-Dispatch*, which had treated Eisenhower's personal diplomacy with more friendliness than many other prominent newspapers, had this to say:

> It is easy, but deceptive, to tell ourselves that President Eisenhower was kept out of Japan only by the violent conduct of a few nasty Communists. If we are going to get at the truth, we must be prepared to admit that while the Communists and their left-wing allies led the riots, they could not have achieved their objectives had not a large body of public opinion been hostile or apathetic to the new military treaty with the United States.

(Apathy may begin at home. Within a day or two of publication of this editorial, a group of over a hundred adult New Yorkers watched in idle horror as a small band of hoodlums stabbed and kicked a teen-ager to death in the streets of America's largest city. When the assailants had run away, somebody called the police.)

Ike flew to the mainland to deliver his speech in Washington the night of June 27. That afternoon, the liberal New York *Post* said, "Please, Mr. President, don't try to fool the country—or yourself. There can be grace and dignity in the acknowledgment of a reversal; it can even be the beginning of wisdom."

Ike had traveled 318,000 miles (including within the U.S.) since taking office in 1953, excluding the preinaugural trip to Korea in 1952. In his speech, the President said:

"The great value resulting from these journeys to twenty-seven nations has been obvious here and abroad. Throughout the world there has been opportunity to emphasize and re-emphasize America's devotion to peace with justice; her determination to sustain freedom and to strengthen free world security through our co-operative programs; her readiness to sacrifice in helping to build the kind of world we want.

"These visits involved, of course, valuable conversations between heads of state and government, as well as the promotion of understanding among peoples.

"However, except for so-called Summits and the NATO heads of government meeting, none of my visits has been planned or carried out solely as a diplomatic mission seeking specific agreements, even though discussions have invariably involved important issues.

"Incidentally, I believe that heads of state and government can, occasionally, and preferably on an informal basis, profitably meet for conversations on broad problems and principles. They can, of course, also convene to give solemn approval to agreements previously prepared by normal diplomatic methods.

"But heads of government meetings are not effective mechanisms for developing detailed provisions of international compacts, and have never been so considered by this government. On the other hand, the good-will aspects of a visit by a head of government can frequently bring about favorable results far transcending those of normal diplomatic conferences. They have resulted in the creation of a more friendly atmosphere and mutual confidence between peoples. They have proved effective in bringing closer together nations that respect human dignity and are dedicated to freedom."

Eisenhower blamed the Communists for having "sought every possible method" to stop his trips because they had reached the conclusion his travels were "of such positive value to the free world as to obstruct Communist imperialism."

He said the Communists in Paris "advanced false and elaborate excuses for canceling my invitation to visit the Soviet Union, when all that was necessary to say was that they found it inconvenient to receive me."

As for Japan:

"With their [Communist] associates in Peiping, they went to great lengths and expense to create disorders in Tokyo that compelled the Japanese government to decide, under conditions then existing, that it should revoke its long-standing invitation for me to visit that sister democracy.

"These disorders were not occasioned by America. We in the United States must not fall into the error of blaming ourselves for what the Communists do; after all, Communists will act like Communists.

"One clear proof of the value, to us, of these visits is the intensity of the opposition the Communists have developed against them."

Reston of the *Times* reacted angrily in his analysis of the speech:

> President Eisenhower has devised a simple procedure for dealing with his critics and his defeats: He simply ignores the critics and claims victories.
>
> That is what he did in his explanation of the U-2 and the Summit incidents last month, and this is what he did in his report on the Japanese situation tonight. The effect of this is serious in a democracy for it confuses the public, infuriates the political opposition and leaves mistakes unexplained and uncorrected.

The Washington *Post* said:

> Undertones of disappointment in the President's speech were obvious. They were all the more pointed because his term of office has less than seven months to run and his good will missions abroad are at an end. It is tragic for the country as well as for himself that the termination has been marked by the collapse of the Summit Conference, the outburst of violence in Japan and a general resumption of the cold war.

The *Wall Street Journal* thought, "The real error we fell into was that of believing that by personal diplomacy we could smooth over all difficulties."

The Des Moines *Register* wanted "hard study, recognition of changes and mistakes" instead of "defense of what has been done." The Richmond *Times-Dispatch* called the report "serious oversimplification of the issues" and said, "Let us hope that he is more fully aware of the difficulties which confront this country than he is willing to admit in public." The Providence *Journal* said the speech was "a dangerous exercise in self-delusion, self-justification and complacency."

Trying to be cheerfully corrective, the New York *Daily News* said:

> P.S. to Democrats who snarl that all of Eisenhower's trips were flops: One of your boys started this whole "personal diplomacy" business. Remember Woodrow Wilson's trip to the Paris peace conference after World War I, and how royally he was taken by Clemenceau, Lloyd George and Orlando. Hah?

And the Atlanta *Journal* said, "We needed a stimulant and got a tranquilizer instead."

Reston followed on June 29 with a brilliantly executed satirical blast at Eisenhower in the form of a letter to Ingemar Johansson on how to explain his flattening at the hands of heavyweight Floyd Patterson in their second fight. Reston wrote to Ingemar:

> I have three suggestions. The best thing is to say nothing. The next best thing is to deny that you ever went to America. But if you have to make a report [to the Swedish people], I suggest that you follow the victory-through-defeat system used by President Eisenhower in his report on Japan. . . .

Time Magazine observed, "What really upsets Columnist Reston is that Eisenhower has stayed popular through thick and thin—and that the people, in his opinion, have stayed so thick."

Albert Ravenholt, writing from Manila for the Philadelphia *Inquirer*, reported on August 31, 1960:

> . . . now, more than two months after Mr. Eisenhower's tumultuous welcome to these islands, it is evident that the President's four-day visit accomplished results which many months of tedious and sometimes acrimonious negotiation failed

fully to achieve. It has placed official relations with 28,000,000 [sic] Filipinos on a more friendly, cooperative course for the first time in several years.

These were the curtain calls as Eisenhower bowed from the international center stage to appear only once again, and that in his own country, before the U.N. General Assembly in New York in the early autumn of 1960.

CHAPTER 19 *WAS IT ALL WORTH IT?*

The pattern of personal diplomacy established by Eisenhower as he traveled the world led to recurrent disputes. The primary point at issue: will it be necessary or advisable for succeeding Presidents to follow this policy of personal diplomacy in times of peace?

There are American leaders of opinion and political action who would argue the point. Some of these disputants are professional wranglers, others are men of responsibility who attempt to shape policies in the best interests of the country. They feel that benefits, if any, from personal diplomacy by a President as represented in extensive foreign travel are outweighed by negative factors.

At my request, Adlai E. Stevenson on May 10, 1960, set forth his opinions of Ike's travels. Stevenson must be regarded as a sincere, serious authority. Few ranking Democrats would be capable of appraising Eisenhower with such careful dispassion and it must be remembered that he wrote his letter at a time when many Americans expected him to be the Democratic presidential nominee for the third time.

Stevenson said (and the letter has not been published before):

> It is a little difficult for me to talk about the President's overseas trip[s] without running the risk of being misunderstood. I have said repeatedly that I think it has been a good thing for the President to use his special talents for communicating our good will and concern for the welfare and security of our friends around the world. But I think that perhaps we

have a tendency to expect too much from these travels and to confuse ceremonial visits with serious diplomacy and the settlement of problems and differences. And I have pointed out that if our expectations from these trips abroad exceed the realities we may be disillusioned as we were after the Geneva Conference in 1955.

As for South America, I think the President's visit helped to reassure our neighbors about our concern for their aspirations and their deeds. But it will take a lot more than good will tours to assure the solidarity of this hemisphere. If his visit created hopes that do not materialize, it could boomerang badly. Many Latins do not fully appreciate the global responsibilities of the United States, and a temporary feeling of better relations and more sympathetic interest could quickly turn to bitterness and disillusion.

Frankly, I have felt that the fact that the President has found this unprecedented use of his great office necessary to reassure and encourage our friends was a reflection of the low level of our prestige, influence and confidence around the world.

And one other thing—I know from my recent trip to South America that there was grave disappointment and bad feeling occasioned in Peru by the failure of the President to visit that country. The same, of course, was true of other countries in Latin America which were left off the President's itinerary. And now I can well understand the inability of our friends in the Philippines to understand why the President should be visiting Japan and Korea in June and not the country which is certainly one of our closest allies in that part of the world. Of course, it is impossible for the President to visit every country which is another reason why I have some misapprehension about the usefulness of these trips.

(After Stevenson's letter, the Philippines were added to Eisenhower's Far Eastern itinerary largely because of the time gap in his schedule created by cancellation of his nine-day visit to Russia. It is interesting that on May 10, Stevenson referred only to Eisenhower's going to Japan and Korea and made no mention of Russia, which was not blasted from the itinerary until May 16

at the Paris Summit conference. Of course, the U-2 plane incident which triggered the Khrushchev action in Paris was much
in the newspapers on May 10 and Stevenson, without intending
to do so consciously in his letter, may have reflected a belief
that the Soviet trip would turn out to be impossible.)

Richard H. Rovere, writing in *Harper's Magazine* after the
President's trip to Asia in the autumn of 1959, had this to say:
"Mr. Eisenhower is certainly using an unspecified power when
he adapts American campaign methods to the creation of good
will among the masses in the underdeveloped nations in Asia,
Africa and South America."

Rovere had more to say about Eisenhower's travels and his
role in personal diplomacy, writing in *The New Yorker* of
June 25, 1960. On this occasion Rovere was writing of what he
called "an American tragedy"; i.e., the fact that anti-American
riots in Tokyo stopped Eisenhower's planned trip to Japan.
The article said in part:

> . . . the late Secretary [John Foster Dulles] left office at a time
> when the President must have been giving serious thought to
> posterity's judgment upon his stewardship. [If Rovere could
> have talked personally with Eisenhower, as others were able to
> do, he would have discovered that this was substantially true.]
> Mr. Eisenhower became, as he had to become, his own Secretary
> of State, and since he is a man who has made some mark on
> posterity in other capacities, it should not perhaps have been
> surprising that he took to personal diplomacy with a zest that
> no earlier President had shown.

The St. Louis *Post-Dispatch* said:

> In his often reiterated willingness to go anywhere in the cause
> of peace, President Eisenhower has pursued a commendable
> policy which his successor will also have to adopt. But it is not
> enough to go somewhere. Tours and summits must be conceived
> as vehicles for a constructive foreign policy which commands

the best thought and the most tireless energy our nation can muster.

And finally:

Because of one setback in Japan, we cannot believe the good will which the President inspired throughout the world has been dispelled. Because mistakes were made in Japan, it does not follow that personal diplomacy must be altogether abandoned.

No less amazing than the millions of Indians and Paks, Spaniards and Scots, Koreans and Chileans who turned out to see Eisenhower was the man himself; the center of a critical storm at home; primary target of Kremlin wrath—a sixty-nine-year-old lame duck who by standards of other years should have been in his White House bedchamber plucking at the political coverlet which seems to cloak most chief executives during their final months in office.

His travels were long overdue in the opinion of many who had wondered about the steady procession of foreign chiefs to American soil without the American President returning the courtesy other than occasional business meetings with the British Prime Minister and so-called Summit conferences which had failed to produce appreciable reduction in the chafing pressures of cold war.

The truth is that Eisenhower for a long time had debated with himself on the advisability of an American President venturing far beyond his own hemisphere. Woodrow Wilson tried it after World War I with disastrous results at home, in that his battle for the League of Nations failed. Herbert Hoover made one trip to South America. Franklin Roosevelt's trips to Africa, the Middle East and Russia were brief although important parts of the World War II emergency. Harry Truman went to Potsdam as the war was ending and was double-crossed by Joseph Stalin.

Ike, too, had a go at summitry in 1955 at Geneva. What was described so roseately as the spirit of Geneva turned out to be a cruel ghost as the Russians, after a seemingly friendly meeting which set high, promising objectives for the foreign ministers, reverted to their policies of truculence and the cold war grew colder.

In the months after Geneva, Eisenhower thought at some length about Russian propaganda moves and the fact that no American chief executive had ever visited Russia, Asia or the Far East. Particularly in the case of Asia, we had spent dollars, blood, time and effort to assure the Asians of our friendship, but no President had taken the time or had the inclination to put foot on the territory of the people for whom we were so otherwise concerned. Our Presidents, when they stirred from this hemisphere, had gone only to Europe and that infrequently. Visits beyond Canada and Mexico were rare.

This stay-over-here policy was somewhat understandable if hard to defend in the twentieth century. It had been only a generation or two since most Americans believed it was against constitutional law for a President to travel outside the continental limits or territories of the United States. As recently as 1947, when President Truman visited Brazil, there was a straight-faced opinion by the Attorney General that official documents signed by the President while outside the country were as legal as the papers he signed daily at his White House desk.

Wilson was attacked so bitterly and with such seeming legal foundation for leaving the country in 1919 to dramatize his fight for the League, publications in his behalf debated the question almost juridically with his critics. In 1919 the *Ladies' Home Journal* devoted a lengthy article to "the curiously common belief that a President may not leave the United States during his term of office." The subject was argued in Congress. Begrudgingly some of the lawmakers agreed with historians of the time that there was no law to stop Wilson from leaving, but

he was advised to undertake no executive formality while out of the country because it might not stand up in court.

Theodore Roosevelt was the first President to travel beyond our borders, and then only to the Canal Zone. Congressional leaders insisted that the Constitution prohibited such travel and there was grave question as to how the federal government could function with Teddy away. He went anyway and somehow the country survived, but the prejudice against presidential foreign travel persisted.

It is difficult for many of us sitting at home today planning a jet excursion for the family this summer in the English country-side to realize that many Americans still prefer their President to remain at home lest he have to bow before some alien monarch or become entrapped in foreign intrigue.

The presidency and the White House legally are the same, situated wherever the President may be. The law moves with him. This in itself adds to the difficulty of travel because he must perform his job at great distances from the White House. But he has been helped immeasurably by jet aircraft and the constant, speedy improvement in communications. No longer is there any physical reason why a President should not ply his trade in any part of the earth.

Eisenhower was well aware of the historic prejudices, the practical disadvantages. But he felt there was definite need for a President to visit such places as India, Russia and Japan long before he did anything about it. What kept him from moving earlier? John Foster Dulles.

No man had more influence with the President than Dulles. And the Secretary, a formidable traveler himself, thought during the first four years of the administration that direct diplomacy was better handled at the ministerial level, with the leaders coming together only at rare intervals to lay down broad lines of policy.

Before his death, however, Dulles changed his mind. He seemed to grasp a new sense of Eisenhower's world popularity and this may have resulted from his own globe-girdling efforts to keep nations talking instead of shooting.

Mitigating this shift, however, was the mother-hen influence of Sherman Adams, who in all sincerity, but with slightly smothering omnipotence, did his best to simplify the presidency for Eisenhower so that the guttier, human aspects of the job were caught in Adams' protective sieve before they could clutter Ike's cadet-clean desk. When Adams, the chief assistant to the President, left, Eisenhower perforce had to dig much more deeply into the minutiae of the presidency. Although he hated the phrase, the President was without question a "new Eisenhower" during the last two years of his second term.

With Dulles sick, Adams out, and the general fortunes of the Republican party in sad shape, his concept of the presidency seemed to change rapidly. One of his closest associates told me, "I think he came to the conclusion that he was *not* doing all he could."

"Doing all he could—for what?" I asked.

"It would have to be pretty broad," he answered. "For the world, for the Western Allies, for the general good of mankind."

"Was he worried about his record in the presidency from the historical point of view?"

"You could put it that way. I wouldn't. I've worked for him since he went into politics, but I'm no blind idolater. It may be boring for some of you to hear him say over and over again that real peace with justice is going to come about only through better international understanding.

"That, however, is no unctuous hooey. He really believes it. When he reached the last half of his second term, he felt a certain amount of new freedom in the presidency. He was on his home stretch. And he began to re-examine the image of America across the world. He did not like much of what he saw and heard and he began to ask himself whether he was doing enough to meet the situation.

"I think, too, he finally came to believe that for too long we had made the heads of other countries come to Washington

almost at our bidding without a comparable gesture by the head of the American government.

"Also, from the time he first entered the White House, he had nursed the idea of returning as President to some of the countries he knew so well during the war."

It was not until after the 1958 by-elections, when the Republicans took such a drubbing in Congress, that Eisenhower's plans for foreign travel began to jell. He charted a rough plan for hitting the highways and jetstreams of the world not as a negotiator, but as a salesman for democracy.

"My trip was not undertaken as a feature of normal diplomatic procedures," he reported on his return from the eleven-nation 1959 tour. "It was not my purpose either to seek specific agreements or to urge any new treaty relationships. My purpose was to improve the climate in which diplomacy might work more successfully; diplomacy that seeks as its basic objective peace with justice for all men."

He found it difficult in some countries to avoid the impression that he was Ike the Bountiful, just arrived with lavish, specific plans for American aid soon to follow, aid of much larger proportions than hitherto extended. This was a recurrent danger point: the danger of expectation without genuine prospect of quick change in long-term American assistance policies, which, after all, were controlled during most of the Eisenhower administration by a Democratic Congress.

To avoid this involvement, Eisenhower tried to keep his mission as simple as possible. He summed up his purposes in one brief statement, uttered in a December rain at Rome's Ciampino Airport with tiny rivulets of water veining over his bald top. Eisenhower said:

"I bring a simple message to you from America. It is this: we want to live in peace and friendship—in freedom. This is the message I shall carry to every country that I visit. It is the message that I hope will be heard in every country where communications are allowed freely."

Quite apart from the impact of his personality on foreign

populations, Eisenhower's travels had an undramatic but far-reaching effect at home.

Thousands of American schoolteachers were able, due to the President's movements, to shift their study courses to follow his itinerary in such a way that geography and history came alive daily not only in the classroom, but at home, too.

Norman Cousins, editor of *Saturday Review*, said no American could be considered educated without direct exposure to the preponderance of the human commonwealth in Asia and Africa. Even with travel facilities increasing, most Americans will never be able to follow Editor Cousins' admirable prescription, but through the travels of a publicity-commanding figure such as their President the chances of Americans learning more about the human commonwealth are decidedly improved.

The reading, viewing and listening of America were dominated by not only the spot news of Eisenhower's travels, but vast amounts of background material concerning the towns and countries and their people. American adults who knew the measurements of Marilyn Monroe and the batting record of Ted Williams began to absorb something about Nehru and Ayub Khan. Whether this new knowledge was deep or permanent was highly debatable, but at least it was learning of a sort, an awareness that could not but contribute something to public understanding of international affairs.

Diplomacy for much too long has been the sacred province of the professionals and this due largely to the public not knowing or not caring. Eisenhower, of course, aroused no great wave of national emotion for the problems of India and Pakistan, but he was responsible for many Americans digging out their atlases for the first time since World War II, when the men in the family were in some mighty odd places, too.

The spark of new interest in history and geography reflected itself at the White House in mounds of mail from teachers and pupils. Thousands of children mailed the President scrapbooks of his trips and teachers by the hundred sent what they con-

sidered to be the better compositions dealing with countries he visited.

The classroom tie-in with Ike's journeys was made possible by the combination of information media. Aside from such sudden news stories as the death of Roosevelt or Eisenhower's heart attack and excluding war, a national election or the resultant inauguration, American newspapers set new records for space devoted to presidential activity when Eisenhower went to Asia.

Most metropolitan newspapers, and hundreds of smaller ones, too, printed elaborate background articles on each of the eleven nations visited, along with pictures, detailed maps and thumbnail analyses of the political situation in each country. Much of this was printed prior to his departure and then updated as he arrived in each country.

The television networks did a masterful job of providing daily film coverage, rushing the footage back to the United States by every available means of air transportation. The networks presented not just the usual newsreel coverage of a day's activities in, for example, Ankara, but extensive background and commentary by trained men on the scene.

This was a godsend to the teachers. Johnny got his history in triple doses as he went from school to living room. The teacher covered the background in class and Johnny went home to see his lessons come alive on the TV screen and spread throughout the newspapers. Many teachers required their pupils to submit daily reports on the President's travels based on stories in newspapers of the previous day.

Even the housewives with little time for studious reading of papers and news magazines were kept abreast of Eisenhower's movements almost hourly on their kitchen radios.

Outside the United States, the story of the President's odyssey was told in thousands of newspapers, thousands of radio stations. Only war or major disaster would have commanded more wordage and attention on the worldwide circuits of the American press associations and the foreign news agencies. Most broadcasting outlets outside the Iron Curtain carried several daily accounts of the trips. Thus, through the travels of a President, the United States was presented in favorable fashion to millions of non-Americans, many of whom were being subjected to a daily diet of anti-United States propaganda.

These informational benefits, these by-products of presidential travel abroad are cumulative in their impact. The results are not dramatic or immediate, but they are clearly present.

The little Pakistani boy, Shahid, who scuttled past the police in Karachi to shove his grubby note of approval into Eisenhower's carriage, the little Turk who crayoned the "Ike Like We" sign in Ankara and the South Carolina sixth grader painfully drawing a map of the President's Far East itinerary had something in common, something no diplomat would think twice about in his trade. These children were learning something of each other's country. The knowledge, of course, had been available to many of them in the normal progress of their education, but a dramatic presidential trip made the textbooks current and transformed what the teacher had to say into something much more interesting and timely.

By human standards which might be more important in the long run, the President's personality on display in foreign lands had an indisputably positive impact. The warmth with which he was received in other countries had to redound to the credit of the United States. There is no evidence that he lost any friends for this country through personal diplomacy and, as dead center as that may seem, it would be a gain in a world whipsawed by the propaganda of controlled societies. In fact, there is reason to believe he made new friends for the United States and he may have paved the way for future Presidents to maintain the momentum.

After the South American venture, the *New York Times* commented editorially: "Hereafter, in the memories of many thousands of Latin Americans, Uncle Sam will look like Presi-

dent Eisenhower—a man who did not pretend good will, but honestly felt it."

Quite aside from domestic political preferences, which invariably color one's acceptance of such an evaluation, and without attempting to assay Eisenhower's over-all performance as chief executive, is not the picture of Uncle Sam as a bald, smiling, familiar figure with his arms stretched high to the applause of millions vastly preferable to the image of a Scrooge-like old scold with glittering dollar marks for eyes?

CHAPTER 20 *THE PRESIDENT SUMS UP*

"Fellow Americans, even if we wanted to, we could not shut out the free world. We cannot escape its troubles. We cannot turn our backs on its hopes. We are an inseparable part of the free world neighborhood."

DWIGHT D. EISENHOWER, May 2, 1960

It was late one summer afternoon in 1960. Eisenhower had completed his foreign travels as President and he was in a mood to be retrospective.

He had been out on the south lawn of the White House hitting golf balls and returned to his office casually dressed in a light tan sports shirt buttoned at the neck, a soft brown jacket and tan slacks.

Congress was preparing to recess for the nominating conventions and a steady stream of legislation was pouring into the White House. Awaiting the President on his desk—he'd been away from it less than thirty minutes—was a new stack of bills and neatly typed intelligence reports with "SECRET" stamped in red across the top.

Naturally Eisenhower looked appreciably older than when he took office nearly eight years earlier, but his posture and movements were decidedly youthful for a man of his age. He still bore facial evidence of the sunny, seaside golf courses of Hawaii and he gave every outward evidence of a man in surprisingly good physical shape.

A late afternoon visitor who also had grown older since 1952 thought the President might be downcast about his record in

personal diplomacy because of his inability to visit Russia and Japan.

Ike scratched his head and slumped down in the high-backed leather chair behind his desk.

No, he didn't feel downcast if the visitor meant dejected. But sure, he was disappointed by the circumstances which made his Japanese trip impossible. Those were good people out there and the rioters did not represent the feelings of the country, not by a long shot.

The visitor suggested that the flareback from the Moscow and Tokyo visits might prejudice the future of personal diplomacy of other Presidents. He would talk of that later, Eisenhower said as he rose from his chair, walked to the window and looked out at the shimmering summer sun on the sloping lawn.

He was quite aware of the criticism of his handling of the Japanese trip and he thought most of it was cockeyed. He rejected quite heatedly the notion that he should have canceled the Tokyo trip when Khrushchev called off his Russian trip. This would have been an awful slap at the Far East, putting those people in the position of being second place or second class; no, that would have been foolish.

In fact, even if the Kishi government had asked him not to come to Tokyo prior to his departure from Washington on June 12, he had been prepared to make a public announcement that he intended to go through with the rest of the trip—to the Philippines, Formosa, Okinawa and Korea.

He thought it would have been a dreadful mistake, even arrogant, to call off the Far Eastern trip because Japan, the largest country on his itinerary, had to be scrubbed. He was aware that some critics underrated his visits to the Philippines, Formosa and Korea because they were friends of ours anyway and what did you accomplish going to places like that? This sort of reasoning was shortsighted and captious; we needed every friend we'd got, the small ones and the large ones.

He felt the Far Eastern trip might have looked differently to the people at home in a nonelection year. He thought some of the criticism at home was purely political. He thought it was not thinking straight to minimize the accomplishments of this trip just because he went to the smaller nations. The United States had a sizable investment in each of those countries and far beyond that, it would be the worst sort of foreign policy to pay attention only to the larger nations.

His feeling was that Kishi, up until about forty-eight hours before the Tokyo visit had to be abandoned, hoped to produce such a large turnout of pro-Western Japanese that the violent dissidents would have been lost in the shuffle, or certainly outnumbered to such an extent that their activities would have been scarcely noticeable. Eisenhower began to worry, however, and so did Kishi, about the disturbing possibility of the good people fighting the bad people in the streets of Tokyo and Eisenhower did not want to be the excuse for internecine conflict, injury and possibly more deaths.

He felt that Kishi's difficulties stemmed from many sources. He thought the Japanese Premier generated trouble for himself the way he rammed the defense treaty with the United States through the lower house of the Diet. He also thought Kishi could not control effectively the activities of the Zengakuren because of basically faulty laws and lax police powers. A share of the blame for this legal situation had to be placed on the United States because these laws were drafted with American blessings during the occupation after the war. It was true, too, that the Japanese people, after many years of a police state, swung too far in the opposite direction in depriving their law enforcement bodies of the proper methods and authority for coping with civil violence.

Originally, Eisenhower wanted to go to Japan later than the scheduled date of June 19, after Congress had adjourned or recessed for the summer, but Kishi held out for his presence in Japan on the nineteenth, the effective date of the treaty.

Even with all the trouble, Eisenhower felt that the treaty was a plus for both countries; he felt strongly that most Japanese still were quite positive toward the United States; that the

incident of his trip should not prejudice the friendship between the two countries nor discourage another President from making a journey to Japan. In fact, he would like to see the next President go to the Orient as soon as practicable.

The President returned to his chair and plopped down in such a slouch that the lapels of his jacket rode up around his chin. Now, about that business in Paris. His face darkened momentarily and he sighed.

Downing the American U-2 plane over Russia on May 1 was the sort of break the Soviets had been waiting for. He accepted with no noticeable rancor that the U-2 case was marked by some bungling in Washington. He was speaking particularly of the manner in which the first reports on the plane being down were treated in official statements (the covering announcement that the U-2 was an unarmed weather observation plane).

He added quickly, however, that he had no apology whatever for the four years of U-2 flights over Soviet territory, but the visitor was somewhat surprised when the President said calmly that he himself became a bit careless with success. The flights were going over Russia without incident, they were returning valuable information on a mighty power and a potential enemy that kept its borders locked to the outside world. Yes, it was true, Eisenhower had become overconfident about the continuing success of the U-2 flights and it did not occur to him to stop them just before the Big Four meeting in Paris.

The U-2 was only part of the story of Paris, however, only part of it. You got all sorts of indications and you were pretty sure in your own mind about these things, but of course, you never could prove them. The President thought that the manner in which Khrushchev conducted himself in the period leading up to the Summit and during their brief contact in Paris indicated that quite aside from the U-2 incident, which was an exceedingly unfortunate break for the United States, the Soviet Premier did not want Eisenhower to come to Russia.

If at any time, before or after the U-2 incident, Khrushchev had indicated, through any number of communications channels open to him, that the visit would be inconvenient or undesired at the time scheduled, the President would have accepted the situation readily. Khrushchev's behavior in Paris was not necessary simply to call off the Eisenhower trip; it was a grandstand play.

Talking easily and casually, possibly because no notes were being taken and possibly because there was no audience ready to grab at every phrase and take it apart for syntax and deeper meaning, Eisenhower spoke with analytic detachment, as though he were speaking perhaps of another President.

He did not know precisely when Khrushchev cooled on the idea of his visiting Russia. It may have happened while Mr. K. was in the United States the previous September. It may have happened when Americans went to Russia to work out actual plans for the trip. It may have been a gradual thing that came to a head with the U-2 affair. But there were other factors aside from the U-2.

Khrushchev may have been burned up by his lukewarm reception in Asia, where he went hard on the heels of Eisenhower. Mr. K. was much more sensitive to public reaction, even in his own country, than many people believed.

Khrushchev was under pressure from Mao and old-line Stalinists to drop his policy of outwardly friendly dealings with the West.

The Soviet Premier's military situation at home was complicated and possibly uncomfortable following his decision to muster out 250,000 Russian Air Force officers and a companionate number of enlisted men.

Khrushchev lapped up his publicity in the United States, his freedom to hold press conferences and appear on television, but once he got home and began to think about having to extend the same sort of privileges to Eisenhower, not only in metropolitan Moscow but in Siberia, too, Mr. K. may have begun to wish he had been a little less lavish with his invitations. Khrushchev was far from immune to influences within his own government and some of the people around him may have disliked

the idea of having the American President spout his ideas from one end of the country to another.

Khrushchev seemed to want Summit meetings only when they suited some immediate purpose of his own, a purpose not always easily visible. For a time, he was more anxious than any of the Western leaders to meet, but then he began to cool.

The President thought it was not entirely a matter of defensive hindsight, but he doubted whether there could have been even a moderately successful Summit in May under any circumstances, even without the U-2 case. This was admitted speculation, but the President thought that if the U-2 incident had not occurred, Khrushchev might have shown up in Paris, gone along with the meeting for a day or two, then raised an issue in such a way that an acceptable solution would have been impossible and the Russian leader would have left Paris in a huff. And Eisenhower's trip to Russia obviously would have been off.

The President speculated that Khrushchev probably would have demanded some impossible sort of Berlin settlement which the West could not have accepted. Mr. K. would have then used this as a lever for breaking up the Paris meeting and making the Eisenhower trip to Russia a virtual impossibility.

For the reasons he mentioned and others he did not voice at the time, Eisenhower felt, and seemed to feel strongly, that Khrushchev never intended for the Paris conference to be successful except from the standpoint of Soviet propaganda.

Eisenhower knew this was not his conclusion alone, but an opinion shared in varying degrees by Macmillan and De Gaulle. The French President told Eisenhower in Paris that he was convinced Mr. K. wanted no dealings with D.D.E., U-2 or no U-2.

The President recalled the one meeting in Paris when the Big Four were together, that thunderous morning in the Élysée Palace. Eisenhower tried to get Khrushchev, following the Russian's lengthy opening blast, to say why he came to Paris in the first place; that if Khrushchev felt so bitterly and wanted to hurl such demands at the United States, why had he come all the way to Paris to do it.

Khrushchev ignored the President's inquiry. He seemed for the moment to brush aside Eisenhower's presence and, as though he had not made a statement at all, the Russian merely reread his long list of grievances against the President and again reiterated, word for word, the reasons why the Russian people would not accept Eisenhower in their country.

The President knew the situation did not call for it, but he could not help smiling as Khrushchev went through his fixed phrases the second time. The way Eisenhower described it, the Russian sounded like a carefully coached witness before a Congressional investigating committee. Eisenhower did feel, however, that Khrushchev's meticulous sticking to the words of his previously prepared statement was interesting; possibly indicative of an understanding with other U.S.S.R. leaders to say his part—and remain ever faithful to the script.

A side door to the President's office opened and Ann Whitman entered with a big smile. She discreetly held out a small slip of yellow paper where only the President could see it.

His face lighted up and he asked the visitor to pardon him for a moment, this was a telephone call of utmost importance. Quickly the chief executive picked up his phone from its base studded with gold stars. It was his granddaughter, Susie, in Gettysburg. A horse was supposed to have been delivered to the farm that afternoon; the animal had not arrived and nine-year-old Susie was worried.

The President assured the child that the matter would be looked into with the greatest dispatch. He put down the telephone and asked Mrs. Whitman would she please try to track down the man with the horse.

The President leafed through some papers on his desk, hunting for a particular envelope. He buzzed for Mrs. Whitman and asked her. Yes, she had it, a letter that had come to him from Manila addressed simply by pasting a picture of his head on the envelope. This one was unusual, but Eisenhower selected it as

an example of the heavy volume of friendly mail he received from the Far East. He was warmed by the number of letters from nongovernment people saying they liked the United States and were either sorry or ashamed over the circumstances in Tokyo.

The visitor mentioned that some ordinarily astute observers of international affairs thought summitry was virtually dead due to Paris and personal diplomacy by a President ill-advised in view of Tokyo. The President took a highly contrary view, regarding such fears or apprehensions as hard to support in a shrinking world.

He felt the new President, Republican or Democrat, could and would participate in future Summit conferences, although for the foreseeable future the results of such meetings were likely to be inconclusive. When one man wants to talk things over with his opposite numbers, you pretty well have to go along with the idea just to maintain a line of communications and get some sort of guidance as to how he's thinking.

Another Summit should not be held until the foreign ministers had come to a fairly substantial agreement on what would be discussed by the principals. The 1955 Summit in Geneva certainly produced no long-lasting results, but another meeting should be organized in about the same way, with the ministerial level getting the spadework done and letting their principals know whether a major meeting would be worth while.

He felt the new President could participate in summitry even with Khrushchev, but he thought it would be next to impossible to have Mr. K. in this country again as the guest of the nation. Eisenhower did not mention the United Nations, which would be something else again, but in the past he had misgivings, although not necessarily final, about having the Big Four meet at U.N. headquarters in New York. This might seem to dilute or depress the importance of the U.N.

He thought it was not necessary or even indicated that a new President inevitably inherit the insults heaped on him by Khrushchev. It was a political summer and he did not go into the personalities of either Kennedy or Nixon. He spoke of the new President only in the neutral third person.

There would undoubtedly be other Summits, but he hoped a new President would proceed slowly, agreeing to a meeting only after the nearest-to-possible ironclad agreement by the foreign ministers on an agenda. If and when the Russians pressed for another meeting, he thought the President should accept the suggestions politely and say something to the effect of, "Let's see how far the ministers can get and then if it looks worth while, we'll give it some serious study."

He thought the American political year had at least something to do with Khrushchev's behavior in Paris. The Russians, even the best of them, do not quite understand our political system, but they apparently know enough about it to realize when a man's term is about to expire. Khrushchev apparently had begun to have his misgivings about Eisenhower anyway, and when the U-2 came along, he decided to exploit the situation as much as he could. Add to this the fact that Khrushchev knew Eisenhower was on the way out of office and, apparently being unable to estimate with any accuracy the residual powers of a President up until inauguration morning, Mr. K. wrote D.D.E. off some months ahead of time.

When Khrushchev spoke at the Élysée Palace in May of possibly trying another Summit in six or eight months, Eisenhower did not believe Mr. K. meant this timing precisely. Taken at his exact words, Khrushchev could have been talking about a meeting between the American election and the inauguration, or one shortly after the inauguration. Eisenhower did not think Mr. K. meant either one. He thought the Russian merely was stating his strong distaste for doing business with D.D.E. again and hoping the heck the new President would be a lot better from the Russian viewpoint.

The visitor, knowing of Eisenhower's frequent consideration of his own role in history, confessed to some surprise that the chief executive did not seem more sorely disappointed or saddened by Paris, Moscow and Tokyo. Without referring to

what these incidents might do to his personal standing with the historians—he had pointed out earlier with a chuckle that there wasn't very much he could do about it if he wanted to—the President spoke of disappointment that world affairs had turned in the direction of new tensions. Much of this could not have been avoided, at least not by him.

He did not believe the U-2, the Summit collapse, the Russian trip and the Tokyo riots necessarily were interlocking. One possibly fueled another. If he had to do it all over again, and by that he meant approach the same series of events, he would make only one change—halting the U-2 flights.

He got up from his chair again, walked over to inspect an oil of a mountain landscape (not his) that he'd seen a thousand times and then returned to his desk.

No, he wasn't dead sure he would do even that, although the loss of that plane was a most fortuitous thing for the Russians if his estimate of the situation was right; that Khrushchev was hunting for an excuse to torpedo the Summit. No, the U-2 flights were valuable and it was also possible to see these things so clearly after they'd happened. It could be argued both ways, but still it might have been better to have stopped the flights and not given Khrushchev the excuse. But we think he probably would have found another one and where would that leave us?

Counting off what he considered to be the salient points on the fingers of one hand, the President reiterated that he had been lulled into overconfidence by the success of the U-2 flights. That was one thing to remember. Another was the fact that the Russians knew about the flights, even before Khrushchev came to Camp David. Why hadn't he said something then? It may have been the hospitality of the situation, but still Khrushchev could have said something to him just before he left the United States. Khrushchev obviously was trying to get one of those planes then, and yet there he was, patting the President's grandchildren on the head at Gettysburg and insisting that they come to Moscow with Ike. The President had planned to go to Russia originally in the fall of 1959, probably in October, and it was

Khrushchev who suggested putting it over until spring or early summer when the weather would be better.

It was interesting, somewhat hard to understand, even mysterious, how, for a few days after the U-2 was brought down, Khrushchev was relatively mild about the affair and he did not warm up to his bombastic denunciations until time for the Paris meeting neared.

Another thing to remember: The fact that Khrushchev came to Paris at all showed that he and the Russian leaders wanted to milk the U-2 incident for the greatest propaganda value and Khrushchev came to Paris with no intention at all, certainly not at that time, of doing business with the West. He came to make trouble for the West, to embarrass the United States more than she was already embarrassed, and in so doing try to frighten and split off Great Britain and France. Khrushchev should have known by then that, while he had a very flashy case, he didn't stand much chance of splitting the Allies. God knows, no one was happy about this thing but Khrushchev wasn't about to scare Macmillan and De Gaulle. In fact, De Gaulle the day before they met tried to talk Khrushchev out of making public his charges against the President simultaneously—that demand for an apology—so the conference could stay in session; at least, keep talking. But no, the Russian knew what he was doing. He was going to blow that meeting sky-high and he did.

The visitor knew the President did not like the 1959-60 label of the "new Eisenhower" and avoided approaching the next phase of the conversation in that light. The President obviously felt that his ventures in personal diplomacy—his good-will trips abroad as differentiated from Summit meetings—were successful in the main.

The visitor pointed out that some felt the world might have been a better place, that there might have been considerably less anti-Americanism, if Eisenhower had started his fabulous junkets during his first term rather than waiting until the concluding phases of his second and final term of office.

As useful as such trips might be, Eisenhower felt that a Presi-

dent had his hands rather full during his first term getting his administration organized and under way, establishing a basic legislative program for the Congress and, of general necessity, concentrating on things at home, including his own re-election.

In his second term, a President had a bit more freedom of movement. Also, there was the very real fact that during his own first term the President had suffered a heart attack and undergone surgery for ileitis.

Aside from his health, what changed things? What got him to traveling the world and talking with other presidents, with dictators and kings?

With the heavy increase in travel of foreign chiefs of state and chiefs of government to these shores, there were always a number of rather nebulous plans about the President going somewhere. But an American President is different, he's unique in that he wears three hats. He is the ceremonial chief of state. He is the operating head of government. He's the head of a political party. And, one may add, the commander-in-chief of the armed forces.

This multiplicity of roles posed obvious difficulties, but Eisenhower began to think less of the difficulties and more of the advantages of informal, personal visits abroad in the late winter of 1959.

As he traced the inception of his period of intensive personal diplomacy, he recalled going in February of 1959 to Acapulco, Mexico, where he had a delightful three-day visit with President Lopez Mateos.

There had been a number of nagging problems between Mexico and the United States, not of the type that breed war talk between other border nations of the world, but still vexing matters involving cotton, oil, airline routes, electric power and some lesser economic involvements.

These constituted the background, not the purpose, of the Acapulco visit. Eisenhower was utterly delighted by his stay in the colorful Mexican resort, going to La Perla one night to dine and watch the native cliff divers, another night to a water ski club for dinner; all with none of the starch and circumstance of usual meetings between heads of state.

Lopez Mateos and Eisenhower got along so well together that after their visit their second and third echelons of government turned to the substantive problems with much more vigor than before.

Acapulco set the broad pattern for Eisenhower's future trips abroad: no direct negotiation between heads of state, but friendly discussion of problems in general terms, leaving the actual negotiation to the ministers and ambassadors. The President found that subordinate officials seemed to work much more effectively when they were convinced of or impressed by close, friendly relationships between the two bosses.

Thus the Acapulco visit, which seemed at the time like little more than a pleasant outing, sold Eisenhower on the idea that similar contacts with other world leaders might be an effective way of strengthening American ties with a number of nations, large and small.

As he got into the business of being a sort of gold-plated traveling salesman, he found the Acapulco type of simplicity was not always possible to achieve. Some foreign cultures and customs would stand for just so much informality and no more. The construction of an itinerary was more complicated and potentially troublesome than he realized at the start.

He could not visit Israel, as many Americans hoped, and he doubted another President would be able to go there in the predictable future without, on the same journey, traveling to all of the Arab nations, including Egypt. Even then, he did not know whether such a trip would be advisable for a future President because of the antagonism between the Jews and the Arabs. To illustrate this difficulty in more detail, he said a trip to Israel would require a trip to Egypt, which would then necessitate going to Saudi Arabia. A President would then find it difficult to arrive at an Arabian cut-off point.

When the Far East trip was shaping up, he had thought of going to Indonesia, but even an entirely unofficial, speculative

suggestion to that effect in the newspapers produced strenuous objections from the Dutch. He had not gone to the Netherlands and here was the prospect of his visiting an area from which the Dutch had departed most reluctantly.

He thought there were many incidental benefits from the good-will trips of a President; benefits that did not show up in the communiqués (the visitor was tempted to say that little of anything showed up in the communiqués) or evidence themselves immediately to those who wanted crisp results.

The President mentioned first the opportunity for fostering good will between two other nations. When he was in India, for example, Nehru told him Iran could solve many of her problems by going ahead with badly needed land reforms. Eisenhower relayed this opinion to the Shah in Teheran, and later the President sent a note to Nehru reporting on his conversation in Iran. Eisenhower was able to report that the Shah would do everything possible to push pending land reform legislation through his Parliament—and he did.

The President realized the touchy situation between India and Afghanistan, but it was not too delicate for him to tell both Nehru and King Zahir that he hoped, and the free world hoped, there would be no trouble on their border.

Eisenhower believed, as independent findings in the preceding chapter would indicate, that much of the pay-off from presidential trips abroad is of such undramatic quality that most of us tend to overlook it. He was speaking particularly of the results of foreign explorations in personal diplomacy on the people at home.

He was reasonably certain that because of his own travels millions of Americans through their newspapers, magazines, radio and television had learned more of other nations than they would have absorbed ordinarily. He thought his trip to Asia and the Middle East was particularly important in this respect as millions of Americans truly for the first time in their lives were exposed to stories and pictures of places known to most of them only as strange lands located vaguely somewhere out there. Afghanistan was a good example. He was there only a few hours, but there probably was more in the newspapers about Afghanistan that day than appears in most secondary school texts.

And how many in the United States had heard of San Carlos de Bariloche before he went to Argentina? Bariloche in itself was not important, but his being there did focus attention on the existence of vast sections of Argentina outside the well-known Buenos Aires. He also knew there were bound to be some miffed feelings in South America because he did not visit more countries, but he regarded as more important the likelihood that he was able to convince a sizable number of South Americans that the United States genuinely cared about them and did not, as many had felt for years, take its neighbors for granted.

What about the future of personal diplomacy, the visitor ventured because the hour was late and the President had devoted considerable time to the discussion. Eisenhower put on his spectacles and looked down at some of the papers on his broad desk. Then he took off his glasses, leaned back in the chair and looked up at the oval ceiling.

Very definitely, he thought the next President should travel outside the United States, possibly not as extensively as he had done within so short a time. But travel, yes. There were bound to be drawbacks, but there were drawbacks to his going even to a dinner two blocks away at the Statler Hotel. With the jet transport due to be even faster than the six hundred miles an hour-plus at which Eisenhower was able to move around the world, future Presidents could travel comfortably over great distances and in a remarkably short time.

He thought the next President might have to space his foreign trips to possibly one major venture a year, i.e., South America this year, Africa the next, Europe the next. And at this point, he mentioned Nixon for the only time in the conversation. The President planned, if Nixon was elected, to

recommend strongly that he undertake a trip to Africa as soon as conditions permitted.

He would have made such a trip himself if his schedule had not made it impossible. He had thought seriously of going to Cameroon. He would be happy to make the suggestion of travel to Africa to any new President, but he doubted he would have the opportunity if a Democrat were chosen to succeed him.

He assumed a new President would do what most recent chief executives have done, pay his first visits outside the country to America's neighbors, Canada and Mexico.

Admittedly he had not thought it out and it seemed to be an idea of the moment, but Eisenhower wondered whether there could be some sort of system or loose understanding whereby a President, operating on the general plan of one major foreign good-will trip a year, would not have to attempt covering most of the world during his tenure if his successor would take up where he left off. He had no thoughts on how such a gentle-man's agreement could be developed, but he felt something of this nature might relieve the pressures on a chief executive to expand his travels beyond what he considered possible and proper at the time.

Eisenhower began tidying up the papers on his desk. Mamie was waiting for him over at the house and there probably were some guests coming in, too. He rose from behind the desk and walked around it to the center of the room.

A discussion of this sort could occupy hours and still not exhaust the subject, but he wanted one thing plain. The new President, of course, could not spend a great deal of his time traveling. There would be the normal pressures of his office, and the man would have a family, a wife and children to think of, and God knows, a man can't go hauling his family around with him everywhere he goes, certainly not in this job; they'd have absolutely no lives of their own.

He hoped, however, that the new President would see things approximately as he did. He knew of no more effective method of convincing other nations of American friendship, or for demonstrating to the leaders of foreign governments our interest in their problems. Chiefs of state and heads of government obviously could not sit down and work out intricately detailed agreements. This was much too involved and generally too time-consuming for the top echelon. But men of responsibility and frequently conflicting ideas, men of markedly different cultures and beliefs would seem to have a vastly better chance of getting along in the world peaceably if they knew something of each other firsthand.

These were the views of one President. His application of them met with mixed success. He thought he was largely successful in his efforts to transmit the idea of American friendship to other lands. Many other people thought so, too. Many thought otherwise, that he could have spent the time better back at the White House and that by heightening expectations of the United States he may have done more harm than good. This is something historians will be debating for years to come.

However the argument comes out, it would be tragic, even cruelly cynical, to think that "out there" those people with strange clothes, faces and voices want us only for our money and our machines. Many of those who ran screaming into their dusty streets to cheer Ike were drawn by the magnetism of an almost legendary war hero. But many foreigners were cheering the United States and what it represented. They'd like some of it for themselves.

ABOUT THE AUTHOR

Merriman Smith, widely regarded as the dean of White House reporters in terms of length of continuous, everyday assignment, has made not only a profession, but a hobby of the Presidency. United Press International assigned him to the White House as a young reporter during the tense period leading up to Pearl Harbor in 1941, and Mr. Smith has been at the same task continuously since then, except for a hiatus of seven months in 1958 when he departed the White House briefly to report the recession and the difficulties of Sherman Adams and Bernard Goldfine.

Few reporters have seen more history in the making than Mr. Smith, from the frightening moments of December 7, 1941, when from the White House he supplied many of the details of the Japanese attack on Pearl Harbor, to the Paris conference of 1960 when he stood in the shadow of Soviet Premier Khrushchev and heard the Russian leader thunder his denunciation of President Eisenhower. Mr. Smith was one of three reporters present at Warm Springs, Georgia, in 1945 when President Roosevelt died suddenly. Mr. Smith went to the Potsdam conference with President Truman, and also to Wake Island. He made all of Eisenhower's foreign trips and is prepared to undertake similar assignments with the new President, the fourth man he has watched from the White House itself.

Mr. Smith has written three earlier books about the presidency—*Thank You, Mr. President, A President Is Many Men,* and *Meet Mister Eisenhower.* Mr. Smith's articles have appeared in most of the major national magazines and he has appeared widely on television.